OLDLAND
AND THE
SURROUNDING PARISHES

BY

IAN S. BISHOP

In Memory of Doreen.

This book is dedicated to my lovely wife and most wonderful companion of Fifty-years, who never lost her love for life, but sadly lost her fight for life.

16th September 2004

CONTENTS

CHAPTER ONE "THE EARLY DAYS"

As its name suggests, Oldland has been in existence for some considerable while, although when it was first laid down as a place of human habitation is now impossible to determine, bearing in mind the complete absence of any written records, and the fact that the original buildings were probably either made of timber, or mud and turf, or probably a combination of both. It is also possible that the name Oldland may have simply referred to an old parcel of cultivated land, as distinct from a place where someone lived. What has been determined from accidental archaeology near to the area of California Road is a number of thinly scattered flint implements, and a socketed axehead of the late Bronze Age period. Regrettably these finds, however interesting they may be, tell us very little about the origins of Oldland, as the items may have simply been dropped by Bronze Age man as he passed through the area, and it is perhaps reasonable to assume that had there been a discernable level of occupation by our Bronze Age ancestors, then more of their discarded possessions would by now have come to light. Not far from St Mary's in Bitton is a Bronze Age round barrow, which probably indicates that these ancestors were not just passing through, but almost certainly there was only a handful of family groups living in the area covered by this book, and that in the main the land on which they lived were little more than rough clearings in the forest, and that that situation probably hardly changed through to the Iron Age and on right through to the Roman invasion in the First Century AD, with the possible exception that more of the land gradually went under the plough and was cultivated for both crops, and the grazing of animals. This action caused, as elsewhere in the country, the local landscape to be affected by human life as our ancestors became more settled, and learned the art of becoming farmers, whilst at the same time all of their hard efforts would have been restricted and directly affected by the surrounding forest, which still dominated a very large area both north and south of the River Avon.

Having invaded these islands of ours during the course of the first century, the Romans gradually moved west, clearing as they went the undergrowth and cutting trees so as to make more habitable space for themselves, more land to cultivate to support a growing population, and more land to build their roads, forts and garrisons as they sought to take more and more control over the indigenous population. At the forefront of the Roman push westward were their legions of well-armed disciplined soldiers, who brought with them a microcosm of their homeland, and wherever the

Roman soldiers stopped, their supporting engineers immediately went to work on constructing a garrison, which, once established, soon created its own small trading community that grew around the stopping point and in one form or another moulded itself on Rome. As for the indigenous population, they either conformed to the law and pattern of life imposed by Rome, or they were outcasts and refugees. For the Romans there was, in travelling west, the bonus of discovering the hot thermal springs, which must have been for the men from the cultivated Mediterranean like finding a small part of paradise in a hostile environment, with warm water in which to bathe, and under floor heating to rid their aching bodies of the discomfort of the dreadful, dull, damp and cold British weather. Having established themselves at *Aquae Sulis* (Bath), the Romans also established a safe harbour as close to Bath as they could; by building a small port near the mouth of the River Avon at a place they called *Abonae,* nowadays known as Sea Mills. To connect both places, the Romans built, in not quite their usual indomitable way, an arterial road that they called *Via Julia* that ran from Weston, Bath over Kelston Round hill, passing Prospect Stile and North Stoke and then down through Bitton. However it should not be forgotten that at the time the road was constructed, there was unlikely to be any sign or indication of the existence of these two subsequent communities, with the hills and dales densely covered by forest trees, with only an occasional habitable clearing. Normally Roman Roads were constructed to connect two places in as straight a line as possible, irrespective of obstacles either man made or natural, but in the case of the *Via Julia* especially that part between Bath and Bitton, the road builders appear to have abandoned those principles and instead used the contours of the surrounding land. Although very little is known of this section of the road, the effort to construct it must have been extremely enormous. A legion or so of military engineers, must have controlled gangs of men, including no doubt a high proportion of slave labour, to excavate and build-up the land through which the road passed. In conjunction with this work there would have been a caravan of soldiers, hundreds of workmen, many of whom would have been Britons, and the many ancillary supporters needed, no doubt with a fair number of camp-followers all living on site and gradually moving along as the road was constructed yard by yard, mile by mile. Stone for surfacing the road would have had to be brought from the rear in heavy wagons drawn by either horse or ox, as would have been the supply of food, tools and equipment. Just dealing with the necessary logistics of such an operation must have taken a great deal of time and effort, and well beyond the abilities of the local indigenous population.

Along this road, that may well have originally been an earlier British trackway, the Romans set up a small military establishment which they called *Trajactus,* and which they probably built mainly of timber, at a place where they needed to cross the River Boyd. Not only was its construction necessary for the safety and control of those who travelled the road, it was also a very useful place to stable fresh horses so that the riders could change their steeds, especially with the climb to and from Bath either just negotiated or about to be negotiated. In addition it was also likely to be a very useful place from which to trade with the local communities, that had by then settled in a place they called BETUNE, or possibly Boyd Town, either of which can quite easily be corrupted in the local vernacular to Bitton. Almost certainly this spot had been chosen, as there was an abundance of fresh water, a fertile valley floor and, with a confluence of two rivers, it was very obviously an important centre of communication, with the waterways being the main highways of the day to travel, and to carry goods, not counting the fact that the rivers were also potentially a source of food. Although there can be no absolute certainty, it is quite feasible that the local inhabitants used a coracle type vessel to travel along the waterways, and from which they could fish, but whatever kind of boat used, it would have enabled them to navigate through the forest to areas we now know as Wick to the north, Saltford or Bath in the east, Hanham and beyond to the west, bearing in mind that at that time the River Avon was certainly tidal right up to Saltford.

From the crossing point, the road continued through what are now the parishes of Bitton; Oldland; Hanham, and St George along a very similar route taken by today's A431 Bath Road, although the direction then taken by the road on its way to Sea Mills is uncertain. It has been suggested in some quarters, that the A4175 Cherry Garden Road was built on the line of Roman Road that ran northward to join the Bath to Cirencester road but there does not appear to be any firm evidence to support this view. To start with there would seem little strategic need for the Romans to build such a road, and its meanderings would just not seem to be their style. With the Roman roads built almost two thousand years ago, there is probably a general acceptance of their existence with little or no regard given as to how the Romans managed to survey the direction of their roads so well. If for a moment we pause upon the construction of just a small section of the road from say Bath to Hanham, how did they ensure that the road ended up in the right spot, how did they prevent the alignment drifting out of line and being miles off course at its termination, particularly when we have to bear in mind the fact that they had to climb over the lower end of the southern Cotswolds, cope with deep valleys, whilst at the same time having their view obscured by a forest covered land. It has been suggested that the military engineers had a team of surveyors who walked over a given stretch of land through which the proposed road was to travel, and by treating each hillock or rise in the ground as a focal point, they lit bonfires on those high points. However, logic would dictate that such a practise would only visually connect one high spot with another, there would be no guarantee that this alignment meant that the plan for the road was going in the correct direction, and it presumes that the surveyors on the other hill actually had a clear direct view of the fire and its location; as basing a survey on the vagaries of rising smoke would not have given the Romans the accuracy they required. Without doubt the Romans must have used surveyors of one description or another, together with some form of mapmakers, so that the surveyed land, and the proposed route could be drawn. In such a way any apparent anomalies in the route could be rectified before the construction work started: in addition it would seem inconceivable that their roads were constructed to the obvious standard they were, without the Romans having instruments of one kind or another to help them in their task.

Apart from the line of the *Via Julia,* little evidence remains of the Roman occupation, but tantalising snippets of confirmation that they were here have been discovered by the finding of Roman tiles and pottery, when a well was being dug in the early 1800's at Castle Inn Farm (Hanham), whilst during 1836, at a site in Oldland Bottom, coins showing the head of Emperor *Valentinian,* and coins of Emperor *Arcadius* were found. More recently in 1954, a large hoard of coins depicting the head of the Roman Emperor, *Constantine* were discovered in the Greenbank Road area of Hanham, whilst during the construction in 1992/93 of the ring road, the remains of a Roman Farmhouse were found at Stonehill. These discoveries, with the exception of the farmhouse, do not automatically mean that the Romans established any long-term civilian habitation in the area covered by the book, and in the main it may have been that the Roman presence was restricted to small military camps or guard posts. That said, across the River Avon there once stood, on the outskirts of what is now Keynsham, a substantial Roman Villa [see my book *Around Keynsham*] and therefore it is just possible that there is one or more such villas to be discovered in and around the Oldland-Bitton area.

Habitation, and the cultivation of the land of one kind or another, certainly existed in this area if for no other reason than it emanates from the study of etymology. Here we have a name that by itself stands alone by saying "old land", and begs the question why should our forefathers have given such a name to a parcel of land if it had only just been won from the forest. Although Oldland is only one name to consider, it is possibly the oldest denomination in the locality, possibly stretching back three to four thousand years, and continuing through the cultural changes of the Roman and the Anglo-Saxon invasions. However, by the logic of etymology, the name could not have been given to the area that far back, and it may well be that the epithet did not come into circulation until the Roman period or, more probably, during the time of the Anglo-Saxons. Certainly by the middle of the eleventh century it is recorded that *Aldeland* was held by *Alfwy* a man of Earl Harold.

It is well recorded that in 1066, Harold lost the Battle of Hastings, and Anglo-Saxon England came partially under the rule of the victorious Normans, headed by William I, although the victory was not as complete as many people think, as it has been said that despite the well told story of Harold being killed by an arrow through his eye, Harold almost certainly survived the battle, and probably conducted an unsuccessful form of guerrilla warfare over the next four or five years. However, in due course the resistance against the Normans failed and when he eventually began his reign and called himself king, William proved to be one of the most able monarchs ever to rule these islands, despite the continued in-fighting and intrigue created by the Barons and Knights who surrounded and occupied his Court. To try and counter-act these problems, and to help raise money needed to pay for loyalty, and to be able to put down the rebellious lords, William required a written record to be made that would establish who owned what, and who held great wealth in the form of large manors, whole villages and many acres of land, as well as gold and silver. Exerting his considerable political power and his undoubted formidable will, William arranged, during 1085, to have those necessary records prepared for the whole of the country, and that once produced they would be kept in a great book to be known as the Domesday Book. Considering the amount of work to be undertaken, and the amount of land and countryside to be covered, it seems quite remarkable that the Domesday Book was completed within two years of the records being started.

From this valuable source of information it can be determined, with reasonable certainty, that there existed at the time of the survey a Manor House at Aldeland, as the area is described as consisting of 2 hides, ~ which equates to around 30 acres ~ farmed by the under tenant, plus there was 1 villager ~ a class of peasant with little land of his own ~ with one plough. In addition 2 slaves ~ landless villagers ~ lived there amongst a further ten acres of meadowland. By any standard a small area, that probably consisted of no more than 40 persons, including women and children, but sufficiently important enough to be included in the records. In addition to these details, the Domesday Book also states "the Bishop of Exeter holds Aldeland". The Very Reverend Osbern, Bishop of Exeter was, before the Conquest, a Norman Chaplain of Edward the Confessor, a rather unusual relationship for a Norman to be chaplain to an Anglo-Saxon king, but Edward had many close ties with Normandy, and was most certainly less belligerent with his relatives across the English Channel than his successor. No doubt motivated by a strong desire for self preservation, Osbern was quite prepared to use as much subterfuge and guile as necessary to ingratiate himself into the Court of William, and before long he had become a favourite of, and Chaplain to the new king.

At this time the forest of Kingswood covered an area of approximately eighteen square miles, extending beyond St George and the environs east of Bristol, and for a considerable distance along the southern side of the River Avon to Brislington. To the north of the river, the forest occupied the present parishes of Hanham; Oldland and Bitton, and may well have also covered Mangotsfield on its way to Pucklechurch. It is therefore possible to imagine Oldland, and some of the other localities covered by this book, as they may have been during the eleventh and twelfth centuries, as a somewhat remote clearing in a vast forest, where few outsiders would willingly venture without the risk of becoming lost or robbed or both, and where the King and his Barons either separately or together would, from time to time, hunt not only the beasts of the forest, but also those who dared trespass in the King's Wood, or even worse poach the King's deer, and such an image might equally apply to the thirteenth and fourteenth centuries. Scattered throughout the forest, at this time, there would be clearings of cultivated land for crops, mainly root vegetables, but also for growing oats or barley, and an even smaller piece of land for a tethered goat, whilst nearby groups of pigs would be allowed to roam the forest undergrowth in a constant search for food. No doubt attached to these family communities would be a pack of dogs, whose reward for being fed scraps of meat, would be to guard and protect the community and their livestock from the less friendly inhabitants of the forest. Either within the clearing, or at its edge, smoke would rise continuously from a wood or furze fire situated in the centre of a one-room hovel built, in some cases with the local pennant stone, but quite often the outer walls consisted of no more than wattle and daub. If he was lucky, the head occupier may have had a small strip of land adjacent to or close to his property, in which he may have had permission from the Lord of the Manor, to grow food for himself and his family, but without any real satisfactory way of preserving foodstuffs, the greatest difficulty of all was to bridge the mid winter months, both for his family, his master and his animals. Within the property, the only light available would have been from the fire that constantly produced clouds of smoke, which despite the many holes and gaps in the structure, hung in layers at head height, and permeated every nook and cranny with its smells whilst depositing a thin layer of soot as it passed. The household may have been sufficiently lucky to possess a straw or more likely a bracken bed, laid on bare earth, and to own a few cooking pots, and wooden platters, a knife or two, and possibly a wooden bench made of unprepared timber from the forest floor and held together with twine or natural creepers. There may also have been an important small area reserved for their animals, as by having such creatures in the house at night, especially a winters night, meant that the humans could share in, and benefit from the warmth provided by the animals although, no doubt, it did little for their own personal hygiene or aroma. Because of the difficulty in having the means to light a fire the family would, wherever possible, keep the fire burning endlessly, although it may at times have been little more than glowing embers of the wood or furze used as fuel. Whether or not they knew of the existence of the local sea-coal; this being the name given to outcrops of coal showing through the forest floor, and its capacity to be used as an alternative fuel can only be speculated upon, but if they did they were unlikely to have risked the wrath of the King or his Sheriff, as everything in the forest belonged to him, and they were not entitled to share in the forest's bounty.

During the hot dry summer months, the air would have been filled not only with the fragrance of the carpets of woodland flowers, but also with a dull red dust, churned up from the local sandstone, which would quickly turn to a red mud whenever it rained. Parts of the forest would have represented open heath land, whilst in other parts, the trees were so thick as to be almost impenetrable, but most of the forest would have consisted of broad leaf English oaks, which spread their majestic boughs over the forest floor, allowing dapple shade to filter through, plus a mixture of tall elm trees, beach, sycamore, elder, hawthorn, and many other varieties, no doubt interspersed with crab apple, walnut and hazel, whilst along the banks of the various rivers and streams there would be an abundance of willow. Within the forest lived the red squirrel, the red and fallow deer, wolves and foxes, wild boar, whilst the waterways would have been home to many otters, water voles, and such other creatures. This was not to say that the forest had all its own way, and well-worn broad paths had been established over the centuries that enabled travellers to pass through the area on their way from places such as Lawford's Gate (Bristol's exit/entrance to or from the east) to Chippenham, or to the monastery at Wynchcombe, or more locally from Bitton through Oldland to the Manor of Gee Moor. This later route certainly existed in medieval times and preceded the present course of Barry Road, as just north of the nursery gardens there exists earthworks which once consisted of up to three concentric banks and ditches enclosing a central area which was probably used for rounding up, and enclosing cattle.

As mentioned above, Bishop Osbern held Aldeland albeit for how long after 1087 is not known, although it could have been for the next ten or fifteen years. After that we have to rely upon Sir Robert Atkyne who in his book *"The Ancient and Present State of Gloucestershire"* first published in 1712, the Manor of Aldeland did afterwards belong to the Damavels, and afterwards to the Mores by marriage of one of the co-heiresses of the Damavel family. Richard de la More became Lord of the Manor as a result of this marriage, which he held from King Edward I, [1272-1307] by service of half a Knight's fee. Upon Richard's death his son Thomas held the Manor, and later Edward I knighted him. Almost certainly Thomas spent most of his time away from Aldeland ~ occasionally during this period of our history variably spelt Eldeland ~ as it is recorded that Thomas lived in the Court of Edward II [1307-1327] and, wrote a "faithful history" of the life and death of that king. It is most likely that Thomas died two years after his beloved king, as by 1329 the Lord of the Manor is shown to be Stephen de la More. Whether this Stephen was the son of Thomas, or a younger brother, or some other relative is not clear, but whatever was the relationship, Stephen appears to have remained Lord of the Manor until around 1341 when, the ownership of the manor changed to a Walter de la More. Although there is no way of determining how Walter obtained his wealth, he was most certainly a man of substance as, not only did he hold Oldland, he also held the Manor of Upton, plus around one hundred acres of Kingswood Forest. In 1350, his son John succeeded Walter to the title, and as far as we can tell, John was the last of the de la Mores to own that privilege. As can be seen from the above, this one family owned the Manor of Oldland for the best part of a century, during which time England had gone through a very dangerous, turbulent and decadent period, when not a single decade passed without Englishmen either being at each others throats or at war with the French, the Welsh or the Scots. How such major events impacted upon the inhabitants of Oldland is not recorded, and it is quite feasible that for many of the hardworking peasants, with their own personal worries taking precedence over their daily lives, the events in the world beyond their imagination probably just passed them by. No doubt they paid heavier taxes, and suffered from the lack of food, adequate clothing, and unsanitary living conditions. In addition they may well have seen some of the fittest of the young men taken off, never to return, or ultimately dumped back into the community with broken bodies and minds but after all, what is new, life has always been hard and unfair particularly for the under privileged.

Some time during the second half of the fourteenth century, the ownership of the manor was in the hands of Nicholas de Berkeley, but his ownership would appear to have been short lived as by 1397, Sir John Denerofe had the privilege, together with forty acres of arable and pasture land in Oldland, within the Manor of Bitton. This may well be the first indication that the village of Oldland was becoming defined, and that the Warmley Brook was being used as the boundary marker between Bitton and Oldland. To understand the significance of this information, it is necessary to remember that Oldland Common is not in the Parish of Oldland but in the Parish of Bitton, and thus all earlier references to the Manor of Oldland must place the building and the land to the west of the Warmley Brook in say the area now known as Longwell Green, rather than in or around the village which is in the Parish of Bitton. Thus Sir John owned the Manor House and land possibly in the area of the large roundabout near to the *Butchers Arms*, although it might just as easily have been in Willsbridge close to the existing *Queen's Head*, or it could have occupied the land around the High Street/West Street area of Oldland Common. We will never be certain of the exact location of Sir John's property, as already in the fourteenth century, Oldland was being identified as two distinct areas.

Apart from the above identification of the Lords of the Manor, there was a further level of hierarchy to be considered, but first it should be understood that despite the original existence of a Norman King and a Norman Court, these estates had gradually become subject to the Anglo-Saxon law of "Frankpledge", a system where each male member of a tithing ~ an area containing ten free families ~ was responsible for the good behaviour of every other member of the community. A Court Leet was held once or twice a year by the steward of the Manor to consider petty crimes, and to inflict whatever punishment was considered necessary. Because the Manor of Oldland had become attached, during the early part of the twelfth-century, to the Manor of Bitton, and therefore the Bitton estates, it had also indirectly become part of the Barony of Berkeley. Now the Barony was itself subject to the control of the superior Lords, the Earls of Gloucester, and thus down through the complex chain of ownership, Oldland became part of the Earl's estates and subject to their jurisdiction.

Henry II held the Oldland honour of Frankpledge as part of the honour of Gloucester, which he then sold to Geoffrey de Mandeville, Earl of Essex. By the time of Edward III, the honour had passed to the Earl of Stafford, but almost certainly all of this ownership was solely on paper, with the monarch or the earls taking little if any interest in the land they owned, and probably if asked would have had difficulty in identifying the exact location of the manors. The Stafford family interest in Oldland came to a sudden and violent end when, on the 21st July 1403 Edmund, Earl of Stafford, was killed on the battlefield of Shrewsbury and, being on the losing side, his advantage was passed on, by Royal decree, to the Duke of Buckingham, whose family held the honour for almost the next one hundred and twenty years. However, in 1521, the then Duke of Buckingham, Edward Stafford, overstepped the mark once too often and was beheaded for High Treason and, as a consequence, all of his estates were forfeited to the Crown. Twenty-six years later, further intrigue, rumour and counter rumour had enabled the Court, and in particular the King to kiss and make-up, as in 1547, Edward VI restored all of the estates back to Edward Stafford's son and heir Henry, and the honour remained in that family until 1776, when the whole honour of Gloucester was sold to Edward, Duke of Norfolk for £24,000, ~ probably equivalent to around £10m in today's figures. As for the inhabitants of Oldland, during this four hundred and fifty year period of their history, they probably lived and died, generation upon generation without having the slightest knowledge that the land on which they toiled and from which they obtained their meagre living had been changing hands in such circumstances or for such fortunes.

Whilst all of the above events were acted well away from Oldland and the knowledge of most if not all of its inhabitants, there was still a manor to be run and controlled, and a lord and master to rule over them. Sir John Denerofe had acquired the Manor of Oldland around 1397, and appears to have held the seat for over twenty years, as by 1419 the ownership had passed to the Wykes, and from that family, via Edward Colthurst, to the Weston family who were then residing at Weston Court, now a very attractive farmhouse just off the Bath Road on the right, as you leave the village for North Common. This was an old and well-established family with connections not only with Oldland but also additionally with Bitton, as well as owning Hanham Hall. The Weston name appears in the Subsidy Rolls, and as early as 1238, a Weston was the Mayor of Bristol.

Historical records tend to concentrate upon the rich and wealthy, and by using their financial influence stories were quite often manipulated for their benefit or the benefit of their family, after all who would listen to the little man who probably could not read or write, and was insufficiently eloquent to speak up for himself.

Accordingly when a small snippet of information becomes available, it can provide a fascinating insight into a minute section of the life of someone whose history would normally have been forgotten. For this reason it is interesting to record at this stage the fact that a Will of one of Oldland's lesser residents, a certain Thomas Smyth, has survived the ravages of time. In his Will, which is dated March 1559, Thomas instructs his Executors to arrange for his burial to take place in the church yard of St Mary the Virgin, Bitton, and that a few shillings be given to the mother church in Gloucester. In addition, he left his *"best crock and broche"* to his son, a flock bed to his daughter, with the residue of his estate to go to his wife Jane. Thomas died in July 1559. Not a great deal of information, but at least we are able to surmise that Thomas was a religious educated man, who could read and write, and as such he could have been a craftsman, although as there is no mention of any tools in the Will, it is more likely that he was a scribe, or clerk. He was certainly not wealthy, but was probably much better off than those who toiled the land, and with his Will having survived for over five hundred years, he has inadvertently opened a small window into his existence.

Not long after Thomas's death in 1571 the Parish Register of births, deaths and marriages began with the first entry, under the general heading "Weddinges," of the marriage of **John Britten** and **Jane Burnell** the service having taken place in St Mary's on the 26th day of June 1571. They appear to be the only couple to have married in the parish during that year, which is perhaps indicative of the size of the population at that time, as even in the following year only two couples, namely **John Henry** and **Marye Strange** on the 3rd May and **Daniell Lane** and **Elsabethe Russell** on the 18th September were married. In comparison, **Annes Britten; Bartholemew Rymer; John Harding; Roger Harding, Byttrice Tibbett, and Robert Gifferie** were all christened during 1572, with there also being four burials during that year.

During 1652, the Manor was sold for £1,854.10.0 (probably around £0.75m in today's terms) to Richard Jones, who also owned Burnt House, better known to us as Londonderry Farm at West Hanham. However by the time of Richards's death in 1697, the estate had been reduced in size with many of its component parts having been sold in a piecemeal fashion, and now consisted of just 15 messuages, 10 gardens and orchards, 300 acres of heath land with common pasture for cattle, plus 200 acres of pasture and wood, and 100 acres of meadow land, well under one thousand acres in total.

In his book published in 1712, Sir Robert Atkyne states that, in the whole of the Parish of Bitton, which includes both villages of Bitton and Oldland, there were probably no more than 320 habitable houses, with about 1,150 residents of whom 37 were freeholders. Although Atkyne provides no specific date for the above information, in a subsequent paragraph, he sets out ~ as reproduced below ~ the details of the tax paid during the first half of the 1690's, and therefore, it is probably safe to assume that the population figures given relate to a similar period in time.

In 1692, Oldland paid £89.6.0 [£89.30 or around £36,000 in present day values] in tax to the Royal Aid, an amount that represented about twenty-five per cent of the total paid by the whole parish.

Two years later in 1694, the amount paid, in what was then called Land Tax, was £116.15 6 [£115.77 or around £46,300 at today's values] this being thirty per cent of the parish total. In addition, the inhabitants also had to pay £27 towards the hated Poll Tax, which for the whole parish amounted to around £100, or approximately £3 per household. By today's standards this would seem to be an insignificant charge to pay, but at that time the £3 probably represented between one-eighth to one tenth of the gross income of each household, perhaps equivalent of between £2,500-3,000 at current levels.

By studying the various tax statistics of the 1690's, it is reasonable to calculate that the village of Oldland had, at that time, a population of around 310 persons living in around 85-90 dwellings. What makes this calculation even more interesting is that, when referring to Weston Court, Atkyne notes that, at the time the seat passed from Nicholas de Weston to John Weston, during the reign of Henry VI, there were 90 houses in Oldland, thus it would appear that for some 250 years to the turn of the eighth century, Oldland as a village remained virtually unchanged in size.

Before moving on, it is perhaps worthwhile pausing to consider the details of two other local Wills, which have fortunately survived the ravages of time and which open for us a small window into the lives of two ordinary folk who lived in Oldland during the seventeenth century. On the 16th November 1670, **William Corbett** the Elder, prepared his last Will and Testament, describing himself as a *"hysbandman"* [farmer] of Oldland, and within the context of the local community, was probably regarded by his contemporaries as being reasonably wealthy. William lived for a further eight years or so before he died in January 1679, and after the Will had been used for probate it was shown that he left his son, also called William, the sum of 1/- [0.05p] together with one great leather girdle with a great brass buckle. In addition he also bequeathed that both **Arthur Hathaway** and **Robert Briant** ~ his overseers ~ should each receive 1/-, as a token of his love, and to enable them to each buy a pair of gloves. As far as the rest of William's property was concerned he left his goods and chattels, plus his cattle, but no mention of there being any further money, to his widow Mary.

Six years after William had prepared his Will, **Pointz Fox,** a coal driver, penned on the 28th October 1676 his last Will and Testament. In it he left all of his wearing apparel and a new piece of cloth containing 3.5 yards of material to his son **Poyntz,** for the making of a suit of clothes. In addition, he also left his son four dishes of pewter, a pewter flagon, a brass clock, and £14 of lawful money, for his use when he takes up an apprenticeship. He then provided for his trustees, **Nicholas Lad** of Acton, and **Reuben Smith** of Oldland, bequeathing to them the sum of 3/- each as a token of his love, and to enable them to buy a pair of gloves. Finally to his wife, Pointz left the residue of his estate, which probably allowed her to become a fairly wealthy widow. At the time that the Will was made, Poyntz Fox was around eleven years of age, and whilst we do not know exactly when his father died, it is probably reasonable to presume that Poyntz Jnr. used the material and money wisely, as we are able to determine that he subsequently married a young lady by the name of Joane, who was some three years younger, and that they lived together until 1732 when, on the 14th February he died and was buried in the churchyard of St Mary Bitton. Joane outlived her husband by thirty years, dying at the ripe old age of ninety-four on the 28th February 1762. As far as can be determined, this couple had at least one child, whom they christened Robert, but neither he or the subsequent generation developed the longevity of his parents, as he died on the 29th September 1739 aged 44, whilst his children, Robert and Elizabeth died aged thirty and nineteen respectively. It will be noted in both Wills, that money was left to a non-family beneficiary for the specific purpose of buying gloves. At present, exactly why such a legacy should be included is something of a mystery, but obviously gloves in the late seventeenth century must have been highly regarded.

It is believed that the ancient Manor House of Oldland once stood on a site overlooking the unmade road that currently leads down to the Willsbridge Mill, but unfortunately its exact location has not been pin pointed. However, it is known that a **Thomas Trye**, who continued to own the property until 1726, when, under an Act of Parliament, he was given permission to sell the whole estate to a Mr. K. Webley of London, originally purchased the house and estate back in 1697. Subsequently, around 1758 the estate passed to Webley's widowed daughter, and in turn she decided to sell the house and land to **James Emerson,** a brass and spelter maker of Hanham who retained the manor until 1803 when it was sold to **Samuel Whittuck.**

Kelston

Approximately three and one half miles from Bath, and almost at the most southerly tip of the Cotswolds, Kelston developed as an important staging post on what was by the tenth century or thereabouts, the main road between that city and its port neighbour Bristol, bearing in mind that the original Roman road joining these two cities and known as the *Via Julia* had probably been abandoned or allowed to degenerate into little more than a trackway by the 6th/7th century. With the lower route, [through what is now Saltford and Keynsham] for most of its length running alongside a river, subject to the vagaries of tides as well as being prone to flooding, and thus frequently making it impassable, left the traveller between these two cities with the more difficult, but normally drier and seasonally longer opened route over the foothills. The horse was, of course, the main source of transport power and accordingly it meant that our equine servants needed to be used as economically as possible, and thus, when they reached Kelston from whichever direction they had taken, the animals would need to be rested from the effects of a long climb. More often than not the horses attached to the vehicle, would be provided with an extra pair of fresh trace horses to assist with the climb, and even if the main animals continued, the trace horses would be taken off to await their next job. Whilst these actions of our forefathers may seem to be very considerate and humane, it was more likely that they were not undertaken with those thoughts in mind, it was just simply a matter of financial expediency, and no doubt many a horse reached the top of the hill with open wounds on its back and rump from the excessive use of the whip. Being as it is, the highest point on the road, Kelston could easily have had an enormous drawback to its very existence if it was not for the fact that several springs exist within the Lansdown Hill that proudly looks down over the cluster of properties that make up the community, and as the water from those springs gradually unite into a brook known as Combesbrook, an adequate and necessary supply of water for both man and beasts existed at Kelston.

Exactly when Kelston, or to give it its earlier titles of, Henstridge, then Kalveston before becoming Kelweston, first developed is not known, but it is suspected that it existed as possibly a clearing in the forest during the Roman occupation. Notwithstanding the existence of the Romans, and the fact that they built roads, it should be noted that the *Via Julia* bypassed the site of the present village of Kelston as it instead climbed up from Weston towards Kelston Tump and onto North Stoke. Thus, apart from the possibility of there being the odd rough stone and timber built dwelling scattered around, no real or established development, or cultivation of the land appears to have taken place during the first five hundred years or so of the new millennium, when the area would most likely have been inhabited by the ancient Britons. Towards the end of the second decade of the sixth century the area covered by this book was beginning to be infiltrated by an invasion of people from the east, as more and more Saxons, no doubt with a goodly sprinkling of Angles and Jutes came in their hundreds and commandeered the fertile land, and dominated the population. In 519, the kingdom of West Saxons was established under King Cerdie, who had defeated the British King Arthur at Chard, and whilst such a significant matter in our history probably passed Kelston by, for the original denizens the changes would almost certainly have gradually engulfed them as a tide engulfs a beach. As in all communities, some would have strongly resisted the imposed changes, whilst others would have been more philosophical and accepted the inevitable. What can be inferred by subsequent events is that in Kelston, and the much wider surrounding area, there was, by the local Britons, a great deal of resistance to these upstart foreigners who were pushing their uninvited way in, bringing upset, confusion and chaos into their stable society, and as such not only were they different to the locals, they additionally had a different language and culture. These broad, but nevertheless, very important differences of opinion and lifestyle, as well as the aggressive nature of both sets of people, came to a head quite locally in 577 when a decisive battle took place between the Britons and the Saxons a few miles away at a place called Derham [Dyrham]. This was however not just a local squabble but a major battle which would determine whether the Britons were to live in their homeland, or be forced to give up all that they cherished and move elsewhere, and so important was the outcome that a number of independent British kingdoms came from afar to stand together shoulder to shoulder on the field of battle. Cealwin, the third king of the West Saxons, led the Saxon armies, and such was his superiority that at least three British kings were killed fighting for the survival of their race, and with their death went a nation, leaving the Saxons free to control of the whole West Saxon area.

As the dust settled, and old hatreds faded with the passage of time, Christianity came to Kelston, and in due course the Saxons constructed, at the western extremity of the village, a church for their settlement. There is no record describing this church, which may well have been a simple construction of wood, as it was not until the later part of the thirteenth century before a more permanent building was constructed of stone, with a nave, chancel and a tower, dedicating the church to St Nicholas. As far as is known, this building, or certainly the bulk of it remained with little or no alteration over the following five hundred years, although by the mid nineteenth century, the construction was in serious need of repair. With a typical Victorian arrogance that they could do much better than their predecessors, they set about in 1860 to rebuild well over three-quarters of the church, although they did decide not to interfere too much with the tower. Thus the building we see today is mainly less than one hundred and fifty years old, including the south aisle that is purely a Victorian invention. The whole cost of the reconstruction came to the magnificent amount of £800, and they were able to include a vestry for just £80.

Returning to the history of the village, there appears to be a lacuna of positive records of Kelston for the Norman period, but this does not mean that it had been abandoned by the Saxons, prior to the Norman Conquest, or that it did not exist in the eleventh/twelfth centuries, more likely it was either overlooked, or more probably, the manor was too insignificant for Kelston to be mentioned, particularly with regard to the Domesday Book. The first positive and retained written evidence of Kelston's existence would appear to be the reference in 1293 that it was part of the lands held by Matilda Gifford, the Abbess of the great Abbey of Shaftesbury, and was valued at around £20, but it is difficult to determine from this valuation the size or wealth of Kelston at that time. In the currency of the time, the Manor of Kelston provided the Abbess with an annual pension of thirty marks, and was therefore an important source of her income, but again trying to measure how big or how small the manor was from that information is impossible to do with any form of accuracy. This somewhat cosy arrangement, certainly as far as the Abbey was concerned lasted the best part of three hundred years until Henry VIII decreed around 1547 that the Abbey of Shaftesbury, together with many other religious houses should be dissolved and their lands and property should be redistributed. With the right of Kings, Henry granted the manor together with those of Bath Easton and Katherine (sic) plus the large house known as Katherine's Court to John and Etheldred Malte, however in this instance, Henry was not simply acting as a regal benefactor. Some twelve years or so previously, Henry had been having an adulteress affair with Joanna Dyngley, alias Dobson, and Etheldred had been conceived. Far from abandoning Joanna to cope with a bastard child on her own, she was given a position in Court, and her daughter grew up within that large circle, and no doubt frequently saw her royal father. It is said that Henry had a special love and regard for the child, and ensured that she was well looked after. John Malte was the king's tailor, and was presumably a reasonably educated man, as Henry required John Malte to be not only her guardian, but also he was appointed to ensure that Etheldred should receive a good education to be funded from the income generated by these three estates. Whilst this arrangement continued, Etheldred was regarded as John Malte's daughter, but within three years of the arrangement being implemented, Etheldred was married to John Harrington, a confidential servant to the king, and with this marriage, the name Harrington became synonymous with Kelston, as John and his wife were the first to settle around 1546, in the partially constructed Kelweston House. Over the years, the great house continued to be built and enlarged and it was not until some twenty-eight years later that their son, also named John, had the house finally constructed, with such refinement that it was considered to be a suitable reception for Queen Elizabeth l, who stayed there during a visit to her Godson. As far as is known, this house stood for about two hundred years, eventually being replaced in 1770 by the existing Kelston Park house, which was designed by John Wood the Younger, at the request of the new "Lord of the Manor" Sir Caesar Hawkins, surgeon general to George II. Sir Caesar, and his family stayed at Kelston Park until 1828, when the house and parklands were sold to Joseph Neeld, then the owner of Grittleton Manor in Wiltshire. Subsequently as a most generous act, he gave the whole of the Estate to his newly acquired son-in-law Lieutenant Colonel William Inigo Jones, as a wedding present. The new owner of Kelston Park, was obviously extremely happy with his new prize, and during his occupation, he became a wonderful benefactor to the village, paying for a school house to be built in 1863, on the site of the old Dower House constructed in 1686 for the Harrington matriarch, and in addition, he also had a number of cottages built and/or restored in the village for estate workers. The particular cottages, which were built and/or restored, can still be identified by the plaque high on the front of the building that shows the initials **IJI**, with the central J wrapped around by the letter A, this being the monogram of Anna-Maria Inigo-Jones, wife of the said Lieutenant Colonel. The village school remained open until around 1922 when Mrs Minnie Walters, the last of the village schoolmistresses retired.

Although, hundreds, if not thousands of people pass through the village today, this has not always been so, and certainly prior to World War Two, its isolation, and inaccessibility meant that it had remained a parochial backwater, with its own village Post Office, its own village police officer, its own lock-up, its own Inn, and its own village shop. Surprisingly, the original Inn was not on today's main road, but was situated in a lovely thatched cottage, now known as *"Tatters,"* and situated towards the bottom of Church Road. After the "*Old Crown Inn*" was created from, it is believed, a rank of old cottages, built during the eighteenth century, and thought not worthy of restoration to habitable conditions, the *"Cock Inn"* closed, and a small part of that building was used for many years as the village post office, before the post office was transferred to number 12 Bath Road. Nearby at number 9 lived the village bobby, who was responsible for the upkeep and maintenance of the village lock-up, also situated on the main road, whilst the shop formed part of house number 15. Overlooking the main road is an impressive tower that forms an integral part of *"Tower House,"* built, it is believed, around 1838 on the site of an earlier house once owned by the Harrington family. The London architect, James Thomson, on behalf of the Estate's owner, Joseph Needs, designed this new house, although, with his estate in Wiltshire, it is doubtful that Joseph ever intended living in that house, more likely he had it designed and built as dower house, ie one where the widow of the Lord of the Manor would live, once her son had taken over his father's position; it could also of course be used to house "unwanted mothers-in-law." Whatever the purpose behind its construction, a great deal of money was spent on the building of the house, with a corbelled staircase around the outside of the tower, a well equipped coach house and stables, and the extensive formal gardens that were seen at their best from the height advantage afforded by the tower.

During the 1840's a gentleman who gave himself the pseudonym "The Church Goer" wrote a number of articles describing his unannounced visits to particular churches in the area, including St Nicholas, and set out below is an extract of the composition he penned on that occasion:

"Kelston is situated on the old upper Bath and Bristol road, about four miles from the former and eight from the latter. The little village itself consists of a group of cottages, with rose-covered fronts and rustic porches. It is very beautifully situated, and, since the opening of the railway has left it to itself, it has a quiet secluded air. Upon my arrival, I asked a heavy lout of a boy, who was leaning his shoulder against the wall, and chewing a long straw in a kind of cloddish rumination, the road to the church. ~ "Go down there," ~ said he, pointing to an ill-kept lane, ~ "and turn to the right."

I did as I was bid; I went down the lane and turned to my right, but my right was not the boy's right, as he then stood, so after describing a semicircle, and walking nearly a quarter of a mile, I found myself back again in the village, but with no Church in view. There was, however, a woman with young girls sitting in the doorway of a cottage close by, and literally under their own vine, and to this patriarchal family I now applied for information.

"The Church sir?" repeated the woman, "This young girl is going close to it, and will show you the way." The girl at once rose and civilly offered her services. "Thank you, child said I as we walked together along the main road. I asked her one or two questions about the parish and the village including, "Have you got any schools?" "Yes" she said, "there's one for girls; it is kept in the Post office, opposite the Crown, mayhap you noticed it; it's a charity school." "Is there not one for boys also," I enquired. "There's just a few boys and they be taught by the Dean in his back kitchen." With that I was about to pass the entrance to a little lane when the girl said, ~ "There's the Church sir," pointing down the lane. As I turn to thank her, I saw the girl disappear into the gateway of a house, which denied me the opportunity of saying Good-bye."

Understandably the community was close-knit, and with the benefit of hindsight and rose tinted glasses, idealistic, but their semi isolation had its drawbacks and of course it's numerous hardships. Although one or two of the more wealthy residents had, after the First World War, purchased their own in-house generators, the bulk of the villagers were still having to cook on open fires, possibly in some instances upgraded to a coal fired range, and to use candles, or possibly oil lamps to provide them with light, as it was not until the mid 1950's that mains electricity reached the village. As useful as the electricity was, it was simply not financially viable to go out to Bath or Bristol, and purchase all the available electrical appliances, and thus it was many years before all of the villagers reaped the benefit of this twentieth-century power. Even then the village was inadequately supplied by spring water mainly channelled down from springs that surfaced on the Mill farm hill, and the luxury of having flush toilets in village houses was not made available until the introduction of mains water and sewerage in 1974, despite Sir John Harrington's invention of the water closet back in the sixteenth century here in Kelston his home village,

Kelston Mills

With Kelston some one hundred and fifty feet or more above the level of the River Avon a small outpost needed to be constructed if the power of the water was to be harnessed, although it must be pointed out that the idea to build a water mill at this place did not come from the residents of Kelston, but from the Warmley based entrepreneur William Champion whose desire to produce copper, and in particular copper implements such as pots and pans drove him to study the river and to see how much use he could make of it. With the river having, in the early eighteenth century, been made much more navigable with the construction of weirs, locks and by-pass channels, Champion decided in the late 1750's that a battery mill could be erected on the River Boyd at Bitton, with a second battery mill being built two miles away at a point where the weir from Saltford reached the opposite bank, and thus was created Kelston Mills. Mr Champion had carried out his survey well, noting that there was a supply of natural building materials in the form of local sandstone, and this was used, together with "imported" bricks, brought in by barge, to build a copper forge, workshops, storage space, plus other buildings, including at least two annealing furnaces, from which stood two large chimneys ~ still extant today ~ and four or five watercourses. Because of the isolation of the site, Champion also had constructed no less than eleven cottages for the workmen to stay on site, and to keep production going twenty-four hours a day.

Although originally intended to work copper, the mill is probably best known for the production of brass sheets, as certainly it was used as a brass battery well into the 1840's. By the latter part of the nineteenth century, Kelston Mills had a distinct air of dilapidation about it, but its one farm was trying to keep going, by providing basic food products, mostly milk, cheese and some meat, and by occasionally stabling horses used to pull the barges between Bristol and Bath. In addition it also operated an extremely important ferry, for those very same animals, as it was at this point along the river where the towpath changed banks, and thus it was necessary to ship horses across from one side to the other. The shallow flat boat was pulled across the river by a chain that was fixed at both banks, and connected to the ferry at both ends. As far as is known the pulling power was simply the ferryman's own personal strength, and it is believed that passengers would be accommodated from time to time, although in due course a smaller passenger ferry was introduced, which either sculled or rowed across. The struggle for survival continued well into the twentieth century, not helped by the ongoing deterioration of the old mill, a significant reduction in the need to convey horses from one side of the river to the other, and a gradual reduction in the number of passengers all culminating in a situation whereby Kelston Mill, in more ways than one, ended up as something of a backwater,

North Stoke

North Stoke's existence may well be due to the construction of the *Via Julia* but it was probably a place of habitation for many years before the arrival of the Roman Legions as, being in the location it is, this small area would have been an ideal place to hide from forest constables and any other undesirables, tucked away as it is from prying eyes, and yet, this elevated piece of ground makes a perfect place to keep a good lookout for those who may be after you, or a perfect place to watch for those who might end up as your victim. Just to the east of the present village there is the remnants of an Iron Age fort, quite often referred to as *Little Down Fort*, whilst a little to the north of the fort there are earthworks that appear to date back to around 5-600 BC. All too often our Iron Age ancestors are conceived as being no better than unintelligent primitive people, who wandered around in a totally nomadic fashion. However, this is an unfair image of these people who were intelligent, dexterous, and courageous as well as being skilful farmers. Although there is evidence of their Celtic existence, what is uncertain is for how long they inhabited the area, and whether or not they were living in and around the existing parish of North Stoke when the Romans arrived. We know that the Romans were there by the evidence of the *Via Julia*, and we know that in due course they settled, as both Roman burials and villas have been unearthed, but whether there was a battle fought as the Celts tried to hold onto their commandeered land, and that they were subsequently conquered, or whether they were appeased in one form or another and subsequently integrated into Roman society as serfs or slaves, will now never be known.

What is known with a great degree of certainty is that North Stoke began its existence long before its Kelston neighbour, but nevertheless would still have been affected by the fighting which took place between the original inhabitants and the invading Angles and Saxons as described in the earlier section. However, with some of the surrounding deforested land producing excellent pasture and fine hay, whilst other land still produced good timber, a manor had been established by around the seventh/eighth century. It is possible that around this time, with Christianity sweeping over the country, that the first church was built in the village during the eighth century, Kenulf, [also spelt Cynewulf] king of the West Saxons in this part of Mercia, presented the manor of North Stoke to the Benedictine monks of Bath, it having previously been held by his sovereign King Offa, the very same king who had been responsible for the construction of the dyke that helped separate Wales from England, and king of the whole of Mercia. It is possible that the monks retained possession of the manor for the next three hundred years, even though the manor does not appear to be recorded in the Domesday Book. However, sometime during the eleventh century there was a claim that the manor had changed hands, having been acquired by a sufficiently powerful family that caused them to either adopt or change their identity to the name of the manor. So strong or so impertinent was the claim that, as so often happens with land ownership disputes, in 1121 the matter ended up in Court, in front of John the Bishop of Bath.

The main protagonist was Modbert de Stoke, who claimed that he had the right to be regarded as the Lord of the Manor, having married the daughter of Grenta de Stoke, who had been the previous Lord of the Manor by hereditary rights, and that the manor of North Stoke, and its title, formed part of the dowry brought by his bride to the wedding table. Despite adding that the ownership of the manor had been in the hands of the de Stoke's family since ancient times, Modbert was unable to supply any or sufficient documentary evidence, or any other proof, to support his claim. No doubt most reluctantly, and we shall never know whether he had a legitimate claim or not, Modbert de Stoke was obliged to give up his claim, leaving the Benedictine monks undisputed owners. To avoid any further claims by the de Stoke family, or any other would-be claimant, the monk's title to the manor was endorsed by Henry I around 1130, and subsequently reaffirmed by King Stephen not long after he came to the throne in 1136.

No further disputes of proprietorship occurred until the suppression of the monasteries, in 1539 when the manor became a Crown Possession until around 1548 when Edward VI granted the manor to William Pauler, to be held on behalf of the Crown, but subsequently during the latter part of the sixteenth century the manor was held by the Earl of Greenwich.

Apart from the conflicts that may well have taken place with the arrival of the advanced guards of the Roman Legions, and the odd encounter over land ownership disputes, North Stoke probably remained a sleepy backwater with history and the outside world passing it by for over fourteen hundred years until July 1643 when it was suddenly and unexpectedly dragged out of its lethargic pastoral existence. During the night of the 4th / 5th July the sleeping villagers were awoken by the passage of the Parliamentary army under the command of Sir William Waller on their way from Bath to the heights of Lansdown. No doubt that which was not already tied down in the village, disappeared during the night, and no doubt little sleep was achieved by the civilians, as the hours past with the continued movement of men, horses and arms. As for the battle itself more will be said later, but with the proximity of the village to the actual battlefield, that days fight between the Royalists and the Parliamentarians could not have passed unnoticed, and it would be surprising if minor skirmishes did not occur in or around the village on that fateful day, to say nothing of the probable treatment of the wounded and dying, and the subsequent plundering of the rich corpses as they lay where they fell.

With the battle over, North Stoke returned to its picturesque sleepy backwater position, where it has in the main been able to remain in a time warp of suspended animation, with the only intrusion coming from the various forms of the internal combustion engine. Visitors stand out as though they are aliens, and fortunately the aggressive hand of twentieth century development has passed this hamlet by, and left it with its attractive old buildings, and marvellous views across the Avon valley, whilst below the rest of the world speeds by.

Despite the above description, it should not be overlooked that for many years, North Stoke was an important agricultural area, supporting a sufficient number of families [the population peaked at around 190 in 1881] for the community to have a school erected in 1833 for no less than forty pupils, although in a relatively short while it became very obvious that the design size of the school had been very much overstated with an average attendance of just fourteen children to be taught by Mrs Elizabeth Blake. Almost certainly there were more than fourteen children of school age in the catchment area, but with no compulsory schooling, many children were kept at home to help out with chores, or even to help out with the family income. Subsequently Mrs Blake left, and was replaced by Miss Louisa Porter, but the economics of keeping a school open for such a small number of children eventually led to its demise, and around 1908, the building closed, and the remaining children were transferred to the school at Upton Cheyney.

Swineford

Swineford, could have just as easily been known to us as Lower North Stoke owing to the fact that it forms part of the parish of North Stoke, almost certainly owes its existence to the simple fact that it was the next location along the River Avon from Saltford, in the direction of the sea, where that river could be conveniently crossed with a reasonable degree of safety, even if it meant that you probably got your feet wet. Before the river was managed by human intervention during the nineteenth century, the Avon was tidal right up to Saltford, and therefore twice a day the flow of water through the countryside we know as Swineford was reduced to little more than that of a village stream, and at Swineford, as at Saltford, it was quite possible for the river to be forded. It is reputed that with the low-lying land frequently flooded by the overflowing river, the land along the river at this point was very marshy and difficult to cultivate, which in turn encouraged wild pigs to congregate in the area. With their continued foraging for food amongst the ground covered vegetation, the animals turned the land along the river into a quagmire of a thick, smelly sticky mud, in which they would revel to their hearts content.

It is also said that in the dim and distant past a local king banished his young son, who went by the name of Bladud, from his court and possibly from his kingdom because he suffered from the dreadful curse of leprosy, and he was shunned by all who came near him for fear that they would catch the disfiguring disease. For a long while, Bladud wandered the countryside in torn rags, hiding from those who would do him harm, scavenging what little food or comfort he could, totally desolate and unwanted. During one long cold winter, Bladud sheltered amongst a herd of pigs that roamed around an area of land adjacent to the river, sharing their food, and at night, without any facilities to make fire, he shared their body warmth as he slept. His illness was not getting any better, and many of the pustular lesions that covered his body would constantly burst and weep, and as the winter changed into spring; it became very obvious that many of the pigs had also caught leprosy. Knowing that it would not be long before the owner of the pigs discovered the unpalatable truth about his sick animals, and the existence of Bladud himself, the prince gathered as much strength his weak body would allow, and began to chase the herd towards and into the river. Whether he intended that the animals, and possibly himself would drown is not clear, but with the tide out, the majority of the pigs, as well as Bladud reached the opposite bank that seemed to consist of a wide expanse of a thick clinging, black mud. Already weak with the leprosy, the exertion of chasing the pigs, and the subsequent wading of the river and the struggle through the embracing mud, the young prince was completely exhausted as he dropped upon the first piece of grass he could find and immediately fell into a deep and long sleep. It is said that pigs are never happier than when they are wallowing in a morass of thick smelly mud, and soon the whole herd was exploring every section of their newfound swine heaven, and with no one to chase them out of the mud they spent many happy days doing what pigs liked best. Eventually, Prince Bladud recovered his senses, and although still feeling extremely debilitated from his illness, and from the lack of nourishment, he began to look along the riverbank for the pigs, some of whom had now exhausted their games in the mud, and were foraging around the adjacent fields looking for grubs, and anything else they fancied. Having gathered together as many as he could, the prince was surprised to notice how healthy they all were, and then realised that those animals that had contracted the leprosy, now appeared to be free of the dreadful disease, and quickly looking at the lesions on his own legs, he was overjoyed to find most of them had stopped weeping and appeared to be getting smaller. And so the healing properties of the mud around the area where the pigs had forded the river became legendary, and the fact that the swineherd had been cured led not only to its fame it also led to its name.

Unfortunately, the Swineford of today is so often seen as a blurred cluster of buildings to traverse, as motorists speed by on their way to and from Bath and in their hurry to reach their destination they tend to overlook the open fields, or the picturesque rank of eighteenth century cottages that include the attractive *Swan Inn*, the sight of Swineford's industrial past, the colour-works; the water-mills; the river traffic, whilst beyond are more cottages, including one that previously was a working ale house known as the "*Old Bath Barge Inn,*" and then, as you are about to leave the village, there is the distinctive metal built Congregational Chapel, built around 1870 as Methodism began to take a much firmer hold on the local community. If you go slowly enough, before you reach the chapel, you might even catch sight of the original milepost hiding in the undergrowth declaring that Bath Town Hall is just 5 miles away. Nevertheless, the hamlet still occasionally floods when the River Avon spills its contents, but for most of the time, the area still retains is rural feel despite the loss of an active farm and its herd of cattle. The pigs have also gone, and so has the marshy land along the riverbank, and so perhaps the claimed healing powers of its mud has also been consigned to the history books and the legends of the past.

Upton Cheyney

As with the other villages mentioned in this book, the origins of Upton Cheyney have never been recorded, or if they were then the details have been lost with the passage of time, all that we are able to do is to make educated guesses and speculate about the probabilities. The land on which the village properties are constructed was once under the sea as a number of marine fossils have been found in and around the existing village. However, if we measure the course of time in hundreds of million years, then ultimately the land rose from the sea and formed the southerly slopes of the Cotswold Hills, which subsequently became part of the Forest of Kingswood, and whilst this does not necessarily mean that the land would have been covered with trees, it is quite possible that trees covered much of the land, particularly the steeper slopes where it would have been more difficult to start cultivating the ground and/or removing the trees. Being within a few miles of each of the other inhabited areas covered by this book, there is likely to be a common history with many similarities, but as far as Upton is concerned no physical evidence has yet been uncovered that would establish beyond reasonable doubt that our ancestors created a pre-Roman settlement in the area of the modern village. Unfortunately, the evidence of Roman habitation is also scant, although it has been suggested from time to time that with a south facing aspect, Upton was an ideal place to grow grapes. Furthermore, with distinct lines of what appears to be south-facing terracing in fields close to North Stoke Lane it has been concluded that the Romans must have planted a vineyard. With a wine drinking army camped a mile or so away at *Trajactus,* plus a number of high ranking civilians living in the surrounding country side, the prospects and desire of a vineyard being established is feasible, but how practical it would be would of course be totally dependant upon local weather conditions, and the skill of the grower. Certainly the suggestion is not that fanciful, especially as vineyards have been re-established in southern England in the recent decades, but as far as Upton is concerned, there is regrettably no positive evidence to support the idea. Similarly, there is no evidence to indicate that Upton and its immediate environs was established by human habitation at the time of the Romans, and thus the terracing may be a natural phenomena and where Upton stands may have just been part of the forest at that time. Alternatively, the Romans might just have established a vineyard and produced wine on those southern slopes above *Trajactus* without the need to create a permanent settlement.

After the Romans left these shores in the fifth century, the country entered what is usually called the Dark Ages, and certainly little if anything is known of that period, but by the time that the Saxons, Angles and Jutes had established themselves in this part of the West Country, the first recorded community at Upton had been constituted, and the name fixed, even though it does not appear in the Domesday record. This may well indicate that the village/manor was too insignificant to warrant inclusion, or it could have been part of a much larger manor, which caused its individual identity to be lost within the records. By the thirteenth century the village formed part of the Barony of Berkeley estate, and was bought in 1350, by a Henry le Chaum, who controlled the estate under the system of "frankpledge" which meant that each group of ten families or tithing, were pledged to act as surety for the peaceful behaviour of the adjoining tithing, or in simple terms, each householder promised to act in a friendly sober manner to his neighbours and would try to ensure that his neighbours acted in a similar fashion. To back up the pledge and the endeavours of the householder, the legalities were regulated by an annually held court-leet, which usually took place in the manor house under the jurisdiction of the Lord of the Manor, or possibly his Steward. This system was not unique to Upton, but applied equally as well to all of the other manors dealt with by this book. It is believed that around this time, ie the second half of the fourteenth century, the name of the village was enlarged to Upton Chaum, and that this title remained in use for some considerable while; however, for reasons which are not totally clear Chaum gradually changed to become Cheyney.

As the de Chaum family did not stay as lord of the manor for much more than eighty years, it is possible that there was a deliberate policy to drop and/or change the second part of the village name, but this is pure speculation, and does not explain why the settlement did not simply revert to the single name of Upton. By 1453, the manor and village was owned by Sir John Barr, of Hanham, which subsequently passed on his death to his widow. After her demise the ownership, for the next one hundred and forty years was with the Bassettt family, and it is believed that it was the third generation of that family who built Upton House during 1608. Eventually, sometime around 1640 the manorial rights, together with lands stretching from the edge of Bitton, on up the hill and over to and including the small hamlet of Beach, as well as the Manor House itself, [now known as Manor Farm] came into the hands of a Mr Brice Seede, after whom Seede Farm was named. [This farm was probably the largest and most important farm in the estate, hence the reason why it was given the lord of the manor's name] Although the exact details of the ensuing events are not clear it is believed that during the 1660's, Brice Seede's daughter Alice married the Reverend Edward Parker, vicar of St Mary's Bitton, and that within ten years or so after this marriage Brice Seede died, and the estate was sold to an Arthur Lacy. Mr Lacy appears to have held the title deeds for around thirty years as in 1701, Edward Parker, the son of the Rev. and Mrs Parker, purchased the whole estate, and began the Parker dynasty that continuously held the manor for the following 245 years.

Almost one hundred and fifty years into the Parker regime, education came to the village in the form of a School House when, after two or three years of debate, particularly by the fathers of the local united Reform Church, it was decided that Upton Cheyney should have a day-school to benefit the many children who lived either in the village, or in surrounding hamlets, and farmsteads. There was sufficient spare land attached to the chapel, and an approach was made to **Thomas Holmes,** a merchant in Bristol, who in addition to being wealthy, was also a good friend of the more affluent members of the village, and in response, he generously donated £100 [around £115,000 by today's values] towards the cost of constructing the appropriate building. With a further £17 coming in the form of donations, the school was opened for business on the 25th June 1849. Whilst the construction was under way, applicants had been interviewed for the prestigious and important task of being the school's first teacher, and in early June a **Miss Haskins** of Kingswood Hill, was appointed at the starting salary of £10 per annum, plus she was to collect as her own, twopence [less than one penny] per week from each pupil, which meant that Miss Haskins had to ensure that she kept going the children's attention and desire to learn, as any truancy or lack of interest would directly cost her money. Fortunately for Miss Haskin, her contract allowed her to live rent-free in the schoolhouse, and on the first day of opening no less than forty pupils turned up for school. Although when viewing this arrangement after a gap of more than 150 years, the twopence per week per child does not seem that expensive, it must be remembered that when the average farm labourer was probably only earning around 8/- [0.40p] per week the school fee, especially if there was more than one child in the family, represented a large slice of any money the parents would have after having paid for food, heating clothing etc.

Whilst the above arrangement worked reasonably well for the next forty years or so, by the early part of the last decade of the nineteenth century, there was the start of mumblings that all was not well particularly with the building, which by now was becoming far too small to accommodate all of the children who wished to attend the school. At a meeting of the School Board held on the 15th September 1892, there was condemnation of the existing school at the Chapel at Upton, which resulted in the decision being taken that a new school would be constructed. Just under one year later in August 1893, it was reported that the work on grubbing out Atwood's orchard trees on land bounded by Lansdown Lane and Marshfield Lane had commenced, despite the fact that many of the trees were still ladened with apples and walnuts; it was also reported that the contract to build the new school had gone to a Mr Long of Longwell Green. Remarkably, the school was completed in a little over six months, with it being officially opened on the 2nd April 1894, by **Aaron Brain, M L Brain,** and **T O Ollis,** with 28 girls and 52 boys attending school on that first day, quite a remarkable achievement when it is borne in mind that the school's catchment area was spread over a wide locality, from Lansdown in the north, to North Stoke in the east, Swineford in the south, and Bitton in the west. Perched as it is high above the valley below, and with no public transport, or facilities for mums to take their children to school by way of 4x4 vehicles, the children in those days had to walk for many miles across fields, along muddy footpaths, and even across the laid out grass of Lansdown racecourse. Not such a bad thing on the nice warm days of summer, but less than pleasant in the dark damp days of winter to the extent that at times the school may have been forced to close due to localised flooding, or heavy falls of snow. A study of the school's log shows an interesting variety of reasons why the school was either closed, or only contained a few pupils.

16 11 1894 Attendance very poor due to bad flooding, school closed for one day.

24 09 1896 Attendance very low for no apparent reason.

14 10 1896 Many senior pupils away from school helping with the walnut harvest.

22 05 1900 Around one quarter or the scholars are absent today mainly due to the opening of the Bath Races at Lansdown, combined with bad weather.

23 05 1900 A few more children have turned up for school this day, but being the second day of the races there is still around a third of the scholars away.

During the first eighteen years and four Head Teachers, the school rooms were heated by open fires, and no doubt certain selected children would not only act as Ink

Monitors, ie those chosen to go around with a jug of permanent black ink and ensure that the small ceramic inkpots on each desk were full, there would be certain older boys chosen to ensure that there was always a scuttle full of coal so that the fire could be kept going throughout the school day. Apart from any safety hazard of having an open fire in a classroom; although those children would have been much more used to such fires than today's more cosseted children; the main drawback with such heating was that those in the front that would of course include the teacher probably roasted, whilst the poor pupils at the back of the class had to endure the cold draughts coming from badly fitted windows and doors, without receiving any real benefit from the heat thrown out by the fire at the front of the room. However, during the summer of 1912, tortoise stoves were introduced to the classrooms, in place of the open fires, and at least such stoves could be placed more centrally, and they were in theory safer to use.

The passage of the First World War appears to have had no great influence on the running of the school, although with so many men being swallowed up by the insatiable appetite of places such as Mons, Passendale and the Somme, everyone was affected by the fact that life would never be the same again. The following snippets, taken from the school log, show that the tentacles of Great War reached out as far as this small community, not by just taking its men, but by changing their day-to-day routines:

18 02 16 Two boys allowed time off from school so that they could help with the farm work now that there is a shortage of farm labourers.
October 1918. For many afternoons, the whole school has been closed, so that the children could be organised into groups and sent along the hedgerow gathering blackberries for sale to the Government Jam Factory, at 3d [just over one new penny] *per pound weight. By the end of the season, the children had gathered a total of 1-ton 355lbs [2,595 pounds, which was probably equivalent to over 5,200 pound pots of jam] and making around £32 for the school.*

With the passing of the Great War, the community gradually came to terms with its loss, whilst the school continued in its normal orderly way, although the log reports that on the 11 June 1923, one of its pupils had to be "Thrashed" for insubordination.

There is no other reference to this instance, and it can only be hoped that the scholar learned from his mistake. During the summer holidays of 1928 the school was thoroughly cleaned and redecorated, and interestingly there is an additional note to the fact that at the same time the floor in the large classroom was levelled, presumably for many years pupils and teachers in that room had to make do with wonky desks and "up-hill writing." It may also surprise the reader to know that although the school had been open for forty years or so, there was no electricity installed until around 1937, and no water sanitations existed until the autumn of 1959. By 1940, the phoney war had ended and, with the fall of France, there was every possibility of Bristol and the surrounding areas coming within the reach of German bombers. Whilst there was little chance of bombs actually falling upon Upton Cheney, they were close enough to their city neighbour to feel the effects of any raids, as demonstrated by the following extracts:

03.04.40 Air raid Wardens come to the school to ensure that all of the children and the staff were correctly carrying the issued gas masks, and that the masks were in working order.
20.07.40 the school day now starts at 10.am to allow the children extra time in bed following the disturbances caused by the night raids.
01.12.41 the school has started serving school dinners, with 31 children receiving a two-course meal at the price of 3½d per head. Mrs Beavis supervises the work, with many of the mothers helping with the preparation of the food, and the clearing up.

Eventually the war came to an end, and once again the Union Jack could be flown from the flagpole that had been erected eleven years earlier, and after the euphoria of peace, the school knuckled down to continue with its excellent education of the local children. In the early part of 1951, the size of the school was reduced when the older boys and girls left to attend a new school at Oldland Common. As previously mentioned the water sanitation was installed in 1960; the school's 75th birthday celebrations were held on the 2nd April 1969; and just over three years later those tortoise stoves, yes the same ones installed fifty-seven years earlier, where taken out of use and replaced by electric night storage heaters, at last the twentieth century had reached Upton Cheyney school!

Over the next seven years or so, the school continued to produce excellent work, but the number of children attending the school was diminishing, whilst the unit cost per pupil was increasing, to the extent that there were rumblings in authority that the school was no longer financially viable. Efforts were made to keep the school open and at the heart of the village, but in the end the accountants got their way, and on the 23 March 1981 **Mrs Joyce Cooper**, the headmistress received notification from the Government that it was the Minister's decision that the school should close for good at the end of the summer term that being the 17th July 1981.

Beach

It is difficult to give a precise or even sketchy history of Beach owing to the fact that due to its size, very few if any events took place there in isolation and thus the history of Upton Cheyney, of Bitton and of North Stoke is the history of Beach. There is no separate mention of it in the Domesday Book, and it is impossible to say with any conviction that there was any form of settlement during pre Roman times. As with the other places within this book, Beach was situated towards the eastern edge of the Kingswood Forest, and may have been a natural or cultivated clearing, and it is possible that a Roman villa was built in the environs of the hamlet, but so far no archaeological evidence has yet been forthcoming. Similarly there is an absence of any Saxon history other than that which affected the whole area, what is known is, that what was originally Beach Farm house [around four hundred years ago] and is now the Grange, used to be part of the prebendal manor of Bitton, and almost certainly the land around the original farm also formed part of the same prebendal manor. In addition Fifteen Acres farm house dates back to the reign of Elizabeth I, and was for some while the home of the Whittington family, a not too distant branch of the Gloucester Whittington's who included Richard the one who found his fortune in London, and subsequently became the Lord Mayor of that city.

Probably the most important historical event to attach itself to Beach was the unsolicited involvement in the Civil War battle of Lansdown, and the fact that one of the lanes leading up to the summit of the hill is known as Slaughter Lane probably speaks volumes when describing the events which took place on the 5th July 1643. Around mid-day, after much fighting between the Royalists, who in this particular engagement were mainly Cornishmen, and the Parliamentarians, the Cornish foot soldiers, ably supported by their makeshift cavalry, were forced by part of the Parliamentary army down from the hill top towards Beach and the surrounding area where, in the language of the time the Royalist claimed that *"When in the bottom they were cruelly gall'd by our ffoote."* The bloodshed did not end with this particular skirmish and with Sir Beville Grenville leading his Cornish pike men back up the hill on more than one occasion, both sides suffered numerous casualties, as well as there being many deserters. Hand to hand fighting with swords, pikes and any other available sharp weapon, with the frequent musket ball thrown in for good measure, can make for an extremely bloody struggle, to which has to be added the tenacity of the participants, particularly the Royalists from Cornwall who, with great gallantry and enormous determination refused to yield ground, with many dying where they stood. Such was the slaughter on that day in the narrow steep confines around Beach, that it was said that blood ran down the lane like a dirty red stream.

The land around Beach was very suitable for raising cattle, and in 1910, Mr Horace Walker started what was to become the famous Beach Jersey Herd, when a few selected animals were taken to Beach Farm, direct from Jersey in the Channel Islands. Over the next few years Mr Walker brought in fresh blood stock from other leading Jersey Herds on both the mainland and on the island, ensuring at all times that no animal was acquired unless it had a good and reputable pedigree. One of the early acquired bulls with the pedigree name *Pallas Noble* was exhibited at the 1914 Royal Agricultural Show, and succeeded in walking off as Championship bull of the show, and later that year, a bull, a cow and a heifer from the Beach Jersey Heard won the King's Cup as the best group of Jersey Cattle, at the Royal Counties Show held at Portsmouth, an extremely prestigious prize that helped to put Mr Walker and his herd in the "top drawer" of Jersey Cattle breeders. Although these were the main highlights, many other more minor awards were achieved during the years leading up to the Great War. With the War having an insatiable appetite for men, the following four years took their toll on Mr Walker who, whilst continuing to drive for excellence, had no shop window in which to exhibit his creation, and accordingly he decided in 1919 to move on and put up the whole herd, 28 cows/calves, and three bulls for sale.

Wick

The general area covered by Wick stretches from Toghill in the east to Bridge Yate in the west, and it is possibly in the extreme west that man first settled, or was drawn to the area, as a site has been identified near the top of Toghill, which is believed to be a flint chipping location of the Mesolithic period. During investigations carried out in 1959, over one thousand shards of flint were found but there appeared to be an absence of any postholes, which might have indicated the construction of a building of one sort or another. Additionally no evidence of fire was found, and this has led to the speculation that those who went to the flint "quarry" were probably nomadic people, and that they probably only visited and/or worked the site during the warmer summer months of their migration, rather than there being any domestic settlement. As the centuries rolled by, more and more people came to the land we now know as Wick, but left little trace of their passing, or indeed of their more permanent stay. South of the village on land belonging to Coldharbour Farm, a Neolithic Barrow has been found together with two or three standing stones, and it is probably reasonable to speculate that both Bronze and Iron Age man settled in the area, and cultivated the rich fertile soil.

With the coming of the Romans, many of the indigenous population were either killed in local skirmishes with the Legionnaires, or simply moved on, or were persuaded by foul means or fair to absorb themselves into the newly created Roman society. Certainly, evidence has been found of the existence of at least one villa, plus a military camp, a burial site and individual stone coffins have been found throughout the parish. None of the findings indicate anything other than the existence of a few isolated Roman families, and/or groups who lived on the fringe of larger establishments, and as such may well have been in the main farmers benefiting from the nearby markets. After the Romans left around 408 AD, Wick and the surrounding areas probably began to revert to nature, as the villas/houses were abandoned, and the old cultivated fields were taken over by a new generation of weeds, brambles and saplings. Behind them the Romans left a rabbit population that they had previously introduced to this country some three hundred years or more ago and now, with the absence of so many human hunters and their dogs, the rabbits were able to proliferate even though they no longer had the advantage of sharing in the harvest from the cultivated fields, but instead they had to rely upon the less appetising plants which had taken over those same fields. In addition the Romans left behind well-built and stylish properties, and well-constructed roads but like the fields, the remaining indigenous population appear to have forfeited the knowledge and skills of their occupiers and, in what might have been something of a pigheaded attitude they totally abandoned the civilization of the past, and reverted back to type. They may of course have been brow beaten by the greater intelligence of the Romans, or perhaps the Romans had a deliberate policy of keeping the locals ignorant as part of their master plan to control their own freedom and peace. Whatever was the cause, the end result would seem that the indigenous population abandoned the fields, the road and the properties, and redeveloped their own lifestyle, based upon old customs, and as such went backwards towards annihilation.

To fill the population gap came three invaders from the east, with the most numerous being the Saxons, and then the Angles, with a sprinkling of Jutes thrown in for good measure, and within one hundred years or so of the departure of the Romans, the number of people living in the area was probably as great if not greater than the size of the Roman community. Whilst there had been two or three hundred years or so of relative peace and stability in the land, the arrival of the new invaders caused old grievances to be settled, and arguments over the ownership of land, property and the female of the species was rarely resolved around a bargaining table. Instead, all sorts of unrest permeated the countryside with few if any settlements being made until many noses had been blooded. Different tribes demanded different satisfaction, and the many conflicts were eventually brought to a head in the decisive battle that took place at Dyrham.

Over the next three or four centuries, Wick remained in something of a backwater, whilst the nearby settlement of Pucklechurch came more and more to prominence. A royal hunting lodge was built, and almost certainly Wick was little more than an insignificant outpost of Pucklechurch in the royal forest, now more frequently known as the Kings Wood. Little if anything changed over the next five hundred years, although it is possible that during this period, or even earlier, there were useful metal deposits in some of the rock formations in the environs of Wick. No mention is made of Wick in the Domesday Book, but within the entry relating to the Pulcrecerce Hundreds, reference is made to the fact that the Abbott of Glastonbury held the estate, and that he was provided with ninety bars of iron per annum as part of his entitlement to payment. With iron ore only found in the rocks around the north of Wick, it is reasonable to assume that at least during the tenth/eleventh centuries, the iron ore was being extracted, and that within the neighbourhood of Wick, the ore was being smelted and turned into a molten state so that bars of iron could be produced. Iron smelting continued in the village well into the nineteenth century, a practice and skill that must have continuously occurred for at least one thousand years.

Quite obviously, as part of the Hundred of Pucklechurch, Wick, variously spelt around this time and over the next few hundred years as Wica, Wycke, and even Berdwic, consisted of little more than a small cluster of cottages grouped around the centre of the hamlet close to where the River Boyd could be conveniently crossed by the original main coach road from Bristol to London. Nearby were other small, but independent hamlets, some of which gradually merged with the main core of cottages, as the natural expansion of the country's population grew, and in doing so lost their own independence and their identity. The older part of the village is mainly situated to the south of the main road, and down the lane opposite the church is the site of a nineteenth-century mill, that ended up grinding corn for the production of animal feedstuffs. From the little bridge, under which flows the stream like River Boyd, it is possible to see a pretty, manmade cascade of water that is the remnants of the old mill system, whilst not far from this spot is the stately Wick Court built during the second decade of seventeenth-century. Almost half way along the main road within the Wick boundary, is the seventeenth-century coaching inn originally known as the *Crown Inn,* but now in its more familiar guise of the *Rose and Crown.* It was here, in 1783, that a John Gully was born, who twenty-five years latter would, as a prizefighter, become the renowned heavyweight champion of the world. Having made a great deal of money from his bare-knuckle activities, he became a Member of Parliament, as well as a successful racehorse owner, with his horses winning the famous Derby race on no less than three separate occasions.

More recently towards the end of the nineteenth century, Wick became famous for the production of iron oxides used in the dyeing industries, particularly the colouring of paint. In addition a variety of other products were mined including Fuller's Earth and Potter's clay. Because of the mined ochre, a fine yellow dust affected the surrounding area, and it is claimed that the origin of the name "Golden Valley" came about as it caused the River Boyd to turn yellow. [For more details on this subject see my book *Around Warmley"]*

Churchley

Like most places, Wick was formed out of a number of small hamlets that originally started out as separate places of habitation but gradually, for reasons of growth, self-defence or economical dependence, merged together to form one unit, with the more dominant partner's name taking an unequal share of prominence so that in due course subsequent generations dropped the old passive names in favour of the ascendant. Land between Wick and Abson was, during the eleventh/twelfth centuries owned by the de Holebroc family, and gradually the area became known as Holbrook, once a separate hamlet in its own right. As for Abson, its church was, until around 1845, the parish church of Wick and its environs, and it is perhaps a little curious that such a small hamlet should have remained free from the clutches of its larger neighbour. Possibly its freedom was ordained by the building during 1845 of a new and separate church much closer to the centre of Wick

Together with Holbrook, Toghill, and Breaches Yate, there was one other constituent part of Wick a hamlet variously known as Church Eight, Churchleigh (used around 1495), Churcheleyght or Churchleight, the latter as spelt in a document dated 1511, but more frequently this small community was identified with the spelling of Churchley. However, irrespective of how the name was spelt, this hamlet, or constituent part of Wick as it would now be, has disappeared inasmuch as no one appears to be able to state with any certainty exactly which part of modern Wick once was the hamlet of Churchley. Various historical references to this hamlet have been noted, but none appear to provide sufficient information to enable the researcher to pinpoint the exact location, particularly as such references seem to dry up around the mid-fifteenth century. The most likely area is somewhere along the boundary between the parishes of Wick and Syston, and more particularly in the general direction of Bridge Yate. Possible clues extracted from the Haynes Papers are that Edward Hall received in April 1674, permission to enclose waste ground at Churchley Hill Lane, and this same lane is mentioned in a mining agreement dated 1727, but here the clue is more useful as the full description is Churchley Hill, Bridgeyate. Thirty years later, a lease allowed Aaron Jefferies and others to dig for coal on land at Breachyate Common and Churchleigh Hill. At this point it may be extremely tempting to connect the modern spelling of Chesley Hill as a corruption of Churchley Hill, and to do so would seem to have a certain strong level of credence but to do so without a note of caution may corrupt history itself, particularly as other sites may also have reasonable claims to make.

Bridge Yate

Originally known as Breaches Yate, the name identifies a particular entrance or gateway into the Kingswood Forest. However, in view of the fact that the forest boundary extended in an easterly direction well past the site of the present Bridge Yate, it must be assumed that if the name, as it appears to do, existed in the eleventh /twelfth.centuries, then either the edge of the forest had been well cut back at that point, or the "gate" represented an entrance into a special/important part of the forest. Certainly there was no physical "gate" as such, either at the forest edge, or someway into the forest, but whatever was there must have clearly identified the passing from one part of the forest to another. Without there being any documentary evidence to clarify the true nature of the name, it can only be assumed, that this particular spot marked a change or possible sanctuary where for example, an animal, or even a human being, being hunted by the royal party could escape the "kill" once it ran past this gateway. Possibly the king had an "inner sanctum" around the royal hunting lodge at Pucklechurch, where only certain privileged allies of the king could go, the outer ring of which was identified by natural markers, or it may have been nothing more involved than at this point there was a natural clearing within the forest, which made it a convenient place for the royal party to gather. All of these assumptions are based upon the belief that the forest extended well beyond the current site of Bridge Yate, but supposing it did not. One other alternative is that although the Forest of Kingswood boundary went well past this site, the actual land to the east consisted of open tracts of heath land, where trees grew less densely and where the ground was occupied not by oaks and elms but by bushes, brambles, gorse and bracken,

Once the earlier kings and their followers gradually lost interest in the sport of hunting everything to extinction, and the royal control of the forest waned, more and more of the forest was lost to the axe, particularly during the reign of the Plantagenet King Henry III (1216-72). Under Henry's kingship, the area was disafforested, which effectively meant that it was removed from the ancient protection of Forest Laws, in fact Henry III went as far as to sign a Charter of Proclamation, which took away from the king's wood the status of being regarded as a forest, and downgraded it to being a Chase. It is reasonable to ask why this action was taken at that particular time, and the answer may well be that by the early thirteenth century, the forest had already been reduced in size by the encroachment of communities, and the clearing of the land for cultivation, and/or mineral extraction. Accordingly, it is quite feasible, that as early as the eleventh century, the forest edge had already been cut back to

Bridge Yate, and that the name was given simply because there was a natural gateway at that point, which led into the Chase.

As mentioned above, Bridge Yate was for hundreds of years regarded as being a hamlet within the parish of Wick, but it has somehow managed to retain its independence, although modern infilling stretching from the outer boundary of Bristol has meant that it is now more associated with Warmley and North Common.

North Common

Until the modern housing estates of the 1970/80's took place, North Common struggled to establish its own identity, frequently being considered part of Oldland Common, occasionally as part of Bridge Yate, and today, postally as part of Warmley, all due to the fact that until the 1850's, North Common formed part of the ecclesiastical parish of Bitton then, with the ever expanding population resulting in the need for increased pastoral support, the decision was made to carve out of Bitton and Syston the new parish of Warmley, centred around the recently constructed St Barnabus church. Chronically over the centuries it formed the same historical backdrop as its adjoining cousins, with life based upon producing enough food and shelter to bring up a family, and accordingly its history is intertwined with that of the area covered by this book. Of note is the fact that during the eighteenth century, as in most of the area, coal was found close to the surface, and over the next three or four decades, this coal was extracted in relatively small quantities. However with the development of the industrial revolution, and more importantly the evolution of the emerging brass industry-taking place not so far away, the importance of the local coal deposits became even more paramount. Geologists had for some while identified the nature of the coal that lay beneath their feet, and in particular the various layers or seams of differing quality coal that lay on top of each other, but in this particular part of the world, the enormous movements within the earth's crust had caused the coal seams to buckle and bend so that at times they came near the surface, whereas in other places the seams were quite deep. Of great importance to the newly developing brass industry in Warmley was coal that burned with the least amount of sulphur as possible, and some 650ft below the surface lay a 20inch seam [50cm] known as Parrot Seam that consisted of coal that was sulphur free, the best coal possible for the brass industry.

Although this coal sold for just 15/- [0.75p] per ton, it was certainly worth the effort and cost of driving the shaft down to reach the Parrot seam and this probably started around 1810 at the pit known as Bull Hall, which occupied land between Nicholetes and Victoria Road, with the pit head somewhere in the middle. Not far away, and at around the same time another pit, Haul Lane Colliery was sunk, also heading for the rich seam below, although both pits would have to drive through and continue to mine the Millgrit seam some three-hundred feet below, then the narrow [18"] Rag Seam, through 250ft of coal free rock, before reaching a 3-4ft thick outcrop of coal known as the Buff Seam, and even then there was a further 80ft of digging before the hard pressed miners reached Parrot Seam. Whilst there was little reward for the 75 men and 30 boys ~ all under the age of 13years, with at least one or two just 7 years of age ~ who toiled night and day, for the owners there was money to be made and to put the 15/- price in perspective, that amount is probably equivalent to around £230 per ton today.

By 1841 the owner of both pits was a **Robert Jefferis** who also owned Cowhorn Hill Colliery, but Mr Jefferis was not a man to throw his money about as despite the depth of the shaft it is believed, that like Haul Lane Colliery, all of his pits, at that time, only used a horse gin for winding, although whether two or more horses were used to bring up the trams of coal is not certain. Probably around 1860, the horse gin was replaced by steam power with a rotative beam engine by either Mr Jefferis or his son, and these engines stayed on site until the pits closed in 1875.

To help take the coal to market, a Dramway was constructed that ran through the length of North Common on its way to the River Avon near Keynsham, and both pits were connected in the early 1830's, further details of which can be obtained from my book *"Coal and the Dramway, [Within Rural Bitton]"* first published in 1999.

The other significant event to happen in North Common was the coming of the railway, when the Midland Railway Company decided to steal a march on their rivals the Great Western Railway. For many years the Midland Railway wanted access to the south coast, so that they could open up new resorts to the large population in the midlands and in the north of England, and they seized their chance when in the 1840's they opened a branch line from Mangotsfield to Bath via North Common although the area was never provided with a station, just a long but impressive embankment that straddles the North Common Valley.

Warmley

For a long time Warmley was just a small, almost forgotten, and certainly frequently overlooked hamlet in the parish of Syston, with neither church nor chapel to its name, placed as it was between the Bridge Yate outpost of Wick parish, and the northern fringes of Bitton parish. It is not mentioned in the Domesday Book, and as such was probably an integral and hardly noticed part of the Kingswood forest for hundreds of years. The oldest known building in Warmley is the sixteenth century Grimsbury Farm house, previously known as the "old Grange," certainly the building or part of it was in existence in 1610, and it was probably constructed around 1550. Apart from this one building, any other contemporary properties in Warmley were likely to have been little more than hovels built in and among the trees, and that position hardly changed for hundreds of years, or at least until the eighteenth century, when Warmley began to give up its hidden wealth in the form of coal. Pits were dug throughout the area, and as the demand for labour increased, so did the number of properties as more and more people took up residence, even though there was still much poverty, and many of the properties were of a temporary nature. With a good supply of water and coal, **John Champion** set up his works in Warmley for the manufacture of copper, brass and zinc, whilst an iron foundry was constructed on behalf of a Mr Gregory. It is impossible to be precise as to when coal was first dug in the area we now know as Warmley, but one of the oldest families associated with coal mining was the Jeffery's. They must have been a financially powerful family in the sixteenth century, as one of the most prominent houses built in the early part of the seventeenth century was called "Jeffery House." Using their financial muscle, they almost certainly helped to "liberate" part of the forest, or if they were not actively involved in this plunder, they certainly aided and abetted those that did, as it is recorded in 1670 that Jefferies ~ [different spelling or simply the plural of Jeffery] ~ possessed coal pits in Lord Stafford's forty-seven acre liberty that was situated south of Grimsbury Lane. Another family by the name of Goldney, owned the Crown Pit, situated alongside the London Road, just past the site of Warmley Station, in the direction of Bridgeyate, whilst others owned about forty to fifty pits in total.

Some time towards the end of the eighteenth century, two men of stature rode into Warmley from Wiltshire, seeking suspected stolen property that they believed had been secreted somewhere in the local area. Having travelled quite a distance from their homes, the men decided to spend a night or two at the *Crown Inn*, which conveniently had room for them both as well as stabling room for their horses. Being thoroughbred animals worth a small fortune, the men paid a night watchman to look after both horses, and having rubbed them down and provided them with food and water, the night watchman settled himself down for a comfortable night upon a bed of straw, ensuring that the stable door was firmly shut, and ensuring that the lanterns had all been turned-off. Once the day visitors to the Inn had made their noisy exit from the hostelry and allowed the landlord to lock up, peace and quiet descended, and it was not long before the night watchman's heavy eyelids tempted him to sleep. Some time after midnight, as best the guard could estimate, he was awakened by a murmuring of voices coming from the stable yard, followed by the breaking of wood as the stable doors were forced open. As he lay huddled in the straw he easily convinced himself that there were at least six men outside, whom, by the noise they were making, now seemed to be even more boisterous and daring in their approach than was originally suspected by the night watchman. There was no doubt in the watchman's opinion that he would not stand a chance against these vicious and undoubtedly armed ruffians, and accordingly he decided that the better part of valour was to hide, even if this did mean that he would be unable to protect the horses in his charge, but in the circumstances what else could he do. As a consequence, and in a rather frightened state he crept in to the darkest corner of the stable, and listened to the dreadful oaths of the men as they led the two valuable horses away from their overnight accommodation.

Waiting an hour or so until he could hear no more unexpected noises coming from the stable or stable yard, the guard crept out from his hiding place and raised the alarm, but despite an extensive search of the area that lasted two or three days, there was no sign of the stolen animals, and no one in the community had any idea of what might have happened, or any idea of who had carried out this dreadful crime.

More than two weeks had passed since the horses had been stolen when, a group of youths with time on their hands, decided to explore the old workings of a nearby abandoned drift mine. Egging each other on, the boys entered the sloping shaft, and gingerly groped their way in trying to use as much of the weak daylight that filtered through the entrance as possible, but eventually they were enveloped in almost total darkness and with the dare complete, were about to return to the safety of the light when one of the group stumbled over a large object on the floor, the horses, or their remains had been found, but why someone should want to steal a pair of fine horses, blindfold them and take them into a pit to kill them appeared to have no logical or sensible explanation, and no one was ever found to elucidate, but one reason may have been that having stolen the horses, those who might have paid the thieves decided that the animals were too identifiable to be passed on through the horse market, and that the risk was too great to be involved, hence rather than return the animals or simply let them loose the thieves decided to destroy the evidence by killing the horses in the abandoned mine. However there may have been a much more sinister explanation, because by coincidence, or perhaps by design, the landlord of the *Crown Inn,* one **Samuel Fussell**, was the local parish constable in addition to being the landlord of that Inn, and he was fatally shot around the time that the discovery of the horses had been made, having previously made the stabling/overnight arrangements with the gentlemen from Wiltshire, and having been the person who recommended the particular night watchman.

By all accounts, a local property owner by the name of **Edward Wilmot**, was in arrears with his tithes; ~ dues to be paid into the parish to assist with the Poor Relief, ~ and knowing that sixty-three year old Wilmot had a short fiery temper, and one who did not readily like parting with his money, the parish overseer, whose job it was to collect the arrears, decided that he needed to take some additional back-up when he went to call on Mr Wilmot and requested that Samuel Fussell, the local constable, should accompany him. Having made no secret of the arrangements being made, or the date and time when both men could conveniently carry out their duty, their joint approach to Wilmot's property was well publicized, which enabled a rather disgruntled Edward Wilmot, to lay in wait as if to ambush both men. Unknown to either men as they approached the property, they were being closely watched by Wilmot, who was standing in a darkened room at the front of the house holding in his right hand a firearm, whilst with his left hand he opened up a gap where the pair of heavy curtains came together, a gap that was sufficient for him to see outside, but with little likelihood of him being seen from the lane. Samuel Fussell was walking a pace or two behind the overseer, who was just about to open the latch of the front gate when he heard, from the direction of the house, a loud noise, which caused him to involuntarily duck and flinch, but whilst doing so he noticed, in that split second, blood spurting from Samuel Fussell's chest, as the constable fell motionless to the floor.

As far as can be certain, Wilmot appears to have targeted Samuel Fussell, as no more shots were fired, and he appears to have taken no action to "run away," although that cannot be said of the overseer who, without waiting to see if Mr Fussell was alive or dead, ran from the scene, as fast as his old legs would take him. Reporting the incident as quickly as he could, he returned to the scene of the shooting, together with two armed constables, and a small crowd of onlookers, to find Edward Wilmot quietly waiting for them. Without further trouble, he surrendered his weapon to the constables and accompanied them to the police station. At his subsequent trial, Wilmot gave no explanation for his actions, or why he had targeted the local constable, and therefore are we left with just a coincidence that the landlord of the Inn, from which two well bred horses were stolen, and mindlessly slaughtered, was himself unfortunately shot not long after the bodies of the two animals were found, or is there a connecting mystery that both men took to their grave ~ Wilmot(t) was hanged at Gloucester Prison on the 14th August 1800.

In the first instance, there is a strong probability that when the Gentlemen from Wiltshire, arrived at the *Crown Inn* to arrange lodgings for themselves, and stabling for their horses, they were on their own, and accordingly the subsequently arranged night watchman was most probably a local man, who no doubt had been recommended by the landlord, as who better to ask than the trusty proprietor. But at this point we need to question why these gentlemen considered that a risk actually existed, and if they genuinely believed their steeds to be in danger, why did they stop at that particular Inn. According to their account, they had travelled from Wiltshire to look for stolen property that they suspected was hidden in the village, but it is not at all clear if the property was theirs or exactly what the property was, however if stolen then the thieves were not going to give up their ill-gotten gains peacefully, thus it might be reasonable to presume that both men knew how to handle themselves. The reason originally given as to why these two men were there may, on the surface, seem quite plausible, but the more the questions are asked, the more the reason seems not to hold-up. Whilst it is possible to have a certain degree of empathy with the night watchman, it has to be asked, why he should have immediately considered his life was in danger because he had heard the murmuring voices outside in the stable yard, even if many of the words being used were blasphemous, why should that alarm the guard, he was, after all in the stables attached to an Inn, where one would imagine that such language was common place. Why did he not go to investigate, and/or call out; he had been employed as a guard, and surely that was his duty, bearing in mind that there were numerous people either sleeping or resting across the yard in the Inn, including of course the owners of these two horses, who may have been gentlemen, but who had both implied by their intended actions that they would and could defend themselves, and presumably their animals.

Whilst in any small close-knit community, word gets around, especially if it relates to two strangers "in the camp," but not everyone in that community is a criminal, thus in a relatively short space of time a "gang" of men would have had to be gathered together, and for arrangements to be made for the capture and subsequent disposal of the animals. It is of course quite possible that the theft of the horses was a job carried out on the "spur of the moment" but they needed tools to be able to enter the stable by force, although it is possible that they may just have happened to find the tools lying around. In addition, it was claimed by the night watchman, that the thieves entered the stable by force, which invariably includes noise, so why was the alarm not raised by someone in the Inn, the breaking if timber doors and the clatter of four pairs of metal shod hooves would have surely made a noise, not counting the human noises that would have accompanied the theft. As far as can be determined, the whole episode appears to have taken place without anyone, other than the watchman, hearing and/or seeing a thing, again a possibility, but not necessarily believable.

The records do not make it clear as to whether the horses were killed, or allowed to starve to death, but why waste such valuable animals, after having gone to the bother, and risk of stealing them, why did no one look in the drift mine entrance, when the search was being undertaken, why did the village gossip not pick up upon the theft, and possible storage of the animals, why was Samuel Fussell shot dead, why was no explanation for his actions ever offered by Edward Wilmot. There are more questions than answers, but surely the two incidents are linked, not by coincidence but by reality, perhaps Fussell and Wilmot were in league with each other, perhaps Wilmot took the risk for an anticipated high financial return, and then felt cheated because Fussell had not done his job correctly to check out the high quality of both animals, and that it was their quality that made them un-sellable in the illegitimate market, perhaps Fussell was an innocent party to the whole affair, but happened to know what was going on, and as the local constable, was about to "tell all." Regrettably with more than two hundred years in between, all that we can do is to speculate on what might or might not have happened, and hope that we do no injustice to the innocent.

Until well into the mid twentieth century, the inhabitants of Warmley were at the bottom of the pile as far as money was concerned, and whilst there was, for the small community, work available, none of it was well paid, and most struggled to earn enough for a very basic subsistence. Bread was a staple part of any meal, and when the volatile price of wheat increased, so did the hardship of the local people. Such a situation occurred during 1800, when a shortage of grain caused by the poor harvest of 1799, pushed up the price of flour to around 8/4d [41p] for a sixteen-pound bag, which in turn meant that a four pound loaf of bread retailed at just under 2/9d [14p]. By today's standards inexpensive, but when an average family then required at least four loaves per week, the price represented around ninety per cent of their total income, an unsustainable level. On one particular day during 1800, a horse drawn cart loaded with sacks of flour approached Warmley from the general direction of Wick. Whilst this was not a particularly unusual event, and one which happened at least once or twice a month, on this particular day, and at this particular moment in time, the cart was seen by a group of ladies from the village who collectively, were feeling extremely frustrated, by the enormous difficulties they were under in trying to make ends meet, and to find scraps of food for the empty bellies of their respective families. Already they had seen the price of bread reach a level that they simply could not afford; and with the leftovers of the winter's root crops almost exhausted, and the new harvest still some months away, they were becoming increasingly desperate. One of the more spirited and much younger women within the group was sixteen year old **Hester Davis** who seeing a sudden opportunity, impulsively called for her friends to stand firm across the road, and prevent the cart from continuing on its journey to Bristol. With a determined strength born in the depths of despair and frustration, the women stood their ground shouting out for the carter to stop, and shaking anything they could get their hands on, to unnerve the horses.

Now the carter was, as his work dictated, a big strong man, who rarely if ever backed down from a fight, and who was not afraid to run his horses through any barrier, but on this occasion the barrier was made up of yelling women, who looked extremely determined, and as rough and ready as he was, there was still a sufficient part of old fashioned chivalry within him, which caused him to pull up his horses a few yards away from the front row of women. Having stopped, he soon found himself surrounded by these ladies from Warmley all of whom seemed to be clamouring for him to go back from where he had come, and some less affable suggestions that even questioned the honesty and state of his parentage, but predominantly he gained the impression that these rather determined females wanted him to leave the cart where it was. Receiving orders did not come easy to the carter, especially when they were being shouted at him by an hysterical cluster of women, and quickly he looked around to see if he should go on, or if there was a suitable and face saving way of backing out of his predicament, after all it was only a bunch of women, and some of them were probably old enough to be his grandmother, but on the other hand there were rather a lot of them, and in any case it was not his flour, which was the main objective of the women's frustration, although the cart was his. Accordingly, having carefully weighed up his choices, the carter decided that a dignified retreat was his best option, until he could return with a few male colleagues who would soon show these wretched women who was the boss. Having climbed down from his cart as dignified as possible, he unhitched the lead horse, and turning it around, he rode off back to his master, with a catcall of cheers hurrahs and something about a yellow streak ringing in his ears.

Having won the hour, and secured the cart, but even more importantly its cargo, Hester Davis climbed up to the drivers seat and, with the help of one of the other women, she lowered a sack to the ground and announced that it was now their time to purchase the flour at a price they could afford. At an agreed price of 2/6 [12p] per sixteen pounds of flour, the women gathered makeshift bags together, and despite there being no available scales, fairly shared out the first two or three sacks, before returning to their homes, whilst at the same time spreading the news of their good fortune so that the opportunity of having flour at a reasonable price could and would become beneficial to the whole community. Within a relatively sort space of time, a pair of scales were found and brought to the cart, and with a mixture of containers, the flour was distributed amongst the populace. Eventually the whole load was sold, and sporting a somewhat dusty overall coating of off white, a somewhat tired Hester Davis and her companion climbed down from the cart, placed a neat pile of coins on the driver's seat, and walked home with her bag of flour.

When the carter, his master and a group of men armed with cudgels, ~ just in case any of the women turned nasty, ~ returned to the cart, they found the horses contentedly eating the adjacent verge and hedgerow, the cart with the flour sacks tidily folded and left on the bed of the cart, whilst on the driver's seat they also found a pile of money, which, when subsequently counted, equated to the cargo of flour having been sold at just over 2/6 per sixteen pounds weight. No action was ever taken against Hester or any of the other women, and it is believed that she lived to the ripe old age of ninety-nine.

Cadbury Heath

This area is probably better known today because of the development of a large post-war housing estate, than for any other reason, and sadly this is also probably due to the fact that Cadbury Heath was for many years something of a backwater, and an area not frequented by too many people and not that often. Probably for over 2,000 years, it was a large open flat space of uncultivated shrub land in the lea of higher ground to the northwest that was roughly in the middle of the King's Wood. As the natural soil was a poor quality few trees would grow there, and there was little if any shelter, either from the hot dry sun of summer, or the wet and cold of winter. Apart from the occasional harvesting of furze [gorse], or the chasing of wild animals in one of the Royal Hunts, there was little reason to go there, or even travel across the area. By around the mid sixteenth century, a large slice of the more southerly area of Cadbury Heath had been acquired by the Newton family, who constructed their country home, and called it Barrs Court, and then set out to cultivate as much of the surrounding land as possible in the form of gardens, parkland, arable and pasture, and whilst economics and/or politics may have a major reason for determining the overall area of the Newton Estate, it can also be said that they ensured that they had liberated the better quality land.

During the following century or two, more and more people began to come into the area, building stone cottages, whilst at the same time clearing small parcels of land for cultivation. Roads and paths began to acquire more importance, if for no other reason than to enable people to go to and from work and, even more importantly, to enable raw materials and goods to reach the market. Coal was being exploited at an ever-increasing rate, which brought in more men and their families in search of work, so that isolated dwellings, soon adopted new neighbours, as clusters of working class hovels began to appear. The much-improved cultivated land was found to be good for growing wheat and oats, interspersed with root crops such as turnip, as well as being ideal for grazing.

For many years, and certainly those up to and throughout the Second World War, Cadbury Heath remained basically the same, with the exception of the two hundred years or so of the exploitation of coal on a commercial basis, and the subsequent effects on much of the populace as gradually the pits closed throughout the nineteenth century. For a period of time there was a thriving pottery business, with the raw material being dug from a large opencast quarry to the east of Tower Road South, and brought to the brick and pipe works in railed tram carts pulled by a mule, up the gradient and under the road in a short tunnel. However, because at this point the gradient became too steep for the four-legged power, the trams were hitched to a wire rope and mechanically pulled the last one hundred yards or so to an area where the contents of the trams could be tipped into a crusher for the start of the raw materials conversion into pipes and bricks. The site of the pottery had previously been where William Champion had set up his Brass Works, and some of the original buildings are extant. As far as the clay pit is concerned, that was used during the 1960's as a landfill site, and now forms the small industrial area known as St Ivel Way. However, long before the closure of this industrial site on the boundary of Cadbury Heath, the remaining area was still very much an agricultural area, although close to the pottery was a cluster of small stone built cottages known as the Batch that had been constructed beside the gently flowing Syston or otherwise Warmley brook. Between the Batch, and the environs of Longwell Green, there were dispersed a handful of "middle class" villas, and a small collection of council houses, strung out along roads that had been constructed in place of the original forest tracks, but unknown to the majority of the residents their local authority, Warmley Rural District Council, had begun to purchase many of the remaining green fields of Cadbury Heath.

The war came to Cadbury Heath and the surrounding area in a much more gentle way than it did in the nearby cities, but for those who lost loved ones the pain was just as great where ever you lived, and of course when enemy aircraft were overhead, living in the countryside was no guarantee that the occasional bomb would not fall upon you. Whilst few if any bombs fell within Cadbury Heath, the village was "invaded" by enemy soldiers when, in the summer of 1944 around seventy-five war-weary Italian soldiers arrived as prisoners of war, having been captured by the Eighth Army in the deserts of North Africa back in 1941, and then taken to prisoner of war camps in Kenya for three years, before being brought to this country and now they found themselves in tented accommodation in Gays Field just off Wraxall Road near to the old Cadbury Heath School. None of these men had shown themselves in any way to be fanatic followers of El Duce and his fascist collaborators and they had been allowed to come to Cadbury Heath to help with the harvest and generally work in the fields. As far as is known they were all well treated by the local inhabitants, there were no recorded problems of confrontation or fights, none of the Italians tried to escape, and a number of friendships were made with these enemy soldiers. However, their stay was relatively short and by the end of September 1944, the small-tented prisoner of war camp had disappeared, with many locals having fond memories of their enforced guests, and could at least now claim that they had been part of the complexities of war.

Within the local authority, plans were being made for a much-improved post-war existence and the desire to see a much greater expansion of the local population and the extra wealth such expansion could bring. The nearby city of Bristol already had a housing problem before the war had exacerbated the position, and spurred on by the ever-increasing demand for new housing, and the fact that the Government were handing out to local authorities generous grants and/or subsidies for the construction of council houses, Warmley RDC initiated an ambitious programme of local authority house building, and offering them to Bristol so that it could relocate some of its inner city citizens. Where to build the many houses required was not a problem, as Warmley already owned many if not all the pleasant green fields of Cadbury Heath, and it was in the late 1940's that the first turf was dug, and the green fields turned into a morass of mud, dust and building materials. Gradually the twist and turns of Earlstone Crescent came into existence as it stretched from one end of Parkwall Road to another, followed by the spurs from Tower Road South, Park Road, and Coronation Road, the latter to commemorate Queen Elizabeth's accession to the throne. There was also Newton Road and Queens Road and then as the fields disappeared forever some of the old field names were handed over to the roads that replaced them, Long Handstones; Great Leaze; Far Handstones, Little and Great Dowles with others named after saints. Part of the estate needed to be left as an open space to avoid any possible ground subsidence resulting from the extraction of coal, whilst almost in the geographical centre a shopping precinct and a new public house was built. Through all of this the construction came families, young and old mainly from the slum and bomb damaged areas of Bristol, to try and weave together a new community that had more than doubled the indigenous population, ~ Cadbury Heath would never be the same again.

Barrs Court

Most people today know of or think of Barrs Court as a 1980/90's housing estate with a few visible foundations of a large barn, and the remnants of a moat, without perhaps realising the full extent of the original manor house and surrounding estates and the history attached thereto. As far as can be determined, the manor house or a manor house existed in the first half of the fourteenth century when the De Bitton family owned it and the surrounding lands, although at that time the property was not known as Barrs Court. The ownership of this estate continued to be held by the De Bitton's for the next hundred years or so, but by around 1450 the male lineage had come to an end, and upon his death the property passed to his sole granddaughter Lady Jane Greyndour, who was then the wife of Robert Greyndour. Fortunately, when he died, a very brief description of the property was recorded, which described the house with a central large "Great Hall" with an attached kitchen, and three chambers above. In addition there were various unidentified outbuildings, probably making the whole manor house a relatively modest; small, draughty, and dreary stone built medieval house, but for the standards of the mid-fifteenth century, it may well have been considered quite desirable. Subsequently, Lady Jane became the wife of Sir John Barre of Rotherwas in Herefordshire, and thus how often Lady Barre and her husband visited her inheritance and whether the property was still habitable and up to her standards, or more likely the standards of her new husband, will now never be known, but presumably she and her husband would have expected a financial return from the estate, and would accordingly have ensured that they had a suitable local agent to act upon their behalf. For around 35 years, Lady Barre retained her ownership of the estate, before it was passed on her death, in 1485, to Sir Thomas Newton, whose descendants and or nominees were to hold onto the estate for almost the next two hundred years. Whether or not Sir Thomas moved straight in to his inheritance, or how he regarded the gift is not recorded, but there is some evidence that apart from the possibility that there were one or two minor alterations to the house and/or estate, it is believed that in the main Sir Thomas was reasonably happy with the existing building, or alternatively he simply did not have the money to spend upon copious changes, and therefore had to put-up with that that had been given to him. Sir Thomas probably died around 1515, and the inheritance went to his son John, who also appears to have done little in the way of enhancing the manor house as in 1540, the property was visited by the Tudor antiquarian, John Leland, who described the house, in his usual minimalist way, as a *"fayre olde mannar place of stone,"* hardly a glowing report but one which may give credence to the possibility that the design, décor and comfort of the house was poor, even to the level of Tudor standards. This visit had been brought about by Henry Vlll, who had empowered his librarian and chaplain John Leland, to travel throughout England in search of antiquities and to explore the libraries of cathedrals and abbeys, and no doubt manor houses for good measure, as such information would give the king a great opportunity of raising more and more taxes, so perhaps for the Newton's it may have been a good thing not to appear to be too ostentatious.

Whilst we have no idea whether it was financial matters that prevented Sir Thomas from refurbishing the house, we can be more positive about the reason why his son did not spend much money on Barrs Court, as around the time of his inheritance, or possibly a little while afterwards, Sir John was financing the final destruction of Richmond Castle, a mile or so from the centre of East Harptree, for the purpose of using the land and recovering the stone for the construction of a new country house.

For the next hundred years or more what happened to the development, maintenance, and/or the restoration of the building and its surrounding estate is not known to us as so much of the information jig-saw is missing. We can piece together the probability that John had at least one son, as there is a record, on the 1st April 1584, of the birth of Theodor Newton, son of Sir Henry Newton, and the death of his daughter Nazereth [sic] in January 1597. Sir Henry himself died towards the end of April 1599, followed nine months later in January 1600, by another of his young daughters, who had also been given the Christian name Nazareth. It is then presumed that Theodor, or possibly an older brother took over the house and estate, and that that person had a son John, and probably a daughter Penelope. The fact that both John and Penelope existed is not in doubt, what is not certain is their respective lineage. John, or Sir John Newton II is identified as being the last of the direct line that had started almost two hundred years previously with Sir Thomas, whilst Penelope is recorded in the Bitton Parish Register as having been buried at St Mary's on the 14th August 1643, being the daughter of Lady Newton of Barrcourt [sic]. That no mention is made of the father probably indicates that he had already died, and that the property had been passed onto Sir John the second, who appears not to have married, and certainly does not appear to have any legitimate heirs.

Knowing that he had no blood heirs, Sir John decided that the house and the estate should remain within the "Newton" family, and accordingly directed in his Last Will and Testament, that the lands and title should be inherited by a completely unrelated Sir John Newton of Hador in Lincolnshire. Accepting his inheritance in 1661, when he was then 35 years of age, Sir John III and his successor occupied Barrs Court, for the next eighty years. Some seventeen years previously when Sir John was eighteen he had married seventeen-year-old Mary, the daughter of Sir Jervase Eyre of Rampton in Nottinghamshire, and over the following twenty years or so she presented him with no less than four sons and thirteen daughters, and she still managed to outlive him by 13 years. However, trying to determine when Sir John and his large family moved into Barrs Court is virtually impossible, and it is conceivable that they never permanently lived there, except that both Sir John, his wife and at least two of their daughters are buried at St Mary's Bitton. On this basis alone it is suspected that on his inheritance, Sir John and his family did not move straight into Barrs Court but probably used it rather like a "holiday home," but gradually began to spend more and more time there as the property became more habitable, certainly it is reasonable to surmise that Sir John lived there for a number of years before his death in 1699, and that Lady Mary stayed there as his widow for a further thirteen years.

The next owner of Barrs Court was another Sir John, presumably son of John and Mary, but this did not mean that he moved back into the house after his father's death, particularly as his mother, the dowager would have still been living there. In fact as far as can be determined he hardly ever set foot in the place, preferring to attend to his much more important Lincolnshire properties, and leaving his Gloucestershire home in the hands of a steward. However, neither the property or the estate were neglected, and maintenance/refurbishing work was carried out over a long period of time, financially controlled at arms length by correspondence as demonstrated by the following copy of the letter written on the 24th August 1720 by the agent to **Sir John Newton**:

Sir, I received yours of ye 28eth of July paste I received Trubody's fine [of] £103 this laste weecke and paid it to esquire Edward the 20eth of this instant. I could not well paie in a sum of mony more as it [was required] by Resen having workmen to pai aboute the house, and harviste workmen; but hope to paie in a sume aboute Michilmus ore vary sone after. I hope the halle will be Done that he will be vary lettell the darkar for walling [in] one lite in eche wendor for thes lits wase 4 lite and the other 3 lite and over the chemly is a hatching oute of walle and that will be carred upe to tacke ye beme thare and it will be handsomer than it wase before and to the others shall youse iren pennes to sequire it and it will be done vary ferme. It is vary toblsom and chargable it being of such a hithe and macking ye schaffols to be safe. Wee had ane axedence this last weeke [when] ye carpendors boye when putting upe one of the peses of tembr, turning hastyly round to give a tole to his master fele of from the tope of ye hall and brocke ye collar bone of his necke and cutes to his hade and squates vary bade. But I thancke god he is licke to doe vary well a gaine. I had him to bristol prasant to a surgante and put him to my daftors (doctors) to safe (save) charges, [however] I muste bage[beg] the favor of your Honar to give me lefe to paie the surgen I beleve I shall macke frands that he will tacke a genny ore 25/- for ye qure because his mother is a pore widow; his father and mother wase bothe sarvants to my ould mastor he have a brother that leves in a gentolmans sarvis that put him to this mastor one termes to gate him a trade and he is a vary actife boye for it.

[It is probable that the *"halle"* mentioned in the letter is still the Great Hall mentioned in Robert Greyndour's Will some three hundred years earlier.

With labour being cheap, and with no Health and Safety to worry about, Sir John probably gave little thought to the injury suffered by the Carpenters boy, and was probably much more concerned about the amount of work still to be carried out, particularly as the work on the property appears to have gone on for at least a further ten years, and probably included the construction of, or refurbishment of, a chapel, a long parlour, as well as two turrets with gilded vanes; in fact it has been suggested that the exterior of the manor house closely resembled Syston Court. Although there is no record of bad workmanship and/or materials, trying to judge the position almost three hundred years later, there is a suspicion that all was not well, and that possibly Sir John relied too heavily on his steward, or was more gullible than he would admit, assuming that the quality of work would be acceptable without the need to travel to Gloucestershire and inspect what he was paying for. It is believed that Sir John died around 1736, and passed the ownership of Barrs Court and its estate to his son Sir Michael Newton. Exactly what happened then is unclear, but it is reasonable to assume that Sir Michael was a much more ruthless man than his father, and may well have been much more prepared to travel. Although there is no documentary evidence that the son ever visited his Gloucestershire inheritance, what is known is that by 1740, Sir Michael had had the house torn down, probably because he never had any intentions of living there himself, and with no heirs to whom the estate could be passed, the cost of refurbishment would have been seen as a total waste of money. Almost certainly more practical than his father, Sir Michael realised that he needed to raise revenue from the estate, and with the encumbrance of the house now removed, he set about creating a working farm.

It is known that for centuries, the manor house, and an area of garden twice the size of the house was surrounded by a moat, with a drawbridge. After the house had been pulled down, any unsalvageable material was used to dam the moat in two places, so that the remaining section of the moat had, from above, the appearance of the letter G without the upright being crossed, and with the top of the G being foreshortened. Here Sir Michael had a fairly large gabled farmhouse constructed, and at right angles to the farmhouse a cruciform shape Barn was built. To the southeast of the barn, the gully, which had been used as the moat's overflow drainage channel, was also dammed and the surrounding area was allowed to flood and thus create one, and possibly two fishponds, which survived for well over two hundred years, only being filled in when Lovell Homes Ltd decided to build houses in Staunton Drive. North of the fishponds was a large, oblong-shaped field known as *The Connigre,* which abutted onto the road or lane that ran alongside the park's boundary wall, and simply referred to as Parkwall, whilst the bottom left-hand corner of the field was adjacent to the barn. As its name implies, this was a field set aside for the "farming" of rabbits, and almost certainly this warren had been established back as far as the fifteenth century providing a very useful addition to the meat requirements of the big house, almost certainly augmented by a dovecote or pigeon house, although the location of the latter is open to speculation. Even though there was no longer a need to supplement the food consumed by the big house, Sir Michael no doubt saw all three-production sites as forming a very useful part of the overall farming revenue. However, farming was not the only source of income for the lord of the manor, because under his land was coal, and coal was becoming a very useful and expensive product, with a growing demand. For Sir Michael had the advantage that his coal was not very deep, although the drawback were the many faults found in the seams, and the seams themselves were quite often less than three feet thick. To extract the coal shallow bell pits would be dug, probably around 12-15feet in diameter, and anything up to twenty-five feet or more deep, depending upon the position of the seam. Having then exhausted the coal in the pit, the miners would tunnel for a distance of around ten feet into the seam on both side of the pit. This aspect was of course totally dependant upon the structure and direction of the seam, and the stability of the surrounding material, as safety was never on the minds of the mine owners, and they spent little if anything upon essentials such as shuttering and/or props, causing many miners to lose their lives as a result of rock falls or flooding. Once the particular bell-pit was exhausted, the miners would start a new set of diggings some twenty feet or so away from the first, in the general direction the seam seemed to take, using the extracted material to fill the abandoned pit. Exactly how many such pits were dug on Sir Michael's estate is not recorded, but before the housing estate was built, the site of a number of backfilled bell pits were identified, particularly to the south of the fishponds. The mining of coal was not confined to the land in the immediate vicinity of the manor house and/or farm, nor was it confined to the tenure of Sir Michael, as his predecessors were not averse to liberating part of the King's wood, and claiming the wealth that the land could provide from what became known as Sir John Newton's "*liberties.*" [see chapter 4] From around 1675, coal was being mined from a deeper *Buff Vein* seam under Newton's estate, and although the exact location of the Barrs Court Pit is not known with any certainty, as it was also known as Hollyguest Pit, and as over 600 tons of coal was uncovered and taken away in April 1993, when the cutting for the ring road ~ the A431 ~ was being excavated in the Stonehill area, it is reasonable to assume that the pit head was in the area now covered by the waste land adjacent to the Homebase Store.

The farmhouse may, in part, have been constructed as early as the fifteenth century, but with the many alterations made to this building, not to say its enlargement, it is impossible to be precise, especially as all that remains are part of the foundations of the enlarged farmhouse. A date stone showing the year 1879 has been found, and it has been suggested that this relates to a cowshed, and possibly the end of the building work, but equally it might relate to the completion of the enlarged farmhouse. By the time that any recorded archaeological work was carried out in the 1970's the condition of the farmhouse was extremely poor having suffered from at least thirty years of neglect, and post-war vandalism, with most of the salvageable stonework having already been robbed, however because of its thicker walls and basic structure, the cruciform shaped barn, has been preserved although it now has a new role in life. The other construction of interest is a semi enclosed rectangular shaped farmyard built just south of the barn. The eastern side of the yard was delineated by two structures containing, at ground level, arcade like openings facing inward, presumably designed to act as winter shelter for livestock, with haylofts above. These arcade structures consisted of segmental arches resting upon substantial rectangular piers, of which a number had, by the nineteenth century, been heavily buttressed, possibly because of subsidence cause by nearby mining, or waterlogged ground unable to support the weight of the piers/arches. A shelter of similar construction existed in an adjoining field, but with the desire to construct housing on the site in the 1970's, these structures were basically in the way, and were demolished, although not before it was recorded that adjoining the base there was a doorway that consisted of two large slabs of a coarse-grain white marble, much too refined for a working farmhouse let alone the outbuildings, and it must be assumed that these items had been recycled from the manor house when it was razed to the ground.

From archaeological work carried out in the 1970's, it would appear that the two-storied Gabled Farmhouse was the best part of 100 feet long, and generally faced northeast. The main entrance was in the middle of the building, with gables either side, whilst the roof behind the gables incorporated the chimneystacks of the kitchen and hall fireplaces. The windows to the main downstairs rooms, and the three upper floor rooms, consisted mainly of casement freestone mouldings, which were matched by the moulding around no less than three doors., one of which led directly into the kitchen area, whilst the third gave access to the dairy. It would seem quite likely that the existing farmhouse structure, and in particular the living quarters were extensively rebuilt with salvaged material when the manor house was destroyed, including, the construction of two wings built either side of the main entrance. Finally it is believed that during the early part of the nineteenth century, a substantial henhouse was built complete with nesting boxes, along side the left-hand wing.

Like a number of Newton's before him Sir Michael also died childless, and passed the ownership to yet another unrelated Newton family, whose interest in Barrs Court was even less, but with an absent landlord, the estate farm continued to thrive for probably the next 140 years, but certainly by the 1930's there was an air of abandonment percolating through the estate, with the Second World War being its death knell, and for the next three decades the farm buildings remained abandoned and free from human habitation, if not the habitation of less desirable creatures, and this, together with the effects of the weather, caused the buildings to deteriorate rapidly, aided and abetted by the new sport of vandalism.

Today the few stone foundations that remain are used as a play area, whilst on the farmland a different form of estate has been built

Gee Moor

The original manor of Gee Moor was situated north of Cock Road, and stretched, in that direction, as far as Newton's lands, and having Kingswood Hill in the west, and Syston Common in the east. It was not a particularly large manor, and formed part of the estates owned at one time by the Weston family of Weston Court. Predominantly this manor was covered by woodland, and it is said that it was the last part of the original Kingswood Forest to come under the blade of the axeman's wonton destruction during the period of disafforestation. Although well forested, a road leading from Warmley to Cock Road Hill known as Grimsbury Lane traversed the manor, and this road passed close to an old farmhouse once the residence of the Woodward family. Subsequently during the early part of the nineteenth century, the house and manor was purchased by a **Samuel Batchellor** and then taken over by his son **Edward** upon his father's death. Being a man of the cloth, Edward was not interested in maintaining the existence of the manor, and in June 1862 split the estate into numerous small parcels of land for sale.

Author's Footnote: Because of the close proximity of the above places, they all tend to share a common history, which only varies according to particular circumstances that may have happened at certain times. Thus standard matters shared throughout the whole area have only been highlighted under one particular heading because it avoids constant repetition, and not because that particular matter only occurred in that one place. For example, reference has been made under the section on Wick, to the introduction by the Romans of rabbits, but that information was just as equally true of the other identified places. Similarly the whole area was part of the king's forest, and was commensurately effected by the thirteenth century disafforestation, which in turn led to there being little if any settled authority until well into the nineteenth century. It should not by any means be overlooked that the removal of the royal prerogative meant that the forest became an open area for free booters to claim sections of the forest, and it was soon recognised as a haven for those who wished or were forced to live outside of the law. It gave the opportunist the ability to poach the red deer to near extinction, to cut down enormous quantities of timber, and to exploit the mineral wealth. As an example it is recorded that in 1325 a Michael de Dune was accused of cutting down, without permission, no less than one hundred oak trees, removing acres of gorse, and killing twelve deer. Whatever happened in general terms to the area of the forest or Chase, as it was officially known from the thirteenth century onward, almost certainly happened throughout the years to some degree or another in the area covered by this book, and accordingly the following points also apply.

The destruction of the forest, as illustrated above, continued during the fourteenth century, with more and more outsiders trespassing into its deeper regions. It is recorded that many persons entered the area without licence and took away quantities of fish, hare, rabbit, pheasant as well as deer and other animals of the forest. In addition they also carried away for their own profit, timber, firewood, gorse and coal. These actions continued for at least the next two hundred years, despite the fact that until around 1585, the Chase was, notionally at least, still part of the estates belonging to the noble Earls of Gloucester and Berkeley. However, around this time, other less noble persons set themselves up as claimants, and the Chase was mapped out into divisions, which were then given the claimants name and the term *liberty* was coined. Thus audaciously not only had the claimants stolen the land and that which stood upon it, they also had the cheek to claim that they were in fact liberating the land from the titled gentry who in essence already held the legal (Crown) right to cut down the timber for their own profit. Furthermore, the usurpers now set up mere-stones around their so-called liberties as boundary markers, and bonds were prepared in an attempt to legalize their spurious claims.

During the following century, many lawsuits took place regarding the legitimacy of these claims, and in 1615 James I issued a proclamation respecting the due observance of all forestlands. This caused great dissatisfaction and forest laws were severely tested with numerous attempts made to try and stop some of the coal pits from operating. In addition, the colliers were prevented from taking, and using for their own benefit, the coal privileges that had previously been granted to them. Further attempts were also made to try and prevent more encroachment in the forest, which resulted in riots taking place. Despite this royal interference, the claimants continued to exploit that which the forest could yield, both above and below the ground. Almost certainly most of the timber in the Chase had all but disappeared by the end of the second decade of the seventeenth century, and over the next few decades the position regarding the liberties and the land claims continued to occupy the minds and pockets of the lawyers and the courts alike but, no doubt, by the early 1640's men's minds were turning to the subject of King or Parliament and, upon deciding whom they should support.

CHAPTER 2 "WAR and SKIRMISHES"

By 1642, England was in the grips of a Civil War and Bristol, the second largest and important city in the kingdom, had decided that it should support the Parliamentarians. In the West Country, the main bulk of the King's support came from Royalist Cornwall, and on the 5th July 1643, Sir Bevill Grenvile's Cornish Pikemen supported by Prince Maurice's cavalry, came face to face with the Parliamentarian Army, which was led by Sir William Waller, on the slopes and heights of Lansdown, Freezing Hill and Tog Hill.

As 1642 changed into 1643 King Charles I, having fled from London with his court, set up his headquarters in the university city of Oxford. Within weeks many influential and wealthy royalist supporters had followed the king and his court, and by mid March there was hardly a lodging available at any price. The academic halls of learning were commandeered; books were piled on top of each other as room was made for just one more family, whilst other halls were used as royal residence as well as a seat of Government. All over the city normal health and cleanliness gradually deteriorated as the ruminants of seventeenth century sanitation became virtually non existent, rubbish and night soil piled up in the streets, and as the weather turned warmer, so did the heat within the king's chambers as despite the massive increase in the fly and insect population, that invaded every aspect of existence he planned, with his Chiefs of Staff, an offensive to recapture London. A pivotal element in the king's plan was centred upon Sir Ralph Hopton's ability to persuade the mainly royalist Cornishmen to leave their homes, and perhaps even more importantly their native County and come and fight for their King. As a sub plot, there were two other matters of concern to the King and his plans, firstly and most importantly was the fact that between the King in Oxford, and what he hoped would be Hopton's army were the cities of Bath, and its high-ranking and influential neighbour Bristol, both currently and willingly held by Parliamentary troops. These troops were commanded by one of the most able of all the Parliamentary generals, Sir William Waller, and this was the other concern to the king, not so much Waller's undoubted ability, but because he was a good and close personal confidant of Hopton, and might therefore try and persuade his friend to join on the side of Parliament. Such is the strange and dreadful nature of a civil war, that frequently brothers as well as friends and extended families found themselves on opposing sides, and at each other's throats. During the early stages of this dreadful war that was tearing England apart, Waller had written to his friend the following:

" To my noble friend Sir Ralphe Hopton.

Sir. The experience I have had of your worth, and the happiness I have enjoyed in your friendship are wounding considerations when I look upon this present distance between us. Certainly my affections to you are so unchangeable, that hostility itself cannot violate my friendship in your person, but I must be true to the cause wherein I serve."

Having completed his letter, the whole of which is too long to reproduce here, Waller completed it with the following: [In all instances the modern spelling has been used].

We are both upon the stage and must act those parts that are assigned us in this tragedy. Let us do it in a way of honour, and without personal animosities whatsoever the issue be, I shall never willingly relinquish the dear title of

Your most affectionate friend and faithful servant.

Signed Wm. Waller

Such was the tragic circumstances of a civil war.

As for the king he needed to have no fears regarding Hopton's loyalty, and his ability in raising a Cornish army. Soon he had over 10,000 men marching across the border into Devon and on through that county and the County of Somerset on its way towards Bradford-on-Avon, whilst always heading and making for Oxford. En route the king's nephew, Prince Maurice and his troop of cavalry joined Hopton, and being of Royal blood, he immediately took command of the Cornish army. This combined royalist army reached the small Wiltshire town during the 2nd July 1643, and being keen to please his uncle, as well as being a little hot headed, Prince Maurice could not resist the temptation of taking the rich prize of Bristol. Surely with the force he now led, there was a golden opportunity to chase the Parliamentary troops out of both Bristol and Bath then, with the king and his forces coming down from Oxford, and Prince Maurice leading the Cornish army up from his success in Bristol, Waller's army would be crushed between both of them.

It is one thing to be of royal blood, and to be able to exert your privileged position with demands, however unreasonable or impracticable they might be, but that does not necessarily mean that you always get your own way, especially if the opposing army has not read the script. Unfortunately for Prince Maurice, Waller had stationed a sizeable part of his Parliamentary army on Claverton Down, and already he had patrols out in the countryside looking for the Royalist Army, and to see whether or not they were likely to engage in battle. Unprepared to enter the field of battle at this precise moment in time, Prince Maurice led the bulk of his troops around Claverton Down, and encamped for the night at Batheaston, although throughout much of the 3rd July, a number of minor skirmishes took place where patrols from both armies surprised each other. During the evening of that day, Prince Maurice held a council of war with his field commanders when it was decided that the Royalist army should take the high ground and occupy the heights of Lansdown on the following day.

Leaving their overnight camp at Batheaston in the early hours of the 4th July, Prince Maurice took the Cornish Pikemen and his cavalry troop along the northern side of the River Avon, around the foot of Little Solsbury Hill, whilst all the while gradually gaining height on his way to the village of Charlcombe. It was probably at around this time that Prince Maurice and his commanders heard the unexpected news that Waller had already anticipated their move, and had outflanked them by moving, undercover of darkness, his Parliamentarians from Bath to the flat open plateau on top of Lansdown, and not only did the enemy occupy the hill, they had had sufficient time to make adequate defensive arrangements for them to confidently face the Royalists should they decide to continue with their approach. This calamitous news caused Prince Maurice and his army to about turn, and head back down the hill to Swainswick, striking north over Charmy Down, and on through the narrow twisting lanes towards Fuddlebrook and then to Marshfield, where they made camp.

Although this move placed the Royalist army north of the Parliamentarians, and therefore there was, or should have been, in theory, a clear road to Oxford, Prince Maurice still had his eyes set on Bristol, and not only that, he could not be certain how easily it might be for Waller to catch up with him, or to push him into another trap. In essence, neither Prince Maurice nor Sir Ralph Hopton had little choice but to seek out and, if possible, destroy the enemy, and tomorrow, the 5th July would have to be the day of their nemesis.

The Royalist army, like many armies before and since, were up as the sun began to rise over the easterly hills, the edge of each pike was honed as best they could with the few available sharpening stones left amongst their number that by now had probably shrunk to a little over 6,000 men. The lucky ones may well have breakfast of hard dry biscuits and watered down beer, although some of the more enterprising men may well have stolen-out during the night and purloined a chicken or two from some hapless nearby villager, supplementing the fowl with whatever vegetables they could find. By six o'clock, the advanced section of the army were marching south, and by around 8a.m. the whole of the Royalist army of footsoldiers and cavalry had reached Tog Hill, and some were beginning to cross over to Freezing Hill. Once again, Waller had out thought the Prince, and by early light had already moved his army across Lansdown, to the edge facing Freezing Hill, and with his typical thoroughness had found time to have his troops throw up defence earthworks from which his musketeers could fire on the approaching army. Although little in the way of fighting happened over the next couple of hours, the occasional musket ball was fired when one side thought that the other side was getting too close, and from time to time there was the odd skirmish between the opposing soldiers. However, a little while past ten o'clock, after what appeared to be a partial tactical withdrawal of some of the Cornish Pikemen, the Parliamentarians began to take the initiative, and a large group of Sir William Waller's troops charged down from the top of Lansdown in an attempt to get amongst the retreating Pikemen. This movement led to around two or three hours of nearly continuous hard, mainly hand-to-hand fighting between both sides, until a combined effort by the Cornishmen on foot, and Carnarvon's horse regiment, drove the Parliamentarians down Tog Hill where they were badly mauled and defeated. Casualties were heavy on both sides, but still the battle raged, and whilst a group of Parliamentarians had been soundly beaten, the bulk of their army still occupied the top of Lansdown.

It was now the turn of Waller's army or certainly part of it to retreat, as they moved off Freezing Hill to the safety of their comrades, and quite deliberately they did not hide the fact that they were withdrawing, as their movements masked the musketeers, who moved down from the top of Lansdown, and took up positions along the hedges, which would flank any advance by the Cornish, led by their kinsman Sir Beville Grenville. The slope up which Sir Beville led his Pikemen was extremely steep, which made their approach painfully slow, and many fell as the musketeers took their toll. On five separate occasions the Cornishmen advanced, and on five separate occasions they were forcibly thrown back, leaving many of their friends and comrades either dead or wounded, including their commander lying on the blood soaked ground mortally wounded. Such was the tenacity of the

Cornishmen, who refused to consider themselves beaten, that with even greater gallantry, they stormed the hill for a sixth time, gained the brow of the hill and seized the earthworks. With the Parliamentarians falling back behind a long stonewall on top of Lansdown, the artillery began to take their share of glory, but with troops on both side utterly exhausted the fighting diminished, and by early evening the battlefields were silent with the exception of the groans from the wounded.

Whilst much of the area covered by this book was not directly affected by the Battle of Lansdown, the proximity of the battle must have had a bearing on all who lived in the area. With the armies of the day living off the land, there would undoubtedly have been the billeting of higher-ranking noblemen upon their contemporaries, whilst food, provisions and shelter for the men, their animals, and the hordes of camp followers, would almost certainly have been given, or more likely taken, in exchange for worthless promissory notes. It is also possible that local men took part in the battle, as relatives fought relatives, plus there would be the spoils of war which would have tempted many of the locals to scavenge the site of the battle during the long hot summer days of July 1643. In addition it has been estimated that a total of at least five hundred men, both royalist and parliamentarians had deserted from their respective armies during the battle, and having decided to run, the most likely way would have been south and west, towards the villages of Wick, Beach, Oldland Bitton etc. Although they may have discarded their weapons, they would still have clearly stood out as soldiers and/or strangers amongst the close-knit parochial society that inhabited these villages, but without their abandoned colour sashes normally used to identify to which side they belonged, they probably stood a reasonable chance of persuading whoever may have been prepared to give them food and shelter, that they were truly on their side, such is the nature of a civil war. Some may have stayed, some may have tried to reach home, but all would have been regarded as hunted animals, never sure whom they could trust.

Two years later the military control of Bristol was now in the hands of Prince Rupert and the Royalists, and in August 1645, Oliver Cromwell and his staff, visited the area in and around Oldland; Warmley and Syston for a number of days, to discuss with Sir Thomas Fairfax the siege of the City. At this time Prince Rupert had at his disposal approximately 3,000 troops to help defend the city and its environs, but unfortunately both Bristol and some of the surrounding villages, were suffering from the extremely harmful effects of the plague, to the extent that it has been estimated that at least one hundred people were dying each week from this malaise, and its related illnesses. During the siege a number of skirmishes took place between royalist raiding parties leaving the relative safety of the city walls, and the advanced parliamentarian troops. For obvious reasons the defenders of Bristol were desperate to lift the siege, and were no doubt equally quite desperate to escape the ravages of the plague and the summer stench of the city. However, despite the bad conditions found in the city, they were a very proud group of people, or certainly their leaders were, who were not going to give up this rich prize of the second most important city in the kingdom to their sworn enemy without accepting the discomforts and putting up a fight. Of course those who made these decisions were not the ones actually suffering the appalling conditions, that scenario was left to the common soldier and the working class citizens. Probably unknown to them, during their period of depravation, Prince Rupert, and his generals received a number of propositions to surrender the City of Bristol to the attackers, but there was usually some form of deadlock that could not be broken by words alone. Quite frequently the problem arose by the numerous amount of procrastination emanating from Prince Rupert, who tried almost every trick in the book in the vain hope that the Parliamentarians would ultimately become bored, and pack up and go home. This was not to be, and the only solution for the attackers was a military one. Cromwell and his staff drew up the necessary plans, and at around 2a.m. on Wednesday the 10th September 1645 the attack was launched on Bristol from the east. Within a relatively short space of time the city fell to the Parliamentarians, and Prince Rupert and his army and followers were run out of the city.

Within two years, Oliver Cromwell was dead, and during 1658 the monarchy was restored to these islands in the guise of Charles II. This brought about great changes with demands made by evicted Royalists, for compensation arising from their Civil War losses, and the restoration of property and land, either previously confiscated, or sold under duress. Within the population, there was still a certain level of unrest and disquiet, and before the seventeenth century drew to a close, there was to take place in the Parish of Oldland, two minor military encounters, which helped to change the course of English history.

King Charles II was at heart a Catholic but, he sat on a Protestant throne, and as a consequence, his reign was one of intrigue and deceit. Fines and arrests, drove many of this Country's citizens into forming secret religious ceremonies and, by continual oppression, the Crown caused its enemies to form a network of tightly bound and devoted Communities, which were subsequently to form the perfect foundation on which to build a revolt. Into this arena of public disquiet stepped James, Duke of Monmouth, the illegitimate and only son of Charles II. Even though his mother, Lucy Barlow, tried to legitimise her son's claim to the throne, by claiming that she had secretly married his father, the King disowned James, and instead named his brother James, Duke of York, as his successor. Thus, upon the death of Charles II in February 1685, it was the autocratic Duke of York who became King James II.

The rebellious population of the West Country just needed a catalyst to turn their dissent into a revolt, and this occurred when the Duke of Monmouth landed at Lyme on the Dorset coast in June 1685. Whilst many men flocked to Monmouth's side out of frustration and the spirit of adventure, all armies, including rebel bands, required money to provide the basic needs of war, such as weapons, food and clothing for the men. Within a week or two of his landing, Monmouth had all but run out of the little money he had started with, and his only hope of raising more would come from his audacious idea of capturing Bristol, and squeezing the money out of its overflowing Customs House, and from the many wealthy citizens, although very obviously some would pay up quite willingly as part of their dues for supporting his cause. Knowing that it had been virtually impossible to take Bristol from the Somerset side, Monmouth decided that he best attack the city from the Gloucestershire side, which in turn would mean having to cross the River Avon, and with there being only one bridge crossing the river between Bristol and Bath, Monmouth's army began the long march from Bridgwater to Keynsham, via Glastonbury, Shepton Mallet, and Pensford, where he arrived on the 25th June 1685.

Alert to the potential danger of an uprising in the west, and the obvious need to prevent Bristol from lending her full support to the rebels, James II needed to station in the city at least a battalion of his loyal troops, but realistically he knew that it would take him longer to get those troops to Bristol, than it would take Monmouth's men to march there from Bridgwater. Having studied the maps, and considered the likely approach Monmouth would make, the King quickly recognised the strategic importance of the County Bridge at Keynsham and, accordingly, sent out an order for the bridge to be destroyed by the local militia.

Having arrived at Pensford during the afternoon of the 25th June and set up camp, Monmouth gathered his senior officers together, and over an early evening meal, it was decided that a troop of cavalry in charge of a captain should undercover of darkness, enter Keynsham, take possession of the bridge, and to carry out necessary repairs to enable Monmouth's main force to cross into Gloucestershire the following day. Whether the king's men intended carrying out a very satisfactory job of destroying the bridge will never be known, but what is known, is that the militia sent to carry out the work soon laid down their tools, and ran off when they heard the approach of Monmouth's cavalry. Finding the only slightly damaged bridge unguarded, and with masonry tools scattered around, the rebel soldiers, who included a number of masons, soon began to repair what little damage the bridge had sustained. With the king's militia nowhere to be seen, the uninterrupted work was carried out so that by dawn the whole of Monmouth's peasant army was able to cross onto Sydenham Meadow on the Gloucestershire side of the River Avon, and into the parish of Oldland.

The intended plan was to carry Bristol by a night assault later that day but, as it was raining quite heavily, causing the swollen river to flood the lower parts of the meadow, and as there was little or no shelter for his troops on that side of the river, Monmouth ordered his army back to Keynsham, where sufficient accommodation and cover had been found, and Monmouth could then use the day allowing the soldiers a chance to rest after days of continuous marching. For security reasons, the Duke instructed cavalry troops to patrol in and around Bitton and Oldland so that they could flush out any Royalist troops. As the wet day wore on, and no doubt, with the nerves of those on patrol reaching breaking point, there occurred during the early evening of the 26th June, two audacious attacks by trained regular Royalist Troopers against the cavalry patrols, not only causing much confusion to the amateurs but also their death. One of these relatively minor skirmishes took place south of Londonderry Farm, and enabled the royalist troops to probe the outer defences of Monmouth's peasant army, whilst the other was nearer Willsbridge, and appears to have involved only horse soldiers on both sides. Neither encounter could hardly be regarded as some of the greatest military events in history, involving as they did probably fewer than three hundred and fifty Royalist regulars, and probably no more than five hundred or so ill trained, and ill equipped rebels but, Monmouth listened and took heed of the many stories that surrounded the aftermath of these two minor events, and like so many unsubstantiated stories told by those who had heard the story from someone else, they began to be exaggerated out of all proportion. His men, with their own fear of a battlefield for which they were ill equipped, never found it difficult to amplify the strength and size of the opposition, which introduced and then heightened the Duke's level of trepidation, and then on top of that there were the stories of those involved from the other side. As so often happens when two opposing forces come face to face with each other, and fighting starts, soldiers on both sides will surrender and be captured, and this occurred during these two encounters, and thus besides listening to his own men exalt the size and strength of the enemy, Monmouth also listened to, and then placed a great deal of credence upon the word of the few captured royalist soldiers, who, for their own safety were very happy to suggest that they were part of a much larger force than existed in reality, and that this large, in fact, very large army was close at hand and ready to do battle.

Any successful general in the field, needs to have considerable belief in his own ability, and in the ability of his men, as well as having a high degree of intelligence relating to the enemy's strength and position. Monmouth knew that his men had enormous amounts of courage, and a certain amount of enthusiasm, but the bulk of them were not trained soldiers, and furthermore many of the weapons they carried could easily have been found on any farm, and in any garden. The fact that some of his men had been killed in two small fights, without inflicting much more than a scratch or two on the enemy, demonstrated to Monmouth that courage and enthusiasm alone would not win his uprising. These doubts manifested themselves in Monmouth's mind more and more as he became quite convinced that the stories he heard were correct, some of which now included the fact that the main part of the King's Army, some four thousand strong, were on their way to do battle, having not long since passed through Hanham. In modern parlance, Monmouth "lost his bottle" on Sydenham Meadow, and convincing himself that not only was there an approaching force, but that its strength was much too great and too powerful for his rebel troops to cope with, he abandoned his dream of capturing Bristol, and instructed his troops to de-camp. In the middle of a miserable wet night, and still without any sign of the four thousand royalist troops having arrived, Monmouth and his pathetic army of men who universally believed that their world needed to be changed, sneaked away towards Bath, and the road which ultimately led to Sedgemoor and the dreadful end of a rebellion.

Unlike the Battle of Lansdown, some forty-two years earlier, the effects of these two skirmishes, and the proximity of not only the rebel army, but also the King's Army, upon the local community, would have been much less. Certainly there are no records of rebels being seen very far from the Gloucestershire side of Sydenham Meadow, nor are there any records of locals having joined Monmouth's cause. The Duke of Beaufort would probably have kept his local Gloucester Militia active in dissuading any of those interested and/or curious to assist the rebel cause from taking any direct action and, probably, one of the main effects of the uprising upon the local inhabitants, would have been the inconvenience of having many more soldiers moving in and out of the area than normal. There were almost certainly pressures put on the landowners/farmers, as the movement of the two armies and the creations of temporary camps, would have caused damage to the land, particularly wet land, and in addition those same landowners/farmers would have been forcibly persuaded to provide food for the troops and their many horses. However, without doubt, the greatest effect on the locals would have been caused by the heavy June rain, which would have dampened their spirits and caused all, but the most inquisitive, to have stayed indoors most of the time. By the end of June, the events at Sydenham Meadows would have been discussed and debated in a variety of ways, and in a variety of establishments, but the most important event of the day would still involve the need to keep body and soul together, to provide food, clothing and shelter for the family and, the return to their humdrum existence and the safety of not being politically involved.

CHAPTER 3 "COAL and the MINERS"

Following the restoration of the monarchy in 1658, numerous petitions were sent to the king from this part of the world by those who were interested in restoring their lands and rights, lost during the time of the Commonwealth. No doubt Charles II was politely reminded of the petitioners' undying support for his cause during and since those troubled times, emphasising the risks that they and their family had taken against the Parliamentarians. Whilst many of the petitions ended up in the waste paper basket, a few were read, considered and granted, including the claim made by Kingswood's Sir Baynham Throckmorton. So successful was his claim that he was additionally appointed head ranger of Kingswood Chase, an honour and an appointment that, from his point of view, came with strings attached. In granting his petition, the king laid down the condition that Sir Baynham should, and this is where the sting was hidden, restock the Chase with deer and to suppress the enclosers at his expense. One must presume that Sir Baynham considered the conditions worthwhile as, having obtained his appointment, he vigorously went to work, and prosecuted many intruders, some of whom were arrested and sent to prison, something which the knighted gentleman was quite happy to do as it increased his standing in the community, that is the higher class community, who after all where not only his friends they were also the local magistrates.

By now there had been established within the forest area, over seventy coalpits of varying size and productivity, the bulk of which had been unofficially opened by the entrepreneurial claimants in their so called liberties. These men who had seen, over the years past, an opportunity of exploiting the natural wealth of the forest, particularly the mineral wealth, and accordingly, had staked their claims, but rarely, if ever, got their own hands dirty, instead they preferred to leave the dirty, dangerous work to the lower classes. It was they who could work in the extremely difficult and uncomfortable dirty conditions, risking cave-ins, unexpected flooding, plus injuries to any part of their body as they crawled along narrow tunnels to earn a few pence, not for them the rich pickings, that was left for the owners to crow over. Although the conditions for the miners were extremely poor, they were a tough, no nonsense close-knit group, who were fully prepared to challenge anyone in authority who tried to take their employment away from them. Similarly, the owners did not like the idea of having their profits interrupted, and thus neither party took too kindly to the high-handed provocative actions currently employed by Sir Baynham. During the next ten years or so, the Chase was restocked with no less than five thousand deer, and Sir Baynham continued with his task of eviction, although it is suspected that some of the entrepreneurs, possibly friends of friends, or friends of influential persons, had less hassle and trouble and were allowed to continue extracting coal. Certainly Sir Baynham stuck to the assignment of trying to legally evict such libertarians as Sir John Newton, Thomas Chester, John Berkeley and William Player, although by the time of his death in 1680, those four men still held their liberties. Although with his passing, his estate was left to his three daughters, there was no-one powerful enough or determined enough to stop the owners of the liberties from arrogantly entering the Chase and taking the law into their own hands, and in doing so showed their complete and utter contempt of the earlier royal decree and chose to totally ignore its existence. Now they were not only prepared to profit from the natural mineral wealth of the forest, they were also prepared to take what they could when they could, and a ready made market for venison was soon established. Realising that they were being "out gunned", the three daughters soon decided to sell their inheritance for as much as they could, and in 1681, they assigned their late father's previously held rights of the forest to a Francis Creswick and others, for the handsome sum of £850, enough money to probably set each of them up for a reasonable and comfortable life.

With there being numerous numbers of coalpits in the area, which were now for the first time being legitimised, the old difficulties of surreptitiously carrying the coal, by packhorses, to the market place over rough forest tracks, could be properly considered. In addition the legalisation, however unofficial it was, meant that more people wanted to become customers, as well as existing customers wanting more and more coal. Thus the existing methods of transportation could not cope with the changing circumstances, and as a consequence proper roads needed to be constructed through the Chase, which in turn led to there being many more gaps appearing amongst the trees and, within a very short space of time, the whole area of the Chase was changed for ever. The many changes that occurred probably affected to a much greater degree, those persons who had inhabited the forest for a number of generations; and whose own culture and way of life had been hewn out of the hard way of life they and their ancestors had grown used to, and who by now, held in high esteem their tough independent stance on life, their loyalty to their fellow foresters, and the fact that whilst they stayed in the forest, they were above, or certainly excluded from the law of the land. To them, although they would not have recognized it as such, the law they lived by was the law of the jungle, with unruly colliers ravaging the woods, searching and taking wood to use as pit props, wood and gorse for burning, stone for building, the deer that were left, occasionally supplemented their more normal diet of boiled hare, rabbit or pigeon, or any other small mammal or rodent that happened to cross their path. At times all these sources of food became scarce, and it was not unknown for the enterprising foresters to turn their lawless skills to a spot of sheep rustling, which like the deer were not only an important source of food to supplement their meagre diets, but the dead animals could also be turned into money, for many a local butcher was prepared to purchase the occasional carcass, for a few pence without the need to ask from where it had come. At least in this way they had some money and sheep, or venison scraps to feed the family. In carrying out these illegal activities, the foresters were taking a huge risk, for if they were caught they did not receive a caution from the local constabulary, or a deferred custodial sentence from the magistrates, instead many a hard working collier, blacksmith, mason and those with other skills, who had fallen upon hard times, found themselves dangling from a rope because the upper class were determined to keep all the benefits for themselves, and make an example of the verminous working classes, even if it meant that the imposed death penalty left penniless widows and fatherless children to die from malnutrition, disease, with little or no hope.

Francis Creswick conveyed his estate to his son, who enjoyed his status during the time when the seventeenth century changed into the eighteenth century, and subsequently this inheritance passed to his son, also christened Francis, in around 1710 who then held the estate for approximately twenty-two years, until his death in 1732. For the next two years the ownership of the estate was in limbo, until 1734 when a new lease was granted to a Mr Onisiphorous Tyndall, a wealthy Drysalter of Bristol. Although Mr Tyndall had high expectations of being able to exercise his control over the land he now leased, and for the wealth that his investment would produce, his self belief was not justified, and throughout his lease, the wealth produced from the exploitation of coal and other minerals became the dominant factor, and ultimately won the long struggle against the indigenous deer and the trees; as for Mt Tyndall, he became a wealthy man and the last tenant of the Chase.

The nearby city of Bristol was, for both domestic and industrial use, heavily dependent on locally produced coal, and in particular that mined in Kingswood, and in fact it is probably true to say that Bristol's prosperity was much more conditional upon the accessibility of the Kingswood coalfield, than Kingswood's wealth was based upon the proximity of Bristol. However, such were the circumstances of the relationship, and of Bristol's dependency, that the name changed from the Kingswood Coalfield, to the Bristol Coalfield. By the end of the seventeenth century, the population in and around the coalfield was growing quite rapidly, and most of those who lived in the area were reliant for a living upon the production of coal in one form or another, either as actual miners, or ancillary workers, or as carriers, or as the family dependents of those workers. With the further development and growth, during the eighteenth century of Bristol's glass and pottery; sugar-refining; brewing; distilling; smelting and soap-making industries, all very highly dependent upon the burning of coal, more and more of this rich mineral product was demanded, and more and more was extracted from the Kingswood area. There was in fact a Royal decree that prevented glassmakers from using wood to heat their furnaces and they had no choice, if they wished to stay in business, other than to use coal.

For those who had to extract the coal this was a period of very primitive conditions and, a great deal of hard work, with little financial reward, much dreaded poverty, and lawlessness to contend with. As for the colliery owners, they saw the ever-increasing demand for coal as a way of becoming extremely rich, without ever having to get their hands dirty, in more ways than one. Despite giving their pits such fanciful quaint names as *Shereoaks; Made for Ever;* and *Thwarting* in Kingswood; *Flashaway;* and *John Jacks* in Syston; *Great Cart;* and *Brandy Bottom* in Parkfield, whilst in Oldland there were pits with names such as *Bull Hall; Haul Lane; Cowhorn Hill,* and *California,* these picturesque titles hid the fact that their owners took little if any care of their employees or of their employees welfare or safety, rarely if ever visiting the source of their wealth, and caring absolutely nothing for the living conditions of the many dependent families. At the beginning, coal was found on the surface, or just under the surface, but by the eighteenth century, all of the coal had to be physically dug out of the ground. Quite often, a twelve-foot wide shaft would be dug down to the coal seam, which could be anything from twenty feet below the surface, and possibly no more than eighteen inches thick. The miners would shore up the side of the pit as best they could, and when they had extracted the coal, they would then start to tunnel into the uncovered seam, for probably a maximum distance of twenty to twenty-five feet, in both directions, or for as long as the seam was exposed, as it should be borne in mind that in the main, the coal seams were more often than not broken and dislocated, having been subjected to the tremendous upheaval and lateral pressure of the earth's movement that had taken place over millions of years. Once the miners had extracted as much of the coal as possible, they took what bearings they could with regard to the likely direction the seam would take and then they moved forty or fifty feet across the surface and started to dig another pit, using the waste material as back fill down the original shaft. Having reached the coal seam the above process would be repeated on a number of occasions. Over each shaft, the wood workers would construct a windlass from which they would hang a large bucket, into which the miners would place all that had been dug, so that the material could be hauled to the surface and sorted and graded, very often by young girls and their mothers. Even when in theory only coal was being dug and sent to the surface, each bucket still needed to be sorted to take out the rogue stone and other foreign bodies which had been shovelled up.

Gradually as the demand for coal grew and grew and grew, the coal seams nearer to the surface became exhausted, and the miners had to dig deeper to find even older seams. Those seams had also been subjected to the millions of years of movement within the earth, and as a consequence there was rarely if ever a seam which could be worked in a standing position, and at most times, the miners, the majority of whom were most unlikely to be more than 5' 2" tall, would have to hack the coal out in a squatting or lying position, from where it had lain for those millions of years,. The deeper the miners went the more hazardous was their work, with one of the main problems with which they had to contend, being sudden and unexpected ingress of water. Other problems were roof falls, sufficient availability of oxygen, not counting the dust, and the many abrasions suffered by the body that had to work in an extremely confined space, surrounded by rough and very often sharp objects. Because clothes were expensive, and because the miners became very hot in their working conditions, many of the men would only wear breeches, leaving their upper body, arms and lower legs to the punishment of abrasions, cuts, scratches and numerous other accidental injuries, most of which would soon be covered in coal dust, that would leave a tell tale bluish coloured scar. However, the one problem that afflicted many miners, firedamp an explosion that occurs when a certain proportion of methane gas is mixed with oxygen did not exist in the Kingswood coalfield, and the miners could quite safely work underground with a lighted candle stuck in their leather helmet.

Having struggled with the underground conditions, the difficulties in bringing the coal to the surface and the problems of having it screened and sorted, there was then the difficult question of getting the product to the customer in either Bristol or Bath, or even occasionally further afield. Bad enough in the dry months, assuming that you could put up with the dust, but certainly not much fun in the wet and winter weather. During the seventeenth and eighteenth centuries, the only way of moving coal to the market place was by horse, either as a packhorse or as a carthorse. The former would probably be unable to carry more than three to four hundred pounds weight per journey, whilst the carthorse would not have been able to draw more than one thousand pounds weight including of course the weight of the cart. With the roads little more than dirt tracks, which worsened in the winter weather, a journey to Bristol from Oldland would probably have taken two days, plus a day and a half for the return journey. Certainly there are strong indications that pits often only worked two or three day weeks during the winter because of transport difficulties, although it is possible that part of the reason was to keep the price high when the demand was high, thus making a much larger profit for the mine owner, but that could be regarded as rather a cynical view. The greater the demand for coal, the greater the transport problems, with the tracks and roads constantly under repair, and quite frequently under water. Such were the difficulties and such was the demand that during the early 1750's, the price of delivered coal increased from 8/- (40p) per ton, to 13/- (65p) per ton, a grossly inflationary increase of sixty-two point five per cent.

Many of the small independent pits, and their owners could not cope with the market changes being forced upon them and, thus, a number of local pits were grouped together under one management umbrella and became known as "works", such as *JOSIAH JEFFERIES WORKS* at Warmley. The main effect of this was that those owners with financial interests elsewhere where able to sell their pits at a reasonable price, and leave the running, of the coal works, and more particularly the marketing of the coal, to the more ruthless professionals, thus preventing the larger users trying to "pick-off" the vulnerable smaller pits and cause a price war. However, the quandary of getting the coal to the market place as cheaply as possible remained over the following decades, with many fanciful solutions being sought including, during the 1782-1793 period, a number of suggestions that the product should be conveyed by water with the construction of suitable canals, but nobody could agree that there was one route which would serve the needs of the majority, and the minority could not raise the money needed to build the canal themselves.

Around this time, pits became mines inasmuch as the men needed to dig deeper and deeper into the mineral wealth of Kingswood. As already stated, the Kingswood area was fortunate to be free of "fire-damp" (methane), although the miner occasionally came across the miniscule pockets of "choke damp" (carbon-monoxide). The absence of the explosive gas should not imply that extracting coal from the Kingswood Coalfield was a doddle, as although the men and children who worked underground may have been able to carry, with reasonable impunity, a naked candle flame through the narrow confined tunnels, as they hacked at the coal and then subsequently transported the material to the base of the shaft, many of those same men and children drowned whilst working in the Kingswood mines. To try and control the problems of flooding, as such incidents were a confounded nuisance to the owners inasmuch as it caused the extraction of the coal to be disrupted, which in turn had an adverse effect upon the level of their profits, a situation that was quite intolerable to the owners, and accordingly it fell upon them to look for ways of preventing the flooding and for the underground water to be removed. The obvious answer was to install pumping machines, which the owners began to introduce with great enthusiasm, not so much with regard to the safety of their employees, but because they soon discovered that by "drying out" one section of the mine, it exposed other seams, particularly those below the water level, which could now be worked, and the more coal extracted meant more money in the pockets of the owners. More money then enabled the owners to invest in bigger and better pumping machines that allowed more areas of the mine to be free of flooding, which in turn exposed more seams, and in due course more money for those who never dirtied their hands, and more death, danger and injury for those whose hands were always dirty. With the insatiable demand for coal, and an insatiable demand for money earned at the expense of others, the mines became bigger, both in depth and spread, whilst at the same time they also became more dangerous, a factor that rarely came into the equation, The only concern for the owner was "is the mine making me money?" If the answer was yes then continue digging, if no then abandon the mine and move elsewhere. The fact that the miners were being exposed to ever-greater dangers with the expansion of the mines was rarely, if ever, a concern of the owners as demonstrated during the year of 1795, when water in a Warmley pit, that had risen

60 feet in less than two hours, caused the death of five trapped miners, most of whom were married men with dependant families, including one man who left a widow and eight children. Despite the scale of the tragedy, no compensation was paid by the owner to the surviving relatives, and no arrangements were made by the owner to look after the future welfare of the surviving relatives, it was as though they simply did not exist, and certainly he appears to have felt no compassion and/or responsibility for those who were left. All that happened was that the miners and colliery workers clubbed together and raised a few pounds out of their meagre earnings, and shared the hardship with the deceased miners' dependants.

As late as May 1839, another major drowning tragedy took place, this time at *Lodge Pit* Kingswood, when water flooded the mine to a depth of one hundred and twenty feet, and caused the premature death of twenty year old, **William Johnson** and the eight young lads in his section, being the three sets of brothers **Joseph & Stephen Goolden; William & George Palmer; William & George Frankom**, plus their companions **John Dursley** and **John Holbrook**. Such was the state of the mine, and the damage caused by the violent inflow of water that it took three months before the mine was finally pumped free of the water, and rescuers could enter the mine with safety, but regardless of their efforts none of the young bodies were ever found.

Although by the eighteenth century water was pumped out from all of the mines with the aid of machinery, the local coal was still brought to the surface by means of a windlass, somewhat similar to that used to draw water from a well, the main difference being that, at the mines, the windlass was considerably larger and usually pulled up more than one bucket at a time. However, by the 1790's a great horizontal drum called a whimsey, around which the winding rope gradually coiled and uncoiled, came more and more into general use, and with it came the ability to introduce a "lift" type cage, so that miners could be taken up and down the shaft in order to proceed to and from their place of work. Although this facility was referred to as a cage, more often than not, it was little more than a platform on which miners stood, having probably no more than two stable sides, and frequently no roof. No doubt its introduction did not fully convince the miners that it was any more safe than the old methods of getting to and from the coalface, and quite often, they would go up and down the shaft using the same buckets as were used to bring up the coal. Probably, they were at times "encouraged" to use this method, particularly when descending, as from the owners point of view, it would be more economical to send down a bucket full of men and boys, rather than to send down an empty bucket.

Prior to the introduction of the cage, the miners were lowered into and out of the pit on a thick rope, which had attached to it loops of thinner rope that were capable of going around the miner's thighs. Thus by reaching out from the edge of the shaft towards the centre of the black void through which the shaft descended, each miner could grab hold of the rope with his hand, and then swing himself across, whilst at the same time manoeuvring his legs through the loops so that he ended up in something akin to a sitting position, although apart from the thin loop, and his grip upon the thicker rope, there was little if anything between him and a rather long drop. The rope and man would then be lowered six feet or so and left to dangle whilst the same process was repeated by the next man, and then the next man until there were approximately ten or twelve men on the rope strung up like onions on a string ready to be lowered into the eternal darkness and down to the working level, and the start of a fourteen hour shift. During the gradual, or not so gradual descent, if the windlass operator lost control of his equipment, the surface light would fade, and within a relatively short space of time the men would find themselves in total darkness. Unwilling to use their expensive candles, the cost of which came out of their own pocket, to light their ride, the miners would need to use their free hand if they wished to avoid being blindly spun around on the rope, and avoid their bodies being dashed against the unlined ragged sides of the shaft. Not only were there men working underground, there was also work for young boys, who may well have gone down the pit at the tender age of six or seven, and if they survived, then they could expect to continue going down the mine for the next thirty years or so. For these young children their first and probably many subsequent journeys down the shaft was a terrifying experience. Choice did not come into the equation, and in those instances where the child was timid and frightened, it was not unknown for the father or an older relative, to put the young boy into a sack and, holding the open end closed, the sack was thrown over the adults back, before leaning out over the shaft and grabbing hold of the main rope. For these men there was no luxury of having a free hand to stop being bounced around the sides of the shaft, they had to rely upon their companions, whilst keeping a firm grip upon their son, or brother or nephew. Once the first man arrived at the bottom of the shaft, he had to disentangle himself from the rope, and hope that the windlass operator knew what he was doing and prevent all of the miners above him ending up in a tangled heap. When all had disembarked, they would strip to the waist, and if worn, they would remove their shoes and stockings to be set-aside in small pathetic piles at the foot of the shaft before stooping/crawling to start a long shift, either digging out the coal, or shovelling the product into a tub, or pulling, on hands and knees, the tub to the bottom of the shaft, or to sit in total darkness, and ensure that the ventilation doors were kept closed after each passage of a tub locally known as a dram, such was the lives of a coal mining family.

Tragically during the history of the Kingswood mines, many men and boys fell to their deaths down the shafts, either by falling or being knocked off the rope, or as a result of a mechanical failure to the equipment, with such instances not being confined to the less sophisticated and safety conscious days of the seventeenth/eighteenth centuries, but remarkably these accidents continued well into the nineteenth century. It was not unknown for frayed and defective rope to be used long after it should have been replaced, and in one instance during April 1810, at **Mr Whittuck's** Whimsey Pit at Soundwell, **Robert Williams,** who was just seventeen years old, and his slightly older companion **James Ball**, who was 34, were both killed when the rope on which they were ascending broke, causing both men to fall a hundred or more feet to their death. If that was not bad enough, some thirty-five years latter at the same pit, more men were to die as a direct result of the excessive and continued use of the old defective rope.

On this particular occasion during October 1845 there was the situation whereby having finished their days work of some twelve hours or more below ground hacking out the coal from a narrow seam, a small group of six, rather tired, miners, crawled back to the bottom of the shaft, and stood up for the very first time in their working day, brushed off, where possible, the dust that clung to their sweaty bodies, dressed and gradually hooked themselves onto the rope, which was to take them up to the surface, fresh air and home. Although there is no certainty as to the order in which they attached themselves to the rope, it is believed that the first man on the rope was **George Britton** who was in his mid thirties. He was then followed by **John Porter** (30); **Benjamin Wiltshire** (33); **Thomas Bird** (41); **William Harris** (60) and last but not least the eldest man in the group **William Bassett** who was probably aged around 67. After spending five or six minutes swinging around, and with the top two or three men adjusting their eyes to the unaccustomed glare of daylight, the rope on which their whole lives depended, jerked as though it was being forcibly stretched, and then broke free of its hold of the windlass and collapsed into the shaft, taking with it the six miners as the end of the rope plunged down upon them. For those men there was nothing that could be done for them as they all fell like stones to be dashed together at the bottom of the shaft, but quite remarkably, as the dust and confusion settled one man, **George Britton**, dazed and in acute pain from a badly broken arm, and with blood spurting from head and back wounds, found that he was the sole survivor in a dark nightmarish world of mangled bodies, bodies who ten minutes or more before had been his friends, his work mates, his companions. With no way out for **George Britton,** until help arrived from above, he stoically sat at the base of the shaft, accepted his pain and discomfort as best he could, reached inside his pocket with his one remaining good arm, took out his pipe, found a small wodge of tobacco, and began to smoke, which it is understood he continued to do until his rescuers brought him to the surface. By then the local doctor, **Henry Mills Grace,** had arrived at the pit head, and seeing amongst the recovered bodies the one sole survivor, he immediately checked him over and, finding that the badly damaged arm was beyond repair, proceeded to amputate it there and then, with little thought of hygiene, and without the benefit, as far as George was concerned, of any anaesthetics. Tobacco must have had many remedial qualities in the nineteenth century which are not recognised today as within minutes of having his arm amputated, George looked across to Dr Grace and, with utmost composure, politely asked if he might again light-up his pipe, and having been given the 'nod', proceeded to fill the surrounding air with clouds of smoke. As far as it is known, **George Britton** made a full recovery from his terrible ordeal and injuries, and lived to a ripe old age.

Although he had survived, there were five men who did not and at their subsequent inquest, the jury were told by an experienced rope maker that, having studied the sample of rope taken from the scene of the accident, he was forced to the conclusion that he had never before seen rope in use, in such bad condition, before adding as a rider, *that he had better quality rope brought into his yard as "old junk".* In giving their verdict, the Jury censured the owner of the mine, **Samuel Whittuck**, and the mine manager, for neglect in not ensuring that the equipment in use was of good quality. However laudable the jury's criticism might have been, it did little or nothing to improve conditions in the mines, and certainly, it produced no real or financial compensation for the relatives of the above men. The comments, nonetheless, did sting the mine owner, which in turn caused him to write to the local newspaper, the *Bristol Mirror,* a letter of explanation. Firstly Mr Whittuck's letter totally rejected all actual or implied criticism of him and his good name, and then went on in great depth to vindicate himself of all blame, claiming, in the form of a casual throwaway of his responsibilities, that he could not be held responsible for the tragedy which had recently taken place at his mine, on the grounds that:

"so little do I concern myself with the works that I seldom go there".

He did not mention of course that he was always very concerned about the mine's ability to produce for him and his family a substantial financial return on his investment, and no doubt made his concerns known to those who were in charge. Thus quite hypocritically, as far as this wealthy owner was concerned, the blame for the accident lay fair and squarely at his manager's doorstep.

Although Samuel Whittuck, probably without realising it, publicly expressed in his offhanded manner his complete contempt and total lack of concern for the miners who worked and died for him, he was not alone as many of his contemporary mine owners placed the safety and the well being of their employees well down the list of priorities, and as a result the history of the Kingswood Miners is littered with the uncaring inquests that continued to sweep the cause of so many deaths under the table. Whilst on rare occasions, the mine owner, or more often than not the mine manager, were chastised by the foreman of the jury, or by the magistrate himself, no one was ever convicted or brought to justice, let alone held responsible for the numerous tragic events.

Another similar incident occurred on Christmas Eve 1854 at the Golden Valley Pit, involving eight males only this time they were on their way to work. At around 5 30am on that cold winters day, **Joseph Attwood,** who was just twenty-one years of age, but nevertheless a seasoned miner with over ten years of experience working underground, left his Hanham home and walked well over four miles through the dark, frost covered lanes in boots that had seen better days and were unlikely to last him through the winter, to the Golden Valley Pithead, where he met up with **Charles Brain** (27), who had, with his young fourteen year old cousin **William Brain,** walked over the hill to work, totally unaffected by the beauty of the surrounding land which had a covering of frost and a sprinkling of snow both of which had shimmered in the pale moonlight as the two of them passed by. As for William, who had had the extra mile or so to walk from North Common, his main concern was trying to keep warm with the limited amount of clothing available to him, and his predicament had not been helped by the fact that having reached Oldland Common, he had had to wait five or six minutes or so for his cousin to arrive. Even though they had hurried over the hill their exertions had hardly raised their body temperature, and with no hot food or drink available to them, they were just going to have to put up with the discomfort. By now the small group had been joined by eleven-year old **Joseph Short** who had come across from Cadbury Heath, and who had, on his way to work, almost on one occasion caught up with his namesake from Hanham, but the man striding ahead, was too strong and quick for him. Also standing in the cold at the pithead was another eleven year old, **Daniel Harding,** and a younger boy of about eight years of age, **Joseph Bawn.** There was just one person missing from this pathetic group of men and boys about to descend into the abject darkness of their employment, and that was **William Powell** (or possibly **Purnell**), who, at thirty-six years of age was the eldest in the group, and the man in charge however, as he lived the closes to the pit, he invariably was the last to arrive, which he did just after 6.45am.

Ensuring that the cart in which they were to descend was in the correct position and, checking to see that the men were carrying sufficient candles, he asked Charles Brain and Joseph Attwood to each light one candle and fix them to their hats, before they clambered into the cart, probably followed by William Brain and Joseph Short, then the group leader, and then the two youngest lads. With all seven safely standing in the cramped conditions of the cart, the instruction to lower away was given, and soon they began their descent into the bowels of the earth, and out of the biting cold. What then went wrong was never established at the inquest, all that was reported was that the crosspiece of the cart suddenly, and apparently without warning broke off causing the cart to violently tilt, throwing the occupants off their feet, and completely throwing the two young boys, Joseph and Daniel out of the cart. With the remaining rope unable to take the whole weight of the cart and its occupants it gave way under the strain, causing the cart with its human baggage to plunge over three hundred feet through total blackness to their death.

With the rope having gone slack at the surface the alarm was raised, and within the hour a rescue party had rigged up ropes down which they were to descend, in the uncertain hope of finding anyone alive, although in the main they expected to do nothing other than to recover the seven bodies. It therefore came as a very great surprise to find over one hundred feet down the shaft the small figure of Daniel Harding, desperately clinging to the side of the shaft. Signalling the surface to stop the descent, they carefully manoeuvred themselves over towards the boy only to hear him cry out:

Don't mind me, Joseph Bawn who is below me is nearly exhausted, but I can hang on a little longer. Save him first!

Unwilling to risk trying to rescue the young boy who at that moment in time had thought more about his younger colleague than himself, the rescuers instructed the winch man to lower them a further ten feet or so down the shaft where, to their great relief they came across a very tired and debilitated Joseph who was literally hanging on by his finger tips.

He was grabbed by the rescuers, and taken to the surface, which meant that the best part of thirty minutes were to pass before they reached Daniel Harding for the second time, and having been assured that Joseph was now on the surface, he allowed himself to be taken into the arms of those who had come to rescue him, and to be taken back to the surface and home.

As far as is known, both Daniel and Joseph lived well into their adulthood, as for the remaining unlucky five, their bodies were recovered over the following days, and were buried together in an unmarked grave in the church yard of St Mary the Virgin, Bitton.

As horrendous as the above two cases, and all the other accidents were, none of them would seem to come anywhere near as sickening as the following case recorded in the Bristol Infirmary notes of 1761/62.

During 1761, a twenty-five year old Kingswood collier was taken to the Bristol Infirmary with a suspected fractured skull, resulting from being hit over the head by a fallen timber beam that had become dislodged. It was there that the incumbent surgeon **Mr Castelman** examined him and found the head wound to be quite extensive and that there was little if any hope that the collier would survive. There are no records that the surgeon carried out any remedial treatment, other than to make the miner as comfortable as possible, and in the early hours of the following morning the collier died. Mr Castelman then examined the collier's well-proportioned young body later that day and, for reasons that were never given, proceeded to remove the young man's head. The torso arms, and legs were then placed in a rough wooden sealed coffin, whilst the head was wrapped in an old surgical cloth, placed in Mr Castelman's bag and taken to the surgeon's home. The following day the family of the deceased, came into Bristol with a small hand cart, took delivery of the body, and walked back to Kingswood, with the full intention of allowing their son's body to rest a day or so in his parents house, before being interred.

As the journey into and out of Bristol had taken up most of the day, the sealed coffin was left overnight on a table in the 'front' room of the parent's house. After the family awoke in the early hours of the following morning, the deceased's father went to work, and it was well into the late evening before he opened the coffin so that he and the rest of the family could say their proper farewells to his son, and in addition the neighbours could also come in and pay their respects to the open coffin. How he must have felt when he looked into the coffin and only saw a headless corpse can only be speculated upon, but whatever those emotions where, they very quickly turned to anger, and resentment. Unable to contain himself, and his anger he quickly decided that he must make every attempt to unite his son's head with his body, which meant that he had to go to Bristol.

Having hurriedly consumed a quart of local ale, father left for Bristol, and walked the eight miles or so to the Infirmary, arriving at the entrance around 3am, Finding the door locked and barred, he began to violently bang on the door first of all with his fists, then his boots, and then, finding no immediate response, with a large stone he just happened to find nearby. Unable to sleep through such a cacophony of noise, Ned Bridges, the Infirmary's apothecary clambered out of the bed he shared with his wife, and in a semi stupor, adjusted his nightcap, yawned on two or three occasions in succession, and crossed the cold wooden floor to the small window that he then opened just enough to enable him to put his head through the opening. With the chill air bringing him a little more to his senses, he half called, half yawned *"What do you want?"* Not at all sure what kind of reply he was likely to receive, he heard, as he pulled his head back into the bedroom a rather harsh, uneducated and somewhat rough country voice say:

"Well ~~ Want, damn thee, why I da want my zun's 'ead I do, and I'll ha un too or else I'll ha thine!!"

Not absolutely certain that he had heard the man correctly, but quickly realising that he was dealing with a very determined person, Bridges decided that his right and only course of action was to humour the man as best he could, and try a little diplomacy and in doing so he would probably be able to appeal to the person's reasonableness and the matter could then best be resolved in the morning. Thus keeping the tone of his voice as calm and as neutral as possible, Ned Bridges suggested to the unseen man standing at the door of the Infirmary, that perhaps there had been a small mistake, and that any such mistake if it had been made would best be dealt with in the morning when the Infirmary was open, and the head, if indeed it was missing could then be found; although why someone should be banging on the hospital door at some unearthly hour of the morning claiming that someone's head was missing completely baffled the sleepy Mr Bridges. Hoping that that was going to be the end of the matter, as far as Ned's disturbed sleep was concern, he withdrew from the open window in anticipation that he would hear from below, a civil acknowledgement of what he considered to be a perfectly reasonable suggestion, after all why should anyone in their right mind want a detached head from the infirmary in the middle of the night. Much to Ned's irritation, the reply from below was nothing like that he had anticipated; instead his ploy to be diplomatic appeared to have backfired as the visitor became more and more angry and vociferous, shouting as loudly as he could:

"Gi I my zun's 'ead or else I'll send a stone through thine and pull the 'firmary about thy ears"

By now the Kingswood father had the apothecary's fullest attention, and despite the time when all good folk should be asleep in their beds, Bridges brain was beginning to work overtime. From the rough country accent of the man at the door, it was obvious that he lived outside of Bristol, and probably somewhere in Kingswood, although the latter part was something of a guess on Bridges part. Kingswood meant miner/colliers, and had there not been such a young man in the infirmary a matter of a few days ago, and had not that young man died of his injuries, despite the efforts of the surgeon. Only Mr Castelman was likely to remove a head from a corpse, he had after all done it before, and therefore the visitor's demands should be addressed to Mr Castelman, not to Mr Bridges, and if that was to happen then Mr Bridges could at least try and get back to sleep. Cautiously putting his head once again through the open window, and hoping against hope that he would not receive a stone in the face, Ned Bridges called down to the man and tried to explain that the person he wanted was Mr Castelman, who happened to live nearby in Duke Street.

"Go and see Mr Castelman," said Bridges *"he is the surgeon and he is the person who will know about any head which might be missing; he was the one who treated the collier brought in from Kingswood"*

Bridges really hoped that this last piece of information might just do the trick and cause the man to go away from the infirmary. Listening as intently as possible, Bridges heard what seemed to be one or two grunts, and something that seemed quite unintelligible, and then came the sound he was waiting for, departing footsteps, which he optimistically believed would bring the night's ordeal to a close, although with his wife now fully awake and well prepared to do battle with anyone who had disturbed her beauty sleep he still had Mrs Bridges to deal with.

With his anger and frustration boiling over, the young man's father walked away from the infirmary with the determination of a man extremely aggrieved with the lack of respect shown to his dead son, and in the dogged certainty that he would find Duke Street and Castelman's house, even if it took him the rest of the night to do so. Although there was the occasional person around none seemed to know, or were too inebriated to know the location of Duke Street, but as luck would have it, his wanderings had taken him in the right direction, and about forty-five minutes or so after he had left the infirmary, he was standing outside Castelman's front door. Without realizing it, the stone that he had used to hammer on the hospital door was still held in his clenched fist, and accordingly was brought into immediate use, and it was not long before the paint on the door became badly cracked, whilst at the same time all in the vicinity must have heard that he wanted to speak with the owner of the property.

Mr Castelman had retired to bed quite late the previous evening, having spent a considerable while in his study, examining the dismembered head of a young man, who had so unfortunately died a day or so previously. Time had not allowed him to start dissecting the head, but he had been able to remove part of the contents, which he had studied under the microscope, and had made copious notes on his findings. Exhausted after a busy day at the infirmary, and the subsequent work he had carried out in his study, plus the after effects of a substantial meal and the three or four glasses of Madeira consumed during the evening, all began to take their toll, and although Castelman was in a deep sleep, his mind appeared to tell him that he somehow he was in the middle of some kind of violent battle, with a great deal of banging going on all around him. As his senses began to take over his sub-conscious mind, he slowly realised that the banging was not some weird and fanciful battle that he had somehow wandered into, but was in fact someone banging loudly on his own front door, despite the ungodly hour of the night. By now he was fully aware of the probability that his skill and services were urgently required and, wrapping his bed cloak around him, he opened the window and called out "*Who's there? Who's there?*"

Although he was not sure what kind of emergency awaited him, he certainly expected a cry for help, however distraught that cry for help might have been, but instead he was totally taken back by a rough, country voice shouting:

"Why, I be 'ere. I be Jack's father and thee's got is ' ead an if thee dussent give UN to I, I'll ha thine!"

With that, Jack's father threw the stone that he had been carrying around with him for the past hour or so in the general direction of Mr Castelman, which fortunately missed the surgeon, but went straight through the unopened window at his side, shattering glass shards all over the bedroom floor.

Undaunted by this action, Castelman decided to lie and shouted down that he could not give the man his son's head as this particular item was at the Infirmary, a statement that did absolutely nothing to quell the father's anger, but instead produced a further verbal onslaught that included a positive threat to break all of the remaining windows in the house plus dire consequences, which might afflict Mr Castelman's body, and to rouse the neighbours and tell them that the nice gentleman living next door had cut off his son's head, that is of course assuming that they were not by now already completely aroused and fully cognizant of the events happening outside Mr Castelman's home.

Being a pillar of the community, it was probably the latter point that struck home, as probably his neighbours would not fully understand or appreciate the scientific value as Mr Castelman did, of his extra curricular activities. Accordingly, looking down from the lofty upstairs window, he said, in as quiet a voice as possible, (there was of course no reason for him to want to broadcast to his neighbours that he did in fact have the head at home), that he would have to go to his surgery to fetch the head, and that he would be with the father in a few moments. Re-lighting the bedroom candle, the surgeon made his way downstairs, and along the cold passageway to his surgery, where he lit another candle, and ferreted around in the semi darkness for the young man's head, and that part of the lower brain, which he had taken out the previous evening with every intention of examining it in detail later that evening. With both located, he reunited the brain with the skull in a fairly crude manner, fully confident in the knowledge that the father would not notice the difference, then wrapped the cranium in a hand towel, that just a few hours previously he had used on a number of occasions, to wipe his blood soaked hands, and which was still damp from its over use. Making sure that he had doused the surgery candle, he went back along the passageway, past the living quarters, and to the front door where the banging had once again started, together with its verbal encore. Having located the key, with help from the light from the bedroom candle, he unbolted the front door and pulled it open, just as a very large fist was about to strike it. Fortunately for the doctor it missed both the door and his face, and he found himself having to steady the man to whom the fist belonged, who had been caught momentarily off balance.

"Beggun your pardon zur, but do e ha Jack's 'ead?

Not wishing to enter in a conversation with the particular uncouth miscreant standing in front of him, Mr Castelman, hastily thrust the towel and its contents into the man's hands, and attempted to close the door, but found that he was unable to do so, now that the man had stepped over the thresh-hold, and was partly leaning against the door, whilst he unwrapped the cloth towel and removed the head. Bending forward as far as he could to gain as much light from the solitary candle held by the surgeon, the father turned the head around, and examined it as best he could to see if he could recognize in the featureless bloody face, his son.

"Aye, Aye, that's Jack' he said after a moment or to of contemplation, but although he had achieved what he had come to Bristol for, he still had much anger inside him, and vented his disgust, his anger and his grief on the doctor who was still trying to close his front door. Quite incredibly for a man who would normally use his fists to settle a debate, on this occasion the anger and frustration was extremely well controlled, although no doubt Mr Castelman had ear ache for a number of subsequent days. Ending his conversation with the comment that should such a thing happen again then he, the father of Jack whose head he now carried home would come back and *"give you a dowse in the chops"* With that the father left Duke Street still muttering under his breath, and started the long way home, but a home where his dearly loved son would, when buried, be complete.

As far as is known, Mr Castelman retired to bed for the second time that night, angry that he had been subjected to such a verbal onslaught, but even more angry that he had been forced to give up the head, after all it was only the head of a young uncouth Kingswood miner.

It is therefore perhaps not so surprising that such examples of injustice, and there were many others, plus the constant body and mind gnawing pain of poverty that was being experienced by the vast majority, added to which was the sheer drudgery of their existence, that many saw themselves as deprived citizens, and as such they were easily persuaded to turn to crime, greed and immorality. Many of the men involved had been brought up under, and lived in, extremely harsh conditions that lacked any form of moral and/or social conscience, and therefore it was easy for the individual to gravitate to like minded persons, and so they grouped together and continued with their huge desire to get back at the establishment, the ruling classes, and basically anyone else who got in their way, and the groups became gangs, which roamed the neighbourhood, bringing fear and terror with their lawless activities. Whilst not all of the participating members were miners or colliers, the majority worked in the coal industry, or auxiliary trades, and as early as 1739, the Methodist leader **John Wesley**, wrote of the notoriety of the colliers, stating that he doubted whether there were more than a few people living in the West Country who had not heard of the colliers of Kingswood and their fame for fearing neither God or King, nor having regard for their fellow man. In an area where there was no established lines of authority, with few if any churches, and few estates with a Lord of the Manor, other than those that had originally been obtained from squatting and by breaking the law, the maintenance, and more importantly the enforcement of law and order, often proved an impossibility. The forest had over the centuries been a haven for those who chose to live outside of the law, and a combination of all of these factors resulted in the miners behaving more or less as they pleased, with little or no fear of any recrimination, and/or punishment from any outside authority. Of course from time to time some were caught and harshly punished, but the chances of being caught outweighed the benefits and pay of the crime. Within the mining and associated trades community, there was a general empathy with others in a similar position, which created a communal social conscience, and an absolute loyalty, and if help was needed elsewhere then the Kingswood miners would more often than not be first in the line, but woe betide any organization who attempted directly or indirectly to impinge upon what the mining community considered was theirs.

During the eighteenth century legal powers had been given to the local turnpike trustees, allowing them to remove furze and heath from any common land for road repairs, without having to pay for that taken. As for the colliers, they saw this as a form of legal highway robbery, with the loss to their community of natural materials used by countless generations for lighting fires on which to cook and, to keep warm plus, the loss of materials used for pasturage and shelter for their meagre livestock. There was in addition one other factor in this dispute that probably stuck in the miners' throats far more deeply than the above complaints, and constantly gnawed at their dislike and mistrust of the upper classes. As far as the miners were concerned, the turnpikes were, in the main, intended to facilitate the passage of wheeled traffic and as a consequence it was the wheeled traffic that caused the bad conditions of the roads, As the majority of wheeled traffic was owned or controlled by the upper classes, many of whom were local landowners, then it was their abuse and constant usage of the road that caused those roads to deteriorate. Accordingly it should be down to the local landowners to provide from their own land, the materials required to repair the road but, and this was the big but as far as the miners were concerned, the local landowners also happened to be the turnpike trustees, and as such they looked after their interests, whilst continuing to squeeze the poor.

Whilst the miners periodically continued with their protests over a range of items, they were in the main protesting against social injustice, as happened during 1709 when their demonstrations were made in support of their fellow workers in the cloth producing industry regarding the unreasonable excessive increases in the price of grain. It should be remembered that in the eighteenth century home grown grain was a basic food commodity required by both the rich as well as the poor but, in the case of the latter, the grain formed a much greater percentage of their staple diet, and thus any increase in the price of wheat; oats or barley had a much greater impact upon them, firstly from the fact that they consumed more grain per family, or certainly would like to, than a middle/upper class family, and secondly, it took more money out of their already meagre budget. The colliers, and more particularly their families, were therefore badly affected by the increase in the price of grain, and their protests were designed to try and secure a just and reasonable price, and to reduce the profiteering that continually went on. At this early stage of the eighteenth century, the miners were not as well organised as they subsequently became, and their 1709 protests had little if any impact upon the price of grain, although that did not prevent the miners from continuing with the argument over the decades to come. As it turned out, the protests of 1709 were a little tame compared with the following events that took place some twenty years later.

The bad harvest of 1728 was followed by a further one in 1729 and these two events greatly increased the huge pressure upon the prices of all basic foodstuffs which were already very high, and which in turn simply added to the intolerable and miserable state of the coal producing workers and their families living in the Kingswood area, although of course, it was not only the colliers, or the area of Kingswood that was affected by the shortage of grain, and the resulting high price of basic foodstuffs. Once again, there were those who were very hungry, and those who were not so hungry, who collectively without consultation, decided to fight back by taking the law into their own hands by carrying out acts of petty theft and robbery. Unfortunately as these crimes increased, the situation within those communities worsened as many of the victims were in fact the same people who were suffering the effects of high food prices. Crime played upon crime with all involved ending up as losers, including those who suffered in silence with their own level of personal dignity keeping them going through these most trying of times. Occasionally, individuals with a common cause came together and formed a group, only then to find that the group was effectively taken over by a dominant few who in turned began to manipulate the majority for their own minority views. Regrettably, the strength of these leaders was not seen as illegal or wrong, but more as a champion acting for the good of all, however that was not the intent, and the groups very often fell in to unison however injudicious were the aims of their leaders. Such events were also occurring closer to Bristol, and in the relatively small suburb of the out-parish of St. Philip's, trouble peaked in early September when a small group of ringleaders and their ardent supporters, possibly strengthened by a quantity of alcohol, went on the rampage, tearing out of their employers' homes many weaving looms, and dragging them in to the street, where they were smashed and set on fire. As bad as this was a much more serious event took place just over three weeks later when, on the 29th September whilst members of the Corporation of Bristol were at church, preparing to swear in **Samuel Stokes** the new mayor, the weavers from the out-parish of St.Philip's walked to Kingswood where, they met up with a group of miners who also considered that they had a grievance with authority to settle. Having no doubt exchanged thoughts, and views and shared opinions about the behaviour and actions of their respective employers over a pint or two of Kingswood's finest ale, they collectively agreed to take action and demonstrate their disgust at the treatment meted out by an upper class only ever interested in looking after their own financial welfare and social status. If we are to be treated as scum, then scum we shall be was the attitude of the weavers and the miners as they marshalled their joint force together to walk back to Bristol. Those who led the march past isolated cottages, market gardens as well as open fields and coppice, towards Lawford's Gate with murder and mayhem in mind decided that they and their compatriots should target the Castle Ditch home of a certain **Stephen Fecham** (also variously spelt **Feacham**).

This particular gentleman was a large local manufacturer of cloth and employed a great number of weavers in his business, and although he had agreed, some weeks previously, with his fellow guildsmen, that the only way to financially survive the depression was to force a wage reduction on all their employees, by paying them just 8/- (40p) per piece of cloth produced, (a reduction of 20%), Mr. Fecham subsequently decided that he would personally go one better than his fellow cohorts and reduce the payment to his weavers by a further 1/- (05p). Very much aware of the fact that his action would potentially make him an exposed target for all kinds of vandalism, and knowing that on the previous Saturday a group of irate workers had not only destroyed a house belonging to another employer, but had also beaten off a small body of soldiers sent to prevent the destruction of that property, Fecham made contingency plans to try and ward off those whom he knew he was antagonizing. Having already been made aware of the Kingswood meeting and the march, Fecham organised the arrival at his home of a larger group of armed soldiers, in strength around twenty men including two sergeants, to stand guard around his property. In addition, Fecham also decided to arm himself and some of his staff with loaded muskets, whilst they awaited the inevitable arrival of, what was to him nothing other than an unruly unintelligent mob.

Faced with a solid ring of armed soldiers and staff around the property, the crowd were at first content to simply hurl abuse and insults in a form of a verbal litany at Fecham and his minders, but gradually with passions aroused, no doubt aided by a further liberal supply of alcohol, and with group courage to the fore, the angry rabble pressed forward and stones began to be thrown at the defenders. For reasons, which were never satisfactorily explained, someone at this point in time, fired his musket from the safety of the house. Acting as a catalyst, this one shot caused the eruption of a number of other muskets to be fired from the house with much more deadly accuracy than the first, as the lead missiles penetrated the crowd, instantly killing five protestors, and mortally wounding two others. In the ensuing and inevitable panic, the trained soldiers were instructed by their sergeants to fire several volleys over the heads of the perceived rioters, but whilst the order was being given, the senior sergeant was hit in the head and killed by a stray shot fired from inside the house. Whether or not the soldiers had been told to load their muskets with shot, or whether they did in fact shoot into the air, is open to speculation but as far as it is known none of the crowd were hit when the military volleys took place. Understandably, the whole affair excited great popular indignation and, at the ensuing inquest into the death of the seven so called rioters, the coroner's jury in the out-parish of St. Philip's returned a verdict of wilful murder against Stephen Fecham.

To try and escape the consequence of his action and the coroner's verdict, Fecham appealed to the Government for protection, citing in his letters to Parliament: *"The coroner of the County of Gloucestershire intends to indite the officers of the out-parish of St. Philip's for not taking me up, so I should be glad if any way can be found to move it out of his power."* No doubt having influential friends in high places can be a very useful asset at times as, it was not long before Mr. Fecham received a King's pardon freeing him from all responsibility for the death of any of the seven protestors. Armed with this important document, Fecham smugly presented himself to the assizes, pleaded with all the amount of insincere innocence he could muster, and not surprisingly was liberated without a single stain on his character and apparently no blood on his conscience, those who died were after all only the weaving scum who worked for him and helped make him rich.

There were unfortunately, no such friends in high places for those who had protested against their poverty and enforced reductions in living standards, which after all had never been anything other than mediocre at the best of times. Nor was there anyone who could or who would be prepared to get up and speak on their behalf, and thus instead they had to face up to the responsibility of their own individual and group actions as stoically as possible, whilst knowing that they had a just cause, that their grievances were justified even though the perpetrator had got away with his actions scot-free. Power in the hands of the privileged can often be a dangerous weapon when used against the unprivileged majority, especially when such power decides it needs to make an example of its authority and that was precisely what happened in this sorry instance of Bristol's history. Not content to pardon the perpetrator and rub the worker's noses in their arrogance, the employers, and the council decided that they needed one or two ringleaders to act as scapegoats and accordingly they picked out **George Bigwood** and one other, both of whom were identified as weavers who happened to be in the crowd outside of Mr. Fecham's house at the time of the shooting, and charged them with riotous behaviour and criminal damage. For George and his companion, there were no influential friends in Parliament to ask for a King's pardon, or even to put forward their case, instead their reward, for simply standing up for their rights, and the rights of their families was the death penalty, and on the 23rd July 1730 they quietly went to meet their maker.

For almost the next ten years, the protests were fairly mild, and localized with little or no organization to bring different groups together, but in 1738, the mine owners, gave the colliers the required impetus their dormancy required when they announced that because times were hard, and that there was little if any profit in mining, that they, the mine owners, would have to take steps to safeguard their investment, and increase their profits by making, well actually, imposing a twenty-five per cent reduction in their employees pay Not surprisingly the miners voiced their objection to these proposals in the only way available to them, but despite their best efforts, the control of prices was, as always, in the hands of the merchants, and as long as they found an outlet for their product at the price they demanded, the poor could shout and rave as much as they liked but few if any, particularly those in authority, were prepared to listen. As soon as one crisis was over, with the lower classes having once again tightened their belts, then worse harvests occurred, and in the uncompromising world of supply and demand, grain prices increased, and the lower classes complained as loudly as they could. Such was the position in 1740, and once more in 1753, when the price of wheat increased to an extent that the local colliers again found themselves in the vanguard of the protest movement.

Whilst it is undoubtedly true that many of the colliers involved in the protests were unruly ruffians, all too quick to get into a fight, without any inhibitions about breaking the law when the circumstances suited them, some, if not all, of the trouble with which they became involved was without doubt socially related, and based upon the simple premise of freedom and rights for the lower classes. They were certainly fully prepared to stand up for that which they perceived were social injustices, and whilst the end cannot always justify the means, the Kingswood miners were probably their own worst enemy, as they allowed their fists to rule their heads, and in doing so obtained a much worse reputation than was necessary for the underlining basic cause for which they fought. Of course for some, the reputation of being uncouth, villainous, and always ready for a fight, suited them down to the ground as it enhanced their own individual stature, and gave those who chose an aura of intimidation, which they used for their own benefit. Within the mining community, the influence of the worst minority occasionally overflowed to the extent that from time to time, the defining difference between demonstrations and riotous behaviour blurred into the background, and when that occurred the more sensible majority were carried along and somehow caught up in the violence.

This certainly appears to have happened during the demonstrations of 1753, when the Kingswood miners went to Bristol to demonstrate their concern over the availability and price of wheat. This was of course a great concern to all those who depended upon bread as a staple part of their diet, and when the news that a quantity of wheat was to be exported from Bristol, the Kingswood colliers, who were never averse to a little bit of physical persuasion, decided that they should be allowed to put over their point of view. Accordingly on the 21st May 1753 many hundreds of miners and supporting labourers entered the city through Lawford's Gate and made their way to the Council House. Having put their case to the Mayor and Aldermen, and being told that their grievance would be looked into, the majority expressed themselves satisfied. However, some of the more militant in the crowd proceeded to the quay where they began to plunder a ship bound for Dublin, and already laden with corn. A running fight then took place with constables armed with staves and, after a brief encounter the colliers withdrew, taking with them some who were quite badly beaten and, leaving others who had been taken prisoner. Hearing of the treatment meted out to their colleagues, those miners who had been prepared to go home without a fight, now went to their aid. Having thrown stones and smashed many windows, the bruised and somewhat battered miners and their allies, left for Kingswood vowing further vengeance. With their threats being taken seriously, a militia was raised and a number of citizens were enrolled as special constables. With both groups of men armed with muskets, they met the colliers of Kingswood at Lawford's Gate on the 24th May and, having taken the fight to the mob soon had it dispersed. Not to be outdone, the miners were back the following day and, together with a horde of weavers and disorderly ruffians from the out-parish of St. Philip's which in total numbered around 900, decided on a slightly different strategy and entered the city by way of Milk Street and advanced to Bridewell where one of Monday's rioters was being detained. Although one of the assailants was shot dead by a warder, the defences were soon breached, the prison rifled, and the prisoner rescued. Having thus achieved their main aim, the next and most pressing problem was to try and get away and this was soon hampered by the arrival of a small troop of dragoons who, having made contact with the mob, immediately began to fire indiscriminately over the heads of the rioters. With panic setting in, the fugitives scattered in small parties causing numerous minor skirmishes to take place in and out of the narrow alleyways with a constant drive towards the anticipated safety of Lawford's Gate and beyond. One group of miners decided to take hostages with them, as possible protection for their own safety and managed to carry off six gentlemen, three of whom, Messrs **Brickdale, Knox** and **Miller** were recaptured by the militia at Lawford's Gate. However, later in that day, the remaining gentlemen found themselves underground in a coal pit where they were held prisoner for a number of days before they were eventually released. Back in the city as the running battles were coming to an end there were four dead colliers, and at least fifty wounded, some of whom would later die of their wounds, and around thirty-five rioters held captive, sorely a case of where perhaps a few hot heads had gone overboard, and taken the more peacefully minded majority with them, with dire consequences.

Whilst many of the miners lived as honest and law abiding existence as possible, there was always going to be that nucleus who, together with other tradesmen and labourers consistently broke the law wherever and whenever they could. Despite the fact that some of the main contributors of that lifestyle were brought to justice, crime continued to increase in the area, thus frustrating the efforts of the authorities who were trying to crack down on the perpetrators. Over the fifteen year period starting in 1796, the more that was done by the authorities to restrict the level of crime, the more the crime rate appeared to increase, due, in the main, to the illegal activities of just one family. (For further details please refer to my book "*The Cock Road Gang [The Story of the Caines family]*" ~ obtainable for £8 + p/p from the author) At the same time that crime was on the increase, the level of poverty suffered by the working colliers and their families also increased, and thus, there may have been a correlation between both events.

At the turn of the nineteenth century, a collier's wage was, on average, around 9/6d [47.5p] per week, but the working week in the early eighteen hundreds was not measured in 30-40 hours, but instead consisted of seventy hours, making the hourly wage equivalent to a rate of just under 0.07p. Furthermore the rate of pay had hardly changed during the past decade or so. In comparison, the price of a major item of his family's staple diet, the quartern loaf of bread had risen to 1/- [0.05p], this being just over one-tenth of the miners total income. Putting these details into context, as a modern large loaf is roughly half the size of a quartern loaf, it would mean that with current average weekly wages in the region of £290, to be on a par with say 1805, two loaves would today cost around £14 each. With such a large slice of the miner's money going on just one staple item, and assuming that the one loaf would have to be sufficient to last most of the week, it is not at all surprising that there was much deprivation, poverty and hunger in the area, with one person in ten receiving parish relief. This was surely a breeding ground for people to take the law into their own hands and risk a harsh sentence should they get caught, especially those who were sufficiently philosophical to believe that their circumstances could not really get any worse. Even though, for those who were unfortunate enough to stand before their accusers, the wealthy landowners and/or employers ensured that any punishment handed out should be as excessive as possible. As an example, in 1812 **Samuel Britton** aged 17 years, was sentenced to two years imprisonment for the "heinous" crime of stealing wheat to the value of 1/- [0.05p], probably no more than a handful of grain.

CHAPTER 4 "OUR DICK BOY"

Whilst most of the crime committed in the area was, if judged by today's standards, little more than petty larceny, and was carried out by shadowy individuals whose identity has for most of them been lost with the passage of time, one or two of those actively involved in the criminal world became well known in their own notoriety. One such local character was **Richard Haynes** who, in his relatively short life gained what some may claim as being the highest accolade of dishonour and disrepute available at the end of the eighteenth century, although from the distance of two hundred years, he could be regarded as a "lovable rogue".

Born in Oldland Green around 1766, Richard, but more frequently known by the shortened name of Dick or Dick Boy, grew up in the harsh reality of a collier's family, which almost certainly included at an early tender age, an initiation ceremony of being taken underground by his father and told to work by opening and closing the ventilation doors at the head of each passage. For reasons which have not been identified, Richard's time working underground cannot be detailed with any form of accuracy, but it is quite likely that he worked in the mine or mines, on and off over a period of six to seven years, probably starting off as a "trapper," this being a small boy whose whole fourteen hour working day underground was to sit in total darkness and act as a door minder, a stiff leather sheet, roughly hinged against one side of the tunnel, and used to control the movement or air so vital for good ventilation. Thus each time a dram, or an individual came through, it was the young boy's job to ensure that the door was properly opened, and then closed, with the minimum of delay. By the age of ten he may well have moved up to being a "tugger" where, on hands and knees, with a leather belt around his waist, and a rope between his legs, he would be expected to pull a cart or dram full of coal and waste from the coal face to the bottom of the shaft. However this part of his life can only be speculated upon, and he may in fact have been a rather weak and sickly child, as at the age of thirteen, he was apprenticed to the more benign and sedate occupation of hat making, at the time an important local industry. Most probably this particular form of employment was also not to his liking and may well have come about as a result of him being orphaned, and that whilst in the care of the Poor Relief Union, they shifted the burden of his expense, to a master, with whom he would be apprenticed for probably seven or eight years. This kind of arrangement certainly suited the master as they were effectively being provided with very cheap labour, veering towards slave labour, and benefited the Union as they had one less mouth to feed from the civic purse. Once again there is considerable speculation as to what happened to young Richard, but in view of the following snippets of information that has filtered through, it is more than likely that for most of his young life he had been brought up by his tough and uncompromising father, who probably died around the time when Richard was twelve years old, causing him to be taken into care by the Poor Relief Union, and then farmed out as an apprentice.

It is almost certainly that at around six to seven years of age, Richard had been thoroughly taught by his father, and had subsequently perfected the accomplished art of stealing food from a hot oven without using the oven door. Many houses in those days had a coal or brush wood fired oven, which was either situated just outside the house or, in some instances, so constructed that the oven door opened within the house, whilst the back end of the oven extended though and beyond the external wall of the house, looking something like a large carbuncle on the outside ground floor rear wall. They were almost certainly built of brick, which was then covered with an insulating layer of clay or mortar that dried and cracked with the internal heat of the oven, and which frequently need to be replaced, if the oven was continually used to its best potential The skill, taught to the young, seven year old Richard by his father was his ability to remove some of the hot outer covering, sufficient to exposed three or four bricks, and then to open the back of the oven by displacing a brick or two, making an adequate hole for him to reach in and extract some if not all of the food being cooked inside, all of which he needed to do whilst at the same time controlling his natural fear of being burned. However, young Richard's ordeal was not yet over as, having taken out the hot food, it was essential that to cover his actions, the bricks had to be put back in place, and the outer lining of clay needed to be replaced in such a way as to appear to all intents and purposes that nothing untoward had taken place, a difficult enough job for an adult, but almost unbelievable for a child to carry out. How much help he had from his father at the time is uncertain, but it would seem almost impossible for the oven break-in to have taken place without the participant getting burned, and we must assume that whilst Richard's antics must have left many a cook wondering why the quantity of food taken out of the oven, was less than the amount put in, he himself had a price to pay for his theft but, perhaps, we should not be surprised what hunger and/or the fear of a beating can force a child to do or endure, however hazardous that job might be.

Hazardous or not, this particular form of theft became something of a party-piece for young Richard as it is recounted that at about ten years of age, he and two other young friends were idling around Oldland looking for something to do, when he noticed through an open door, one of the village women preparing to put some whitepot and puddings into the "outdoor" oven. Drawing his companions to the events going on in the cottage, he asked, in a whispered voice, whether they would like some whitepot and pudding themselves in an hour or so, both eagerly said yes, knowing, as children do, all about Richard's ability. Deciding that they would walk down to the brook to kill time, they eventually made their way back to the cottage, with increasing hunger pains being aggravated by the mouth-watering aroma, which now pervaded the mid-day air. Concealing themselves as best they could they watched Richard climb through to the back of the cottage, remove part of the outer casing of the oven, and plunder some of its contents, which he then carried to the hedge passing the hot whitepot and puddings through to his companions, before returning to the oven, where he mended the breach. The three lads had consumed most of the food, by the time that the unsuspecting housewife returned to her cooking duties, and in a short while she had opened the door of her oven. Taking a disbelieving step back, she again looked into the oven void to confirm what she had just previously seen with the exclamation *"I am sure this bin done by a witch"* much to the obvious amusement of the three lads.

A few years after this particular incident, Richard found himself caught up with the law, when he was apprehended for stealing a quantity of provisions and wearing apparel from a house in Beach, but before he could be brought to justice, the local constable was surrounded by a mob of young men, most of whom were either friends or acquaintances of Richard, and in the interest of his safety, the constable took the wise precaution of letting Richard go with a warning that next time things would be different. With the warning long forgotten, Richard continued to steal food and clothing, and the occasional item of wealth, and soon he had paired up with his lifelong friend **John Carey,** and together they began to widen the scope of their criminal activities, as on the occasion when along the road which led from Bridge Yate through Oldland Common, they came across a man who sold gin, whom they stopped and entered into conversation, asking the vendor if he could direct them to Hanham. Whilst being distracted, as he gave the necessary directions to the two strangers, from his cart and its contents, Richard and John each purloined a bottle of the fiery liquid and ran in the opposite direction to where the gin seller was pointing. However, they did not run far enough, and with the help of two or three villagers, both lads were apprehended and handed over to the constable, who arranged for them to be sent to Gloucester Gaol to await trial. However before the trial could take place, it would be necessary for the constable to obtain a sworn statement from the victim accusing the young men of the theft of his property, and for this statement to be produced in court. Accordingly, a day or so after the event in Barry Road, the constable arrived at the Gin Seller's home to obtain the said statement, but was ushered away with the comment that he, the Gin Seller, may have made a mistake after all, and upon reflection, he was quite sure that the lads had in fact paid for the two bottles of gin, and therefore they had not been stolen as he first mistakenly thought. No sworn affidavit meant there was no case to answer, and within the week the two young men were free and back in Oldland. What had caused the Gin Seller to change his mind can only be guessed at, but almost certainly it involved the exchange of money, no doubt supported by one or two threats to the person of the travelling salesman, on the other hand perhaps the Gin Seller was not quite so honest as he might have been, when it came to accounting for the duty on the gin.

Undoubtedly, Richard's upbringing taught him to be strong, tough and self-assured, and as he developed into adolescence, he created a strong and supple body, chiselled out of the knocks and bumps and scars of his childhood. As he was about to enter his teenage years, his strength and self-assurance meant that he felt more able to "take-on" his father and it is recorded that on one occasion he challenged his father to a race around the lanes of Oldland and Beach. Having decided upon a "circular" route through these lanes, Richard's challenge was that with father and son starting at the same place, he would run around the route in a clockwise direction, whilst his father ran the same route in the opposite direction, with the winner being the one who had got the furthest around the circuit measured to the point where both met, having in the meanwhile taken every opportunity of individually attacking and robbing the first person unfortunately happened to be in their way. Despite the obvious age difference, Richard's father was still keen to show his son that he was the stronger and fitter of the two, and accordingly had no hesitation in accepting the challenge. Being much younger and, as it turned out, much fitter than his father, Richard was more than half way round the course before he spotted through the hedgerow and across the field, his first unfortunate victim. As he continued to run it seemed to

Richard that he was quite easily gaining ground on this person, and he therefore very quickly decided that he would conceal himself behind a large tree that bordered a bend in the lane ahead of him, and wait for the unsuspecting victim to come to him, certain in the knowledge that the approaching man had not yet spotted Richard. Crouching in his very useful, if temporary, hiding place, he could hear the laboured breath of the approaching person, and then, as quick as a flash, Richard sprang from his position, completely knocking the victim off his feet with such force as the poor man rolled to the side of the lane totally dazed and disorientated and that immediately gave Richard the upper hand. With the advantage his, Richard went over to his victim, and lashed out with his boot, kicking the poor unfortunate passer-by in the back, the ribs, and stamping on the head, causing a wound to open up and turning the grey hair red. Although dazed by the fall, and in terrible pain from the kicking, the old man tried as best he could to shield himself from the vicious onslaught, and rolling away from the swinging bloodied boot into the ditch, where it was much more difficult for the attacker to continue with his frenzy, the victim held up his arms as well as he could, and feebly cried out *Dick! ~ OUR DICK! For God's sake it's your Father."* Richard, who was just about to put the boot in for the umpteenth time, heard the pathetic cry, but more importantly recognizing his name and what seemed to be his father's voice, he fell on his knees, in a fit of remorse with the sudden realisation of what he had done, and the probable injuries he had inflicted. With blood streaming down his father's face and neck, and with bruising already appearing on the exposed parts of his arms and body, twelve-year-old Richard burst into tears, and asked his father for forgiveness. No one had of course witnessed the incident, and no one was around to give assistance, and thus with tears running down his cheeks, Richard dragged his father out of the ditch and carried him the three miles home, where he tended the injuries as best he could.

Whether or not the father recovered from these injuries is not known, but with Richard's apprenticeship in the locally important hat making, arising when he was thirteen years of age, it is quite possible that his father died around this time, and even possibly from the beating he had received from his son, thus making Richard an orphan, and setting in motion this new employment. To say he liked the work would be a gross exaggeration, as he was frequently in trouble with his new employer, who saw Richard simply as a child and as an irritating form of cheap labour, who rarely if ever did what he was told. The amount of food provided for this fit and still growing young man was always insufficient, and despite his skills of being able to steal food from a hot oven, the opportunities to do so were extremely restricted, as the master operated from home, and ensured that Richard hardly ever had any time off, or away from the home. As the months went by, the arguments between Richard and his master intensified, and eventually the inevitable happened, when the adolescent, unable to control his anger any longer, assaulted his master, a heinous crime in the eyes of the law, and left Richard with just one option, and that was to abscond, and go on the run away from Oldland, away from the area he knew best, but an area where he could be easily recognized. Although still in his early teens, Richard had been taught well by his father, and was perfectly capable of looking after himself, even if it meant that at all times Richard lived outside of the law. For probably the first time in his relatively short life this young man felt, at ease with himself, he was independent, and by using his own aptitude, and ability, he was very capable of surviving these difficulties and in addition he had time in which he could master new talents, and hone them to perfection, or certainly the perfection of his own standards. During the next three or four years he wandered, around southern England, and throughout much of Wales, accompanied by his childhood friend and teenage accomplice, John Carey. They had been born within a year of each other, and both had fathers who had worked underground, and had accordingly experienced an early harsh, tough life of poverty, hunger and cruelty, but now they were independent of those horrors, they were free to meander where they chose, to eat when and what they liked and by combining their purloining skills, their ingenuity, plus the recklessness of youth, they had, all that they desired. Either through the inefficiencies of the uncoordinated constabulary of the day, or sheer luck arising out of bravado, or their constant moving from one place to another, or possibly a combination of any of these reasons, both Dick Boy and his close friend John Carey appear to have enjoyed many years of living the lives of outlaws, as no records have yet come to light which would suggest that they appeared in front of a magistrate. Still only teenagers they ranged all around the southern counties of England, flirted with the Midlands, and spent a great deal of time in Wales, and whilst their lives were much better than anything they had previously experienced, living rough with just their wits to keep them alive and free gradually took its toll, and frequently they would return to the area of their birth where they still had family living, but always knowing that they could so easily be recognized, and turned over to the magistrates.

On one of their sojourns home, around 1784, the inevitable happened, when Richard was arrested and brought before the local magistrate, charged with having stolen provisions and clothing from a house in Beach. Undoubtedly, Richard was a wily character, having learned over the past few years to live on his passion for subterfuge, and those skills did not let him down on this occasion, as with insufficient evidence he was acquitted of the charge. This acquittal, and others that subsequently followed over the next few years, increased Richard's self-belief in himself, in his prowess and possibly his arrogance to live beyond the law but best of all, to get away with it. By late 1786 or early 1787, Richard's confidence was at an all time high, and his confidence easily spread to his friend and companion, but John was, by nature, a more cautious young man, although he would not have admitted as much to his best friend, particularly now that Richard was becoming more and more enthusiastic about highway robbery. They had both robbed isolated travellers in the past, including a gentleman near Saltford, from whom they had taken a watch and five shillings [25p] in coin of the realm, but as demonstrated by the poor result of the Saltford incident, they had only toyed with the idea, apart from the fact that it was much more difficult to be a highwayman when you did not have a horse to ride up to your victims. On one or two occasions in the past, they had been thwarted in their attempts to rob a traveller, by the traveller simply spurring or whipping his horse out of the way, leaving both men looking a little foolish, with their intended victim a hundred yards or so away, and travelling at a pace which they could not hope to match on foot. However, all that had changed now that their past achievements had enabled them both to acquire a steed, and whilst neither beast would win a race, they allowed Richard and John to look the part, and would help with the intimidation so necessary for a successful highway robbery. To add weight to their appearance, and to demonstrate that they meant business, Richard had obtained an old pistol, which he proudly wore tucked into his belt.

Practise makes perfect, and Richard and John carried out a number of successful attacks in and around the Oldland area, but in the main they chose travellers who carried little money, and the financial rewards for all of their efforts, hardly inspired them to bigger and better things. John was probably prepared to give up the romantic notion of being a highwayman, but Richard was not going to be deterred by one or two minor setbacks, but decided that they should turn their attention away from the local farmers and the occasional traveller who might wander through the parishes of Bitton and Oldland, and seek out more lucrative victims, and accordingly went to Downend, where he felt sure there were better pickings to be found.

Having found a suitable position along the road from Chipping Sodbury, both men lay in wait and were soon rewarded with the sight of what appeared to be a wealthy merchant ridding towards them. Hiding their faces behind makeshift scarves, and with the gun drawn from Richard's belt, and a cutlass from John's belt, they spurred their mounts forward to block the merchant, a certain **Mr Crach's,** path, and told him, in no uncertain manner, to stop and to hand over all of his money and valuables. Faced with two armed and desperate men, most travellers would have stopped and carried out the instructions shouted at them, but Mr Crach was made of sterner stuff, and not only that, he was very much a miser, who was rarely parted from his money. Accordingly without hesitation or thought Crach bravely, if somewhat foolishly, attempted to resist the highwaymen's threats, aimed his whip at the nearest of the two robbers, whilst at the same time tried to turn his Arab horse in the vain hope of trying to out gallop the poor specimens on which the two men were sitting. Neither action worked as the whip was too short and missed its intended target, whilst in his haste to escape, by turning his horse around, the reins slipped through his gloved hand allowing the horse to ignore his master's instructions and to take charge of the situation by moving across to a tasty patch of grass that happened to be growing at that spot. Despite his failure to escape, the mere fact that he had attempted to do so further enraged the highwaymen, particularly Richard, whose adrenalin was now working overtime, and in his annoyance and frustration he repeated his threats in an even more menacing voice, endorsing his verbal threat by him raising his pistol and aiming it at Mr Crach's head. With his victim still defiant, and with Richard unprepared to back down there was only one possible outcome to the impasse; Richard squeezed the trigger expecting any moment, when the gunpowder smoke had thinned, to see the blooded merchant slump in his saddle, if not fall to the ground. There was certainly a flash, but then relative silence, as Richard was left holding a miss-fired pistol, whilst the merchant was, with mixed feelings of relief and terror discovering, as he raised himself upright and back in his saddle, that his nightmare was not yet over. By now the initial indignity and anger felt by Dick Boy, was being fuelled by the impertinence of the merchant who appeared to be sneering at him, and the incompetence of his gun, which, although it had not fired was still a weapon in the highwayman's hand. Digging his heels into the horse's rump, Richard manoeuvred his horse forward so that it went alongside the merchant's horse whilst at the same time changing his hold on the pistol from the butt to the barrel. As soon as he was close enough, Richard leaned forward and using the butt of the gun, delivered a fearsome blow across his victim's head that almost certainly fractured the poor unfortunate merchant's skull.

Having carried out this dastardly deed, a complete change of emotions came over Richard, and for the first time he heard, or understood, his best friend John, calling him to stop, and to come away. Whilst he watched, in a sense of numbed shock and disbelief, as Mr Crach slowly fell from his horse to remain motionless on the floor, his mind was being re-focused on the reality of the events that had just taken place, and the mayhem that was around him. By now John was shouting that they were both in serious trouble and needed to get way before anyone came along, and without even a second thought of remorse, Richard pulled his horse's head around and both incompetent highwaymen fled the scene, living a badly injured traveller dying in a pool of his own blood.

There were of course, no witnesses to this attack, and it was the following morning before Mr Crach's lifeless body was found, by which time both Richard and John were long gone, safe in the knowledge that there was no one who could identify them as the killers, as surely that is what they had become, and it was most unlikely that anyone would come after them.

During the following months, the two men roamed the countryside of Gloucestershire, Wiltshire, and Somerset, but at no time did they ever venture far from home, and with the unsustainable confidence of youth, and in particular of young men who have got away with their actions for all too long, they continued to seek adventure in their own backdoor. Having carried out various depredations throughout the remainder of 1787 and on into 1788, Haynes and Carey found themselves on one particular day travelling backward and forwards along the Kelston road seeking an outlet for their criminal activities. After an hour or two they came across a middle aged man travelling alone, whom they confronted and took from his person a silver watch, and one guinea [£1.05p] in coin of the realm. Both men then took off across the fields and lanes back towards Oldland, leaving the frightened but also angry man to head for Kelston where he raised the alarm. Within a few days both Haynes and Carey were arrested in Somerset on the charge of highway robbery, and were sent to prison awaiting trial at Taunton Assizes. During the period of their incarceration, Richard Haynes, alias Dick Boy, stood firm and was not intimidated by either the surroundings or, by the thought of his impending conviction. However, the same could not be said about the more timid Carey who for reasons best known to him, confessed to being involved in a great number of thefts and highway robberies, and the murder of Mr Crach. Although he was unable to live with his own guilt, he remained absolute in his determination to remain loyal, and at no time did he ever incriminate his best friend and co-conspirator Richard Haynes. Whether John Carey had some form of misplaced loyalty for his friend or whether there was some other reason(s) for making the confession will now never be known, but it could simply have been that Carey took a calculated gamble that by doing so he could divert attention from his friend, and at the same time end up with nothing more than a custodial sentence. That said, John was not the most intelligent person in the world, and once he had started to confess, he failed to know where to stop, and included in his avowal that together with two other men he had robbed **James Chapple** the butcher from the village of Brislington. Almost certainly at this time John was feeling extremely guilt ridden and remorseful, particularly since he had recently discovered that at the previous Somerset Assizes, an unfortunate individual by the name of **Jenkins** had been wrongly charged and convicted of being involved with the robbery of the Brislington butcher and, having been found guilty, was duly hanged, despite all of his, and his family's, protestations of being innocent, which of course John Carey knew to be true.

John Carey was summoned to appear before the magistrates at the summer assizes held in the small market town of Ilchester, and there the prosecution lawyer read out his confession. For John there was no lawyer to speak in his defence, or to plead his case, there was just John a less than educated man, to mumble through his fear that he did not mean to carryout the robberies, and pleading mitigation, all to no avail as within at matter of minutes, the magistrates proclaimed that John Carey was guilty of the charge, and that he was to be taken to a place of execution and hanged by the neck until he was dead. Within a matter of days, it was on the 25th August 1787 that twenty year old John Carey took the long and difficult walk within the walls of Ilchester prison, to the hangman's noose and there he painfully met his maker.

In the meanwhile Dick Boy had kept his nerve, and said and did nothing to incriminate himself, and when he appeared at his trial, which also took place at Ilchester, on the same day as his friends, he even managed to successfully convince the magistrates that he had nothing to do with the crime with which he was charged, and after deliberation, he was acquitted and set free. Knowing of the potential sacrifice made by his friend, and knowing that there was nothing he could do to stop his friend's inevitable demise, Richard found a cheap and cheerful hostelry near to the prison gates, and stayed for the next few nights, until the 26th August, when he went to the prison and claimed John Carey's body, from the shallow grave in which it and others, who had been hung the previous day, had been thrown. Arranging for the body to be washed, and finding some relatively clean clothes, Richard "borrowed" a hand cart on which he carefully place his companion's body, and pushed it back home to Oldland, for a proper Christian burial. However, some months later after he heard that John Carey had confessed to the murder of Mr Crach, he was overheard to exclaim that had he known about this confession at an earlier date then he would have thrown his friend's body in the river.

Over the next year or so, Richard, alias Dick Boy, managed by foul means or fair, to keep one step ahead of the law, but continued with his depredations throughout most of southern England, until the inevitable happened, and his luck ran out when he was caught robbing a man on Westminster Bridge. Perhaps the London Magistrates were less swayed by a bribe, or that they were simply better at their job than their more countrified contempories, or possibly they just did not like the idea of "uneducated peasants" robbing the wealthy London citizen, will have to be left as just possibilities, but at the London Assizes, Richard met his match, and for the first time in his life he was not only found guilty, he also had the dubious pleasure of having to face up to real harsh punishment, as the magistrates would have no truck with him, and decided that the seriousness of the crime was for Richard Haynes to be transported for life to the renowned penal colony of Botany Bay.

This may well have been the end of the story as far as our knowledge of Richard Haynes, alias Dick Boy, born in Oldland some 23-25 years previously, but for a remarkable twist of fate that happened to this young man that enables his story to continue.

Although there is no absolute certainty, it is believed that Haynes was sent to one of the many prison hulks that existed around the coastline of southern England and there he was held until a berth was found on one of the ships that regularly sailed between England and Australia with their human cargo of the homeland's dregs and throwaways. In due course, Richard Haynes arrived at the penal colony known as Botany Bay. [Positioned south of Sydney, close to the main airport for that city] Little if anything is known about the sea journey or what Haynes was required to do over the next three or four years but, it would seem that he behaved himself sufficiently well enough to be given a fair amount of latitude as it appears that he obtained his liberty together with another man to go fishing in a canoe, and that not only did he obtain permission to go fishing, the authorities agreed that he could take about three days provisions and go on a long trip. No doubt using the many inlets at his disposal, it is probable that he was, within a matter of hours, out of sight of the penal colony, which then enabled him to put his dastardly plan into action, which was to kill and dispose of his companion. Using the remaining provisions as economically as possible, Richard took the canoe and his own fate to sea, although that may well have still been within the outer limits of Botany Bay itself. After paddling around for three or four days, and with his provisions almost exhausted, an extremely tired Richard came across a small island where he landed, and having dragged the canoe up onto the sandy beach he soon found himself surrounded by an inquisitive group of the local indigenous men, whilst behind them was a smaller group of women and children. Fortunately for Richard, none of the island's inhabitants were hostile, and apart from the women and children, none appeared to be frightened by his dishevelled appearance, or his sun reddened skin. Believing him to be a ship-wrecked sailor, he was taken back to their village where food was provided. After resting for a day or two, and being extremely grateful for the hospitality shown him, Richard returned to the canoe and continued with his escape.

Over the next week or so, Richard's solitary journey took him past other islands, some of which were inhabited and some of which were not, but in all cases he was able to stop, rest and replenish his food stock, content with the thought that as each day passed, he was one day further away from the penal colony. Eventually more by luck than by judgment, he landed on a larger island, with a greater level of civilisation, and contact with the outside world. Here large cargo ships came and went, and Richard mingled with their sailors as much as he could in the hope that he could merge into the background, whilst at the same time finding out as much as he could about the individual ship's destination. After waiting for about a month, and deliberately not wanting to pick an English ship, Richard came across a ship bound for Holland that also happened to be in need of an extra deckhand.

Approximately a year or so after he had escaped from the Botany Bay Penal colony, Richard stepped ashore on mainland Europe, to all intents and purposes a free man. The undoubted hardships he had incurred since his arrest in London did little to curb his passion for living outside the law, and within hours of leaving the ship, he was up to his old tricks. However, within a relatively short space of time, a new and quite different facet of Richard's life took place when, having been told that just over the German/Dutch border there was living an Englishman who was in need of a servant/bodyguard, and still being young and muscular, Richard decided that this position would suit him. He accordingly travelled to the town, made enquiries of the whereabouts of the English Gentleman, and applied for the job. For the first time in over ten years Richard had proper employment, but no doubt there was an ulterior motive behind his actions, as true to form, within ten weeks of taking up the appointment, Richard was on the run having robbed his master of a considerable amount of money and valuables. With the ensuing hue and cry, Richard decided that it was too hot to stay around, and travelled west towards France, and subsequently crossed the Channel back to England.

Exactly what Richard then did is not known but during 1793 Richard, like the proverbial bad penny, arrived back in Oldland with a wife on his arm and, perhaps with a smirk on his face, he introduced his lady as the daughter of a wealthy German nobleman, whom he had met on his homeward travels. Needless to say this announcement was either part of Richard's fertile imagination, or the result of Mrs Haynes wishing to enact, for a wider audience, a personal fantasy, or more likely a joint desire to fool the local inhabitants. It is not clear whether Mrs Haynes put on an accent, but with very few residents of Oldland having had contact of any kind with a lady, let alone the daughter of a German nobleman, she probably had little difficulty in pulling the wool over their eyes, even though she was in fact a native of Westerleigh, a village just a few mile away. Again it is not clear how long the charades lasted and whether or not the deception was ever discovered, but the continued play acting role in rural Oldland was not to Mrs Haynes liking as within a matter of a month or so, she disappeared, having travelled on her own to London where once again she lived of her wit's, and criminal activities, which ultimately led to her death in 1794, when she was found guilty of the charge of robbery and sentenced to be hanged.

It is believed that Richard also went to London around the same time and in fact they may have left Oldland together, certainly during the same year that his wife, if that is what she was, was hanged, Richard had become acquainted with the notorious pugilist known as *Big Ben.* Seeing that money could be made out of fighting for a purse, and being well built and well able to handle himself, Richard spent the next few years fighting as a bruiser earning himself a formidable reputation as well as earning a fair amount of money, of course in between fights he was able to continue with his criminal activities, which helped to supplement his high outgoings of gambling, drink and women, although not necessary in that order. Un-refereed bare-knuckle fighting gradually took its toll, and toward the end of 1798, Richard threw in the towel, and returned to the place of his birth, with money jingling in his pockets. Despite his awesome reputation, and being easy to recognise, Richard took up residence in the village and settled down, happy in the knowledge that he was unlikely to be betrayed by anyone living in or around Oldland.

Old habits die hard, and Richard still needed to enjoy the thrill of a robbery, and/or the money that usually arose from such activity and where better to fulfil those desires than in Bristol, where the pickings would have a higher value, but where he also ran a greater risk of being recognised by someone who did not have the misplaced loyalty or intimidation as the locals of Oldland apparently had. Inevitably, it was during one of those trips into Bristol in July 1799 that he was seen and identified by a local police officer, who single-handed, bravely tried to apprehend the notorious *Dick Boy,* on suspicion of stealing a silver tankard. During the melee, Haynes drew his pistol and shot at **PC John Driver** and wounded him in the arm. By now quite a crowd had gathered, and seeing that the police officer was hurt and therefore at a great disadvantage to the powerfully built Richard, some of the bystanders went to Driver's aid, and this time there was no escape for Our Dick Boy. Charged with robbery and the wounding of the police constable whilst resisting arrest, Richard Haynes was committed for trial at Bristol Assizes, found guilty and sentenced to death.

It was therefore around mid-day on Friday the 25th April 1800 that thirty-four year old Richard Haynes, otherwise known as *Dick Boy,* declared to the community at large that he had no ill feelings against anyone and began the last journey of his life from Newgate Prison, close to the centre of Bristol, to the gallows on St Michael's Hill. According to an article in the Felix Farley's Bristol Journal dated, 26th April 1800, and to the One-Penny booklet published by W Matthews of Broad Mead on the life and adventures of Richard Haynes, the **Rev. Walcam** (the Ordinary of Newgate Prison) accompanied the prisoner to the gallows, although unlike a **Mr Bundy** who sat beside Richard Haynes in the prison cart throughout the journey through the streets of Bristol, the Rev. Walcam rode in style aboard the coach which brought up the rear. Twenty-four hours previously, the Rev. Walcam had gone to the cell occupied by Richard, and having found the prisoner to be mild and gentle of manner stayed with him until 5am on the morning of the execution. During this time the reverend gentleman encouraged Richard to spend his last few hours on this earth singing hymns, praying, and exhorting his worldly thoughts so that he could meet his Redeemer, washed and cleansed of all his sins. Later that day a Mr Bundy joined both men and added his weight to the religious events, joining in with the singing of the hymns and the reciting of the prayers. Whether he was religious or not, Richard appears to have satisfied the men of his genuine remorse, and as the sun was beginning to rise, they left the cell and retired to the Governor's room for breakfast.

Certain that their efforts to have the sinner redeemed were not being wasted, both men having enjoyed a large breakfast, returned to Richard's cell, for more prayer and singing. Eventually it was time for Richard to begin the one-way journey to St Michael's Hill and, with arms and legs suitably shackled, he was placed in the prison's open cart, with Mr Bundy sitting alongside him, whilst the ordinary of the

Prison decided to ride in the more comfortable surroundings of a coach. Despite there being at least two vehicles involved in the journey, the Rev Walcam was a big enough man with a big enough voice to ensure that he could continue conducting the religious service from his coach-seat. Thus as the small convoy made its way over the drawbridge, and struggled up Steep Street the deep resonate voice of the Ordinary boomed out across the city, whilst slightly behind and out of key could be heard the two other voices. Having arrived at the site of the gallows, where a large audience had now gathered, Richard shuffled his way on to the platform and standing as erect as his bonds would allow him expressed his desire not to have a long delay, but for the execution to take place as quickly as possible. Whether or not the Rev. Walcam heard Richard cannot be said, but the Ordinary of Newgate Prison was not a man to miss the pious opportunity of speaking to a captive audience, and having followed Richard onto the platform, he turned to the spectators just as Richard repeated his request. Somewhat cut-off in his prime, the Rev. Walcam began his speech by stating that it had been his intention to address the watching crowd in a discourse suitable to the melancholy occasion, but having heard the prisoner's desire, and the apparent inclemency of the weather, meant that he would now have to curtail his sermon. Standing before you, the Ordinary said, is a criminal, but not just a criminal, but also a redeemed criminal, who had expressed his desire to redeem his soul, whilst at the same time had shown great gentleness and good behaviour not only to him but at all times to his fellow helper in the Lord, and had made his peace with God. Yes this man standing before you has done dreadful things, but God had the power to forgive all sinners, including those amongst you. "*Let us pray.*" The Rev Walcam then said a prayer, and gave the final benediction, and then making affectionate farewells, including embracing Richard, returned to his coach where, he fell upon his knees and continued the loud litany of prayer until the hanging took place when he exclaimed "*Lord Jesus, receive his spirit.*" For his part, Richard continued to encourage the Rev. Walcam by joining in with the prayers right up to the last moment

After hanging by the neck for a number of hours, Richard's body was removed and placed in a hearse. It was then carried to the parish church of St Michaels, where it was buried on Sunday the 27 April 1800. Thus ended the life of one of Oldland's more notorious sons, who, in just thirty-four years, created such a bad reputation, and yet was sufficiently a likable rogue, that it was considered worthwhile to have a penny pamphlet printed about his life, or certainly his life as recalled to W Matthews, printer of Broad Mead, by an unknown person who claimed that he had known Richard since his infancy, and who had heard Richard relate the tales at different times. Who ever that person was, or if he ever truly existed will just have to remain a mystery, but it is suspected that the printer and author, Matthews, simply used the comment to add authenticity to the story, authenticity that probably never existed in the first place. Richard Haynes certainly existed, had the alias of Dick

Boy, lived a life of crime, and was hanged in Bristol on the 25th April 1800; it's the bits in between which may have important elements of doubt about them.

Richard Haynes was not the only eighteenth century criminal to have been born in or around Oldland, many families such as Britton, Peacock, England, Willmott, (various spellings) Fry, Brain, Cook(e), Whitting and many others were involved, but the most prominent criminal family in the area was the Caines, and if you wish to find out more about this and the other families, and the lives they led during the eighteenth century, you are recommended to read my book *"The Cock Road Gang (The Story of the Caines Family)"* priced £8.

CHAPTER 5 "DOMESTIC VIOLENCE"

Although domestic violence happened all too frequently in the harsh uncompromising, poverty stricken world, little if any details were ever recorded, the law allowed the husband to beat his wife and his children, and for hundreds and hundreds of years women were regarded simply as chattel. All that can be used today is our imagination of the hardships married women underwent where poverty ruled their daily lives, where they had to attend to their husband's needs, plus the demands put on them by bearing numerous children, and their subsequent upbringing, and the constant need to find food to keep them alive. With little or no affordable medical support, the women had to resort to "grannies recipes for common ailments", and somehow had to be able to turn their hand to nursing when sickness frequently visited their home. Even if their husband was good and kind, their daily humdrum lives would leave them with little pleasure in life, but any added mental torture, or physical violence, from which they could not escape, would leave them in total despair.

However, although it was more often then not that women were at the receiving end, this was not exclusively a female club, and from time to time the tables were turned. One of the more serious domestic crimes that has been recorded, where the wife was more violent than the husband occurred in April 1820, when **Thomas Worlock,** having just returned home to his humble stone cottage on the turnpike road in Oldland after a hard days work, which had been aggravated by a long and tiring, hot walk home, flopped into the only, but somewhat bedraggled, armchair in the house, and shouted for his eleven year old daughter **Mary Ann Worlock** to come to him. Pressing a few coppers into her dirty hand, he instructed her to collect the chipped jug from the scullery, and to run across the road to the *Chequers Inn* for a quart of ale, and to be quick about it; he also gave her a gentle clip about her ears, and told her not to spill any, as he had an almighty thirst.

Having paid for the ale the daughter, carefully holding the jug with two hands, left the only bar of the Inn, crossed the dusty road, being chary not to step, but more particularly not to slip in the various and strategically placed piles left by passing animals, and returned to her home, where she was met by her mother, who surprisingly took the jug from her. Holding her finger against he lips, to indicate to her daughter not to make a noise, **Rebecca Worlock**, **(nee Flower)** in a whispered voice told her daughter to go back out and find her brother, **John** and sister **Honor,** and to stay with them until she called. As soon as the daughter left, and Rebecca was on her own in the scullery, she surreptitiously took a small packet down from the top of the dresser, and emptied rat poisoning in the jug, stirring the contents with her finger, which she then carefully wiped in her none too clean apron, and with a smile took the jug of ale to her husband, who was dozing in the armchair. Hearing his wife come into the room, Thomas opened his eyes, stuck out his right arm, and snatched the jug from his wife, with a grunt and a comment, to really no one in particular that surely it should not have taken that long to simply fetch a jug of ale from just across the road, whilst looking into the jug with the satisfaction of knowing that this was the best part of the day. He had an insatiable thirst that had not been helped by the long walk home, and now was not the time for niceties, as with one movement the jug was at his lips, and the bulk of the ale was going down his throat without even tasting it, although quite a bit had escaped around his mouth, and now ran down his lower cheeks, and onto his smock. Used to the habits and bad manners of her man, Rebecca unemotionally looked on, and nonchalantly commented that "you look like you needed that". With well over three-quarters of the jugs contents now gone, Thomas withdrew the jug from his lips, stood up, looked into the container, belched, pulled a face, and exclaimed that there was something wrong with that ale, "it must have been off." With another powerful belch, Thomas staggered and held his ample stomach, as a searing pain shot through his abdomen and before he had time to take another breath, he was violently sick over the parlour floor.

Without any outward sign of anxiety or concern, Rebecca casually took the jug away from her husband's grasp, and went back to the scullery, where she calmly threw away the remaining contents of the jug and rinsed it out. She then returned to the parlour with a bowl of water and broom, and proceeded to swill and sweep the disgorged fluid, across the flagstone floor and out through the back door, commenting to her husband, as she reached the open door, *"it must 'ave been somfink you ate"*

Unable to find any sympathy from his wife of thirteen years, but still suffering acute abdominal pains, Thomas half crawled, half stumbled his way up the narrow twisting stairs to the matrimonial bedroom, where he rolled onto the bed in the hope of finding a little bit of relief and comfort from the terrible cramps in his stomach. After an extremely fretful night during the hours of darkness with frequent use of an overflowing chamber pot, Thomas rose from the bed just as the sun began to bring light and warmth to the surrounding area, at which time he sent one of his children to a nearby friend with the request that the friend came to see him as soon as possible. Although still in much pain, and weak from the numerous vomiting, Thomas persuaded his friend to help him walk to the nearest doctor at Keynsham, this being the same doctor who Thomas had had to visit on two or three separate occasions in the recent past, when he had complained of stomach pains, and a general degree of lethargy. After a painful and slow journey to Keynsham that took the best part of two hours, they reached the doctor's home, and were let in, whereupon Thomas described the acute pains and sickness suffered over the past twelve hours or so, and explained that the symptoms were much more worse than those he had previously experienced, and that he was now quite certain that he had been poisoned. Having patiently listened to his patient and given him a cursory examination, the doctor dismissed Thomas's own prognosis in an authoritative manner and decided that he was probably suffering from an unknown ailment that was most certainly not life threatening, and that the best treatment was for Thomas to return home, retire to bed, and try a little gruel later that day. There appears to have been nothing prescribed by the doctor to alleviate the pain, and Thomas was left to walk the three miles or so back home, without having received any medical help. Perhaps in fairness to the doctor, he may have considered the combination of all of Thomas's visits to be nothing more than someone wanting attention, and was therefore wasting his time, and someone whose imagination grew with each visit, furthermore the doctor would have been conscious of the fact that Thomas would have had little money to pay him for extensive treatment, and therefore did not want to unnecessarily waste his precious time. In addition there was probably very little that the doctor could have done in 1820 to prescribe any medication that would have reversed the effects of the poison or relieved the associated pains.

As suggested, Thomas retired to his bed and spent the next four days in absolute tormented agony, with alternating bouts of extreme sweating, bouts of shivering, occasional sleep, and further vomiting, until in the early hours of the fifth morning relief eventually came to Thomas in the form of death, as his soul left his body in a frozen contorted shape. Two days later, an inquest was held into Thomas's death, where it was established that despite the doctors earlier diagnosis, Thomas had indeed been poisoned, and shortly afterwards, his widow, Rebecca was arrested and charged with her husband's murder.

During the trial held at the Gloucester Assize Courts, on the 14th August 1820, it was established that Rebecca had, some weeks prior to her husband's death, visited Mrs Stephens, the apothecary on Kingswood Hill, with a view to purchasing a quantity of rat poison, but had been thwarted by the proprietor's rule not to sell one person on their own any such poisons. Having been refused, the disappointed Rebecca left the shop uncertain what to do, but equally determined that by hook or by crook she would obtain the poison. Suddenly the chance to do so was in front of her, as walking up the hill with a large bundle of washing over her relatively young shoulders was **Sarah Jenkins.** Seizing the presented opportunity, Rebecca stood in front of the young woman and clutching her arm, she asked, in a rather plaintive voice, if Sarah could assister her in getting rid of a rat. She then explained that she had tried to purchase some rat poison, but that the "old bag" in the apothecary shop had stopped her because she wouldn't sell poison to somebody who was on her own. If, said Rebecca, Sarah was a good Christian woman, then she would help her fellow creature, and come into the shop so that she could buy the poison. Always willing to help and only seeing the good in people, Sarah agreed, and accompanied Rebecca as she went back into the shop, and explained that Sarah was a friend she just happened to meet outside, and who had agreed to act as a witness, if that was what was required. Mrs Stephens had no reason to doubt the honesty of the statement, and accordingly opened the jar containing the grey/white powder, tipped around two ounces onto a set of scales, and from there placed the poison in the centre of a sheet of thick paper, which was carefully folded so that none of the powder could escape, received the few pence that it cost and the transaction was complete. Both Rebecca and Sarah left the shop together, and with a cursory 'thank you' from the former, both women went their separate ways, but not before the immense pleasure of having "gotten one over the rotten old apothecary" got the better of Rebecca. With the great relief of having the desired poison in her possession, Rebecca almost felt a little light headed, and told the somewhat gullible Sarah, that the real reason why she wanted the poison was because she lived with a hell of a man, who was unkind to her, kept her short of money, and who was the plague of her humdrum existence, and that she had had enough, and was going to take the first opportunity she could to put this man asleep and be rid of him for good. With a sudden realisation of what she had blurted out, Rebecca, gave a silly false laugh and quickly said to Sarah that she was just joking, and had bought the poison to kill rats, not her husband. *Oh just forget what I said,* said Rebecca, *its just the ramblings of a silly woman. Here have this threepence and buy yourself a pint of ale on me, oh, and by the way there's no need is there to repeat what I've just said to anyone else.* With that, they parted company, with Rebecca trying to forget what she had blurted out, but convinced that the threepence given to Sarah was enough to keep her mouth shut, whilst Sarah continued her homeward journey up the hill with an urgency in her step, as she hurried home to tell her mother what had just happened and in particular what this strange women had said to her.

Having gained the above information from the two witnesses, Mrs Stephens, and Miss Jenkins, the jury were then told that despite what Rebecca had said to Sarah Jenkins about her husband and her marriage, there was another side to her character, inasmuch as for some while Rebecca had participated in a number of relationships with other men, and her infidelity, being known to her husband, was a major cause of their many rows. The fact that Thomas had not thrown his unfaithful wife out of their matrimonial home was credit to his own loyalty, and it seemed very obvious to the prosecution that Rebecca's premeditated act of killing her husband, was simply to remove him from the scene so that her current lover could move in, in his place. With such damning 'evidence', the jury only took four or five minutes to find the defendant guilty of the foul murder of her husband by poisoning and, as a consequence, she was sentenced to death by hanging, with the added decree that after her body was removed from the scaffold. It should be handed over to the local surgeons for dissection.

Taken down to the cells, Rebecca soon found herself the sole occupant of the condemned cell, whilst at the same time she was under constant surveillance from the Prison Warders. The only contact she had with the outside world occurred on the day following her trial, when she received a visit from the Rev. Ellacombe, the incumbent at St Mary's Bitton, who came to pray for her soul, and to ask for her redemption.

In the early hours of the following day, Wednesday 16th August 1820, a large crowd, many of them from the general area of Oldland and Bitton, began to gather outside the main gate of Gloucester Prison, jostling for position, and ensuring that they and their children had the best view possible of the room constructed upon the open arch high above the gatehouse, and in particular, the open area immediately beneath that room. Some people had brought food, and many had brought jugs of ale, and even flagons of gin, and soon all were enjoying the fare, and the warming summer sunshine with the frolicking atmosphere of a country fair, indeed, some of the travelling hawkers had already set up their stalls, and expected to do a roaring trade as the crowd waiting with high anticipation of an excellent show.

In her cell, Rebecca could hear the distant hum of expectancy, knowing that the gathering people had come for just one thing, and that was to see her, in less than an hours time, dance to the hangman's tune; she had picked at the breakfast left for her, and had sipped a little water, as she washed her face and combed her unruly hair. Rebecca was never considered to be a beautiful woman, but certainly in her younger days, there had been an aura of gentleness in her features that had enhanced her looks and made her pleasantly attractive, but today as Rebecca stared at the reflection in the water, she shuddered at what she saw, life had been hard on her, and the effects of the trial, and the forthcoming events of the day, had taken their terrible toll, and this morning it was difficult to recognize the rippled face that stared back at her. As she tried to make the best of a bad job, brushing down, with her hands, her rough prison dress, the door of the cell opened to admit the Rev. Ellacombe and the Prison Chaplain, accompanied by two warders, while a few steps behind came the hangman appointed for that day. With knees trembling, Rebecca felt that she was about to collapse, but before she fell, the stout arms of the two warders held her arms, and kept a sagging body upright. In the background Rebecca could faintly hear the mumblings of the two men of the cloth praying for her soul, and imploring her to make her peace with God before it was too late. Without her having realised it, the hangman had in the meanwhile, already stepped into the room, and had manacled Rebecca's hands and feet, and now the time had come for Rebecca to make the one journey in her life that she was most reluctant to take. With the Prison Chaplain, reading the burial service, leading the way to the empty room over the gatehouse, an extremely frightened Rebecca, ably supported by the female warders followed on behind to be followed herself by the Rev. Ellacombe with the hangman bringing up the rear. Gradually through the dimly lit stone corridors, this pathetic party made their way to a room that was devoid of all furniture and/or decoration, had two small windows built high into the outside wall, just the one door, and a wooden floor in the centre of which the boards had been cut and hinged so that by pulling the adjacent bolt, both sides of the trapdoor would swing on their hinges and drop down to expose a ten-foot gap to the roof of the actual gatehouse below. The more observant of those who entered this cold and eerie room would also have noticed that across the room just below the height of the ceiling was a large sturdy wooden beam, from which dangled a stout knotted rope, and almost certainly of all of the rooms limited attributes, this was the one aspect upon which Rebecca would have focused as she entered that room for the first and last time in her life.

At present the waiting crowds had little knowledge of what was going on behind the scenes, all they knew was that Rebecca Worlock was supposed to be hanged at eight o'clock that morning, and for those who could tell the time, and for those who could not, there was already a buoyant attitude pervading all those who were gathered which could only mean one thing, Rebecca's performance was nigh. They may not have the pleasure of seeing the hangman place the noose about her neck, or the pleasure of seeing her trembling and wetting herself as she stood upon the trapdoor, but because the new gatehouse had been constructed in the way it had they would certainly see her fall, twitch and dangle as she appeared below the top room into the space below. The excitement increased as the prison authorities allowed the outside set of double gates to be opened causing a multitude of watchers, many of whom were latecomers to the party, to leave their picnics, and their chosen spots and to surge forward, elbowing and pushing their way towards the gatehouse so that they and their family could obtain a better view. Fights broke out as neighbours fought for their favourite or chosen place, but suddenly there was an unnatural hush that fell over the crowd as a distant church clock began to strike eight, and with that Rebecca made her final appearance in this world, and to publicly announce the event, a prison warder raised the black flag above the prison entrance. Rarely if ever did the noose of those days break the victims neck as gravity took charge of their body, and accordingly most were asphyxiated by the rope throttling the life from them, and this is certainly true of Rebecca, who was left dangling at the end of the rope for the next hour or so to ensure her death, whilst at the same time allowing more and more of the crowd to gape at her earthly remains, in the knowledge that they had witnessed the fact that justice had been done.

So ended one particular domestic tragedy that came to Oldland, and although perhaps not as spectacular, there were probably many other such instances, some of which were recorded, whilst many were carried out without the crime ever coming to the notice of the authorities, who were, to say the least, more interested in upper class scandals, and what went on in their elite circle, than the domestic inconveniencies of the working class.

Footnote:
Thomas, who was born in 1779, is believed to have been the eldest son of **John Worlock** and his wife **Martha (nee Prigg).** Certainly they were his parents, but having married on the 5th May 1779, there is a possibility that Mrs Worlock gave birth to Thomas before the wedding. Thomas married Rebecca Flower on the 7th October 1807 at St Mary's Bitton

An inquest was held at the *Queen's Head* Willsbridge on the 26th March 1804 with regard to the recent discovery of human remains in property belonging to Thomas Pearsall esquire. It was understood that the body of a newly born male child had been found the previous day by one of Mr Pearsall's servants in the privy or necessary house in the grounds of Willsbridge Castle, and that one of the domestic servants, a **Mary Marsh** who was around twenty-three years of age, was believed to be the mother of that child. In front of the local Coroner, a jury of twelve men, who were undoubtedly influenced by the large number of unexplained infant deaths, which constantly happened throughout the country, spent six hours questioning a very frightened Mary Marsh concerning whether or not she was the mother of this bastard male child, who the father was, and had she killed her child. Having carried out this full and intimidating investigation, against the unrepresented female, the twelve men came to the unanimous verdict that twenty-three year old Mary Marsh, a single woman had, on her own, given birth to the child in the privy, and that she should be sent to Gloucester to await trial at the next available Assizes, charged with the wilful murder of her newly born son.

At her trial medical evidence was submitted that the child was probably still born, or certainly died not long after birth, although the exact cause of death could not be determined. Accordingly, Mary was acquitted of the charge of murder, but was found guilty of "secreting ye birth of ye child" and was sentenced to twelve months imprisonment.

Sometime during the first decade of the nineteenth century in the parish of Bitton an **Arthur Roberts** was born to less than wealthy, but undeniably hardworking parents, although this was certainly nothing special or particularly different to the many other children born at the same time. As the decade rolled by, Arthur struggled, in his formative years to obtain a modicum of education which was unfortunately hampered by the fact that quite often he found himself in trouble with authority due to the somewhat morose side to his character and his tendency of having a rather quick-fired temper. Ultimately, at the age of around twelve years, Arthur left school and its many frustrations, and became an apprentice in the local hat making industry, and in particular was taught the way of making felt. Maturity brought with it less melancholy moods, and a better control of his childish tantrum's, but it also brought with it the strength of a man who was now more difficult to control. In due course Arthur met and subsequently married and set up home with **Margaret,** but events were to show that she received the worst side of the bargain, and soon began to feel the effects of her husband's mood swings, and of his fists. As the marriage progressed Arthur seemed to find more and more faults with his wife, and his possessiveness brought with it feelings of unfounded jealousy that in turn led to Margaret being the innocent victim of his moods, his tantrums, and worst of all his beatings.

Despite his wife's total and truthful denial of any unfaithfulness, Arthur saw demons in every corner and every sentence of her repudiations, and ultimately towards the end of 1827, in a fit of rage born out of his uncontrollable jealousy; he beat his wife about her head, blackening both her eyes, breaking her jaw and nose, and as she cried out with pain for him to stop, he grabbed hold of her neck and squeezed it in an attempt to prevent her screaming. With Margaret falling into a state of unconsciousness, Arthur relaxed his grip, and allowed his battered, and blood covered wife to slump to the floor then, with little or no remorse, Arthur washed his wife's blood from his hands and having bathed his grazed knuckles, went into the garden for no other reason than to potter around and to sort out in his mind his next course of action.

The commotion had been heard by the Robert's next door neighbours, and although they had heard the shouting, and screaming before, there was something more sinister and chilling about today's episode that led them to want to interfere in a domestic dispute that seemed to have got out of hand. As he entered Roberts' garden **William Short,** with his wife closely following behind him, was greeted by the sight of his neighbour in a blood stained shirt, wandering about and mumbling to himself. *"What ever has happened"?* Said William as he approached Roberts, not knowing what to expect from his volatile neighbour. *"I reckon I've done for her this time,"* came the reply. In the meanwhile, a pregnant Mrs Short had gone past her husband and through the back door where, on the kitchen floor she found the semi-conscious battered body of Margaret Roberts lying where she had fallen. Using what little water was left in the bucket, Mrs Short tried to clean the blood from her neighbour's bruised and swollen face, calling out at the same time to her husband, to fetch the doctor. By now some other neighbours had arrived, and it was decided, that Margaret Roberts should not be left where she lay, and was carried into Mrs Short's house, to await the doctor, and the local constable who had also been summoned. Although the doctor could diagnose what had happened, he could do little for Mrs Roberts until the swelling had gone down, and agreed to call back the following day which he did noting that Margaret Robert's condition had deteriorated overnight, and she was having difficulty in breathing. Unfortunately, the patient's plight did not get any better, and two days after her beating Margaret Roberts passed away due, according to the surgeon who subsequently carried out the post mortem examination, to throat injuries brought about by strangulation.

Arthur Roberts was duly arrested, and sentenced to be tried at the next available Gloucester Assizes on the charge of murdering his wife, and in the circumstances it would seem to be an open and shut case, with William Short, the principal witness at the trial stating that:

"Mrs Roberts was in her habits, a very simple woman who would regularly attend Sunday school to improve her own inadequate education, by trying to learn to read from the scriptures. On these occasions she would go alone, as her husband did not encourage her learning, as according to the witnesses' opinion, he was concerned that his wife might end up being better than him, and that would certainly not sit well upon his shoulder. In her daily life she never troubled herself about other people's business, and that neither he nor his wife, had ever heard her talk ill of anyone. She kept herself to herself, rarely speaking of her own achievements or misfortunes, with the exception that on a number of occasions over the recent year or so, she would hint or speak openly about her husband's temper, and his miss-use of her. It was a situation that she seemed to have accepted as part of her married life, and she seldom complained, although he ~ Mr Short ~ felt that she had every right to complain."

Both the attending doctor and the local constable gave evidence, but although Mrs Short had gone to Gloucester with her husband to give corroboratory evidence, she was unable to attend the hearing as she had gone into labour, and giving birth the day before the hearing took place. With Arthur Roberts void of any defence other than that he did not mean to kill his wife, the magistrates had the relatively simple task of hearing what had happened, although it had to be admitted that there were no independent witnesses to the actual beating/strangulation. Having heard the witness's statement, and Robert's response they pronounced their verdict to a somewhat hushed Court when the senior magistrate announced that the defendant was not guilty of murder, but was guilty of the lesser charge of manslaughter, and that Roberts' punishment would be eighteen months hard labour.

Such a fairly lenient sentence given to a husband whose actions has caused his wife's death, whether or not he had meant that to have happened, demonstrates how in the nineteenth century authority, particularly Court Authority, placed a greater emphasis on property over human life, or more certainly that group of human life that made up the lower classes, especially the working class. To illustrate this point it needs to be recorded, that at the same assizes, two men were sentenced to be hanged for a crime of highway robbery, and a further twenty-seven were sent to the gallows for crimes ranging from house breaking or theft. In none of those twenty-nine cases was anyone physically harmed, what was, in the eyes of the magistrates, so heinous about the crimes committed and now before them was that these miserable creatures had had the audacity of trying to steal goods and chattels from their contempories in the upper class, and that simply could not go unpunished. The fact that a husband from that lower class had killed his wife was really nothing more than a trifle, as it did not really matter, it was just not that important, but the thought of those poor people, the gentry of the land who, whilst travelling in their own coaches, had been humiliated by having their progress halted at gun point and made to hand over their valuables, or equally those whose homes had been violated, did not bear thinking about, and thus the perpetrators must receive the full weight of the law. Also at the same assizes was a poor unfortunate woman who, to help clothe her family, had accepted some articles of clothing, knowing them to have been stolen. She was found guilty and sentenced to 14 years transportation, which in reality was a life sentence, as the chance of her ever seeing her family again, was virtually zero. Similarly, a man received 14 years transportation for stealing a gun and a pig; the latter intended to provide meat for a number of his family and friends. But from whom had these items been stolen, not the poor, but from the rich, and that had to be punished.

The total cost to the parish of bringing Arthur Roberts to trial was £22.12s 9d [£22.64p], and this included paying a fee of £10 to the Counsel for the Prosecution; £3.50p for the cost of Mrs Short's lying in, (confinement) whilst staying at an inn in Gloucester, and a 30p payment to an **Edith Jeffery** the local "midwife."

Although the ensuing items do not strictly come under the heading of domestic violence, the following extracts from contemporary journals give us an insight into crime in general, and the punishment meted out on local criminals, at the turn of the nineteenth century.

Gloucester Assizes 30 June 1800:

Our assizes were not concluded till eleven o'clock on Saturday night. Four criminals were capitally convicted and were left for execution viz. **William Sheppard, John Roberts, John Hawkins** and **Benjamin Gullick.** They were all brought before the bench, on the charge that they had broken into the house of **George Jones,** a horse dealer of Hanham nr. Bristol, and having forcibly gained unlawful entrance, they stole cash and bills to the amount of more than £150, (probably equivalent in today's value of around £75-80,000) It was put before the Magistrates that the accused Sheppard and a certain **Mr Palmer** had hatched the idea of the robbery, based upon the grounds that they knew that Jones was a successful horse dealer, and a man of property, and that when he returned, on the evening of the 17th March from the fair that was being held that day, he would have a considerable amount of money about his person. The plan was that Sheppard and Palmer, together with extra muscle power supplied by Gullick, Roberts and Hawkins, would waylay George Jones in an isolated place, and encourage him to part with his money, as he returned to the stables situated some distance from his house. The plan of course assumed that Jones would co-operate and take the path to the stables, and that he would give up his money to the five ruffians, but like so many plans, there was no contingency for changes which might be forced upon them, and thus the men were somewhat surprised, and a little confused, when George Jones did not come along the path leading to the stable, but instead continued his journey to the large house. This meant that the intended thieves either had to go home empty handed, or to take the greater risk of breaking into the victim's own home. They took the gamble, and stole the money, but not before their identity had been compromised. With the resulting hue and cry, which was being orchestrated by Jones and his wealthy land owning friends in full flow, Palmer, who had been previously identified as being one of the "gang," decided that his best course of action was to turn King's Evidence, which in due course led to the arrest of the four accused men.

Having turned King's Evidence, Palmer sentence was quite minimal, whereas the death penalty was imposed upon Sheppard, with Gullick, Roberts and Hawkins having their sentence reduced to transportation

Gloucester Journal 1804

Local men **George Fry** and **John Ferryty** were brought before the autumn assize courts on the charge of highway robbery. Fry was capitally convicted; Ferryty's sentence was reprieved.

Gloucester Journal April 1817

Sitting at the Gloucester Lent Assizes, the Magistrate found the following local men guilty as charged:

Thomas Sweet ~ unlawfully breaking into a house in Bitton, and stealing there from. Sentenced to be hanged, although it would appear that the sentence was subsequently changed to imprisonment, as there is no record of a Thomas Sweet having been hanged or transported. It is also possible that Sweet had an accomplice as **Richard Moreton** appeared in the same Court at the same time on the charge of having committed a burglary in Bitton. Likewise he was also found guilty and sentenced to death, and similarly there is no record of a Moreton having been hanged, certainly both men together with **George Wilmot, Giles Wilmot, Edward Peacock** and **Henry Moreton** were all inmates of the Gloucester gaol during 1817. All of these men were contemporaries of the Caines family, and the infamous Cock Road Gang. (See my book "*The Cock Road Gang [The story of the Caines family"]* ~ available from local shops and/or the author priced £8)

Benjamin Caines also appeared at the same assizes and was similarly charged with burglary of the Bitton home of the elderly **Sarah Prigg**. As with Sweet and Moreton, Caines was found guilty, and sentenced to death, but unlike the other two, Benjamin was a Caines, and as such there would be no reprieve for him, and was subsequently hanged on Saturday the 6th September 1817.

During 1816, there had been an affray in Bitton regarding the local constables, and a group of men and women, who wished to rescue one of their comrades from the clutches of the law. Amongst those arrested were **Henry** and **Ambrose Willis.** Both men were charged with having obstructed the constables of Bitton in the execution of their duties and, having been found guilty, Henry received a sentence of two years imprisonment at Tewkesbury jail, and Ambrose one year in the same place of correction.

Gloucester Journal August 1825

The calendar contained the names of no less than 53 prisoners for the County, plus two in respect of the city. The Court dealt with all 55 prisoners by the end of Saturday night and passed the death sentence upon the following:

Francis Caines alias **Bush** and **Samuel Nedds** found guilty of the charge of highway robbery in Bitton against the person of **Abraham Golding** and stealing there from a silver watch a hat and a handkerchief.

Francis Caines Bush was the second illegitimate son of Elizabeth [Betty] Caines and Timothy Bush, being born in 1807. His elder brother James Caines Bush, born two years previously was, in due course to be indited, with six other men for the wilful murder of Isaac Garden outside of the *Tennis Court Inn* on the 27th November 1824.

Elizabeth was the eldest daughter of Benjamin and Ann Caines and sister to a number of brothers who, together with cousins and friends collectively become known as the Cock Road Gang. As a result of the strong family ties, and the fact that Timothy Bush, the father of the two boys, was transported, on the charge of horse stealing, to the colonies in 1813, both boys gradually dropped their father's family name, and chose to be known as Caines. As Caines they may have had more influence or power in the community, but the drawback was that Magistrates were less than forgiving when a Caines was brought before them. Certainly this appears to have happened in the case of James ~ please see my book "*The Cock Road Gang (The Story of the Caines family)*" and may well have also occurred when Francis was brought before them. Thus for poor Betty, she was to lose her two eldest sons to the work of the hangman in the same year.

It would be wrong to suggest or even imply that the area covered by this book was, during the early part of the nineteenth century a hot bed of crime. It was certainly an area of high poverty, and the majority of the available employment was tough, very often dangerous and poorly paid, and these factors may have contributed to a small portion ~ probably less than ten per cent ~ of the population turning to crime, much of which would, by today's standards be regarded as fairly minor or petty crime.

CHAPTER 6 "PICTURESQUE VILLAGE RAMBLES"

During the mid 1890's a Mrs L Wheatcroft undertook forty rambles around Bath, and described each one in detail in individual articles that were published in the weekly *"The Bath and County Graphic"* The three particular articles where her destination was a village covered by this book are faithfully reproduced below, so that today we can have a glimpse into a world that was very different one hundred years ago.

KELSTON

Two miles from Upper Weston, 4 from Bath

....

There is a train to this quiet little village, but the pedestrian will prefer the walk over the fields from Weston. Leaving the Firs at the end of the village we come to two roads, the one to the right leading to North Stoke the subject of the next ramble, and that to the left to Kelston. We first pass Weston Lodge, a charming old house with a pretty garden, and very soon are in what may be styled a Devonshire lane; it is steep, and its high banks and trees overhead have all the characteristics of the lovely lanes in the neighbouring county. Looking back the rambler has delightful peeps of distant Bath at one point, while Beckford's Tower looms in the landscape. Summerhill and the Wesleyan College on Lansdown gradually appear as in a moving panorama. The pedestrian will continue on this road till he comes to one leading through a field to a farmhouse; avoid the white gate just below overlooking the kennels. This road, which is at first broad enough for a cart, gradually gets

Kelston Church as seen through the eyes of an artist

less and less wide as you proceed over the fields, and after passing the farmhouse on the left it is so narrow as to be scarcely visible, but the path in the centre of the field must still be followed. A stile has then to be crossed and a meadow skirted by a coppice in which numerous rabbits gambol about. From the next small field a very good view may be obtained of the park and mansion, the residence of Colonel and Mrs Inigo Jones. The fourth and last pasture brings the rambler to a lane, which after a few moments walk terminates in the village of Kelston, or Kelweston, as it was called in olden days.

On reaching Kelston Lodge a road to the left leads to the Church and Vicarage. The Rev. Francis J. Poynton, the rector, has kindly permitted me to make some notes from his very interesting book entitled "Memoranda, Historical and Genealogical, relating to the Parish of Kelston," which may be interesting to some who have not had an opportunity of perusing that work From the same source I am also indebted for the illustrations of the early remains:

"That a chapel or church was in existence here in Saxon times cannot be doubted because several stone carvings of a pre-Norman character are extant to this day. Again, a circular-plate of bronze metal of undeniable Saxon character as to its ornamentation, marked with the Christian emblems of the Cross, besides Saxon pellets and other quaint emblems peculiar to the style, was found by the writer in some soil thrown from the church when it was undergoing restoration in 1860. Surely such relics as these are stubborn facts, and prove unmistakeably that this spot where I am writing was in the occupation of the Saxons, and that after their conversion to Christ they worshipped where Kelston Church now stands."

"The date of one Saxon fragment is probably the 11th Century. The style has advanced from the mere coil and rude letters of the Runes, and sets forth *The Three of Knowledge of Good and Evil."*

It is the remains of an old cross, which probably formerly stood by the old Cross House, now pulled down. The portion here illustrated has been built into the chancel wall. In the belfry is a black lettered board of Commandments with the following inscribed at the bottom: - *"This is the way walk ye in it."* There is some beautiful

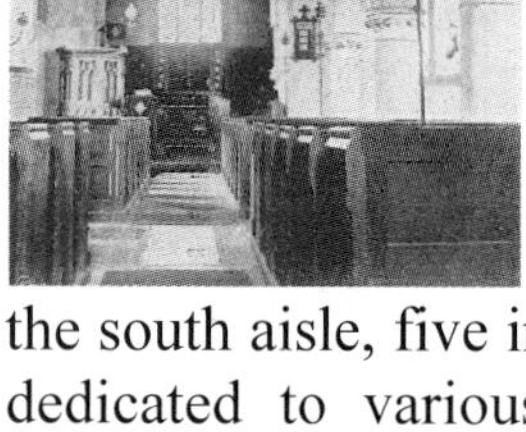

old glass in the windows, date uncertain. St Barbara, the subject of one, is rarely represented; the only other place in which this saint is found is in the Triptych at Winchester. All the windows of the church are of stained glass; those within the Communion rail, by Wailes of Newcastle (1863), are to the memory of the Harrington and Hudlestone families. Those in the south aisle, five in number, are by Hardman of London and Birmingham, and are dedicated to various members of Colonel Inigo Jones's family. All the other windows contain old stained glass presented to the Rector (and caused by him to be adjusted to Kelston windows) by the late Mr Pratt, an antiquarian dealer of Bond Street, London, who in his lifetime paid frequent visits to Kelston prior to the restoration of the church. His connection with Kelston was through his marriage with a Miss Randolph, niece of "good churchwarden" William Jones, of that parish. There was no stained glass in Kelston Old Church.

During the restoration of the church in 1860 several pieces of fluted Roman tile were unearthed from the floor of the chancel, some of which are still in the possession of the Rector; and some were carried into Bath by **Mr Harries,** surgeon, of Walcot Parade, who took much interest in the church. Possibly they are still preserved. The Rector was also informed by the late **Mr Arthur Weston,** of Charles Street, that some Roman coins were dug up when his father's grave was made in the south porch of the old church. The dish-like top of a Roman votive altar, found during the excavations, is preserved in the porch of the present church. It is strange that no tomb was ever erected to the memory of **Sir John Harrington** or of his son, John, who held office under the Commonwealth, and was a Somerset County MP.

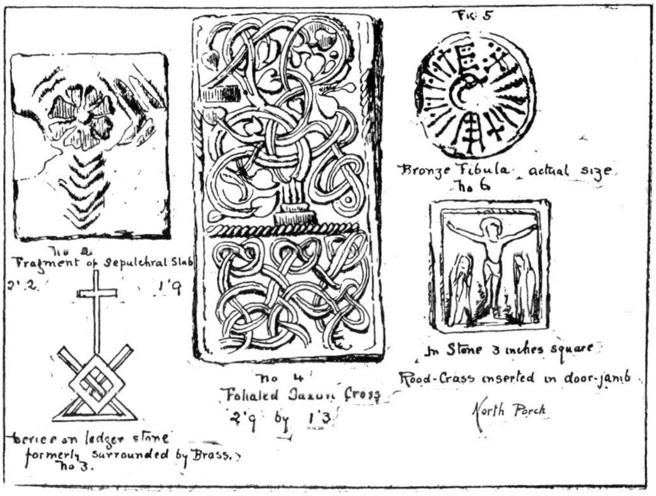

Amongst the many quaint monuments is a musical one on brass. It is let into a border of white marble, and is a composition in three parts adapted to the words ~ "Blessed are the dead which die in the Lord."

The churchyard, like that of Weston, seems to have been a favourite resting place. Monumental records are to be seen, pertaining to persons, mostly invalid visitors to the hot springs of Bath, whose only connection with Kelston has been to drive out there, and then ultimately to desire to be buried in this rural spot. Coming out of the churchyard we are in the midst of the old monastic buildings, and this drawing on the right gives an illustration of the Manorial Barn before Henry VIII confiscated Church property. There is one of the largest dovecotes in the country here, not so picturesque as the one adjoining Old Widcombe Manor House, but well worth inspection.

Leaving the farm buildings we pass the Rectory, where the antiquarian, should he be favoured with the opportunity, will much enjoy a chat with the Rev. F J Poynton, who has made a life study of ancient remains; the keys of the church are also here. From the gate a turn in the road reveals one of our picturesque thatched cottages said to have been "The Old Cock Inn," now the residence of **Mr James Steager**, (see illustration below). A spiral staircase inside is not often found in a cottage

The Old Cock Inn

The village school with its sixteenth century porch is very picturesque, and contains in the schoolroom, two fireplaces very much like, and apparently of the same period as the one I hope to find when I visit North Stoke.

A ramble to Kelston would not be complete without mention of the Harrington family, who lived here for many generations. Unfortunately their house is now pulled down, and only one small portion remains, which was carefully preserved by the late Colonel Inigo Jones. An illustration of the house is given in Mr Poynton's book.

The Manor of Kelston was given to **Ethelred Malte** by Henry VIII, when she married **John Harrington.** His son, who was to become the celebrated **John Harrington,** is stated by Collinson to have been born at Kelston, but this is rather doubtful, as there is no entry of his baptism in the Parish Register.

The want of a proper residence for an important family, on a Manor, which for centuries had simply been farmed on a lease from the Abbey of Shaftesbury, is another argument against this supposition. The father had a residence in London or Lambeth, and it is probable that the son was born there. Queen Elizabeth and the Duke of Norfolk were two of his sponsors. Her Majesty is said to have made a gift of a miniature golden font, which was long afterwards treasured among the family plate. Unfortunately at a later date it was lost in the siege and surrender of Bristol Castle, to which fortress the plate had been sent for greater security.

Lord Burleigh was distantly related to the Harrington's of South Witham, in Lincoln, and seems to have taken an interest in the youthful scion of a kindred house. Perhaps he may have been solicited to write to him by the Queen herself, but certainly many letters passed. In writing he styles him "Dear Boy Jack," which soubriquet seems to have clung to him, for he himself tells us many years afterwards that when he appeared at Court, after taking his M. A. degree, Her Majesty caused him to be written to as follows:

"Boy Jack, ~ I have made a clerk write fair my poor words (her opening speech in Parliament that year) *for thy use; as it cannot be that such striplings have entry into Parliament Assembly yet. Ponder then in thy hours of leisure, and play with them till they enter thy understanding; so shalt thou hereafter, perchance, find some good fruits hereof, when thy god-mother is only a remembrance. And I do this because thy father was ready to serve and love us in trouble and thrall.*

A short walk through fields brings us to the railway station, or a longer one may be taken by the high road, both equally enjoyable, but the latter may be preferred by the timid who would rather avoid the cows generally to be met with in the meadows.

NORTHSTOKE

Distance from Upper Weston 2.5 miles. From Kelston station, via Kelston Mills, 1.75 miles.

One of the charms of this old village is that it is far away from other human habitation, and has, therefore, escaped the hands of the modern builder. It is difficult to find, so much so that it is only recently I have been able to get there. From past experience I thought before making another attempt it would be wiser to apply to head-quarters for direction, and the Rector kindly sent the following route: -

"The way from Upper Weston and Northstoke by the *Via Julia* is easy enough, if you know it, up the zig-zag (sic) and straight on by the path that lies about midway between Kelston Round Hill, and Prospect Stile. People new to the road almost invariably get (sic) wrong, so that if you come from Upper Weston it would be well for you to have a guide."

The Rector afterwards told me of a visit from the School Inspector, who was deposited by the cab at the bottom of the zig-zag before mentioned, with instructions to go straight on and he would see the village on the other side; to make matters worse, and to add to his subsequent misfortunes, it was raining heavily. However, on he went, and on and on, but no village could he see, and after wandering for hours he managed to get into the Kelston road, and he made his way at last to the desired haven. If the scholars had a bad time of it, it was not to be wondered at. Now, as I do not want my readers to vanish into unknown space I will make my instructions as clear and direct as possible.

There are two ways to Northstoke, one via Kelston, the other by Upper Weston. We shall go by the latter and return by the former. As there is plenty to see at the village it will be advisable to take an omnibus to Upper Weston or Combe Park, the former if possible; we then proceed, as we did previously on our journey to Kelston, to *"The Firs,"* at the bottom of the village of Weston, a sketch of which appeared in an earlier ramble; here then, are two turnings, the one to the right is Lansdown Lane, which we must take, and proceed along for a short distance till another turning to the left leads to Broadmoor Lane. Along this we go, passing Broadmoor Farm and Westbrook Cottages; keep to this lane, passing other cottages, till you come to a point where the lane divided into a fork, at this point turn to the right. Here I would caution the pedestrian not to ask the way, as he will be most likely directed, as I often have been, by a longer and more circuitous road, which has always led me away from, instead of to, the place. Well, having turned to the right we go along the lane till we reach a field with a gate; through this we pass, and as we may see other fields with gates en route, the right one may be discovered by a signboard with **"Trespassers off the path will be prosecuted"** written on it. The footpath, which bears towards the left side of the field leads to a gate, where the traveller can sit and rest for a time before commencing the walk up the zig-zag already mentioned.

Tithe Barn

On arriving at the top of the zig-zag [sic] come the crucial point where the School Inspector was lost and where the *Via Julia* is found. A grass-grown road scarcely perceptible is the direct road to Northstoke. On the day that I made its discovery it was covered with brushwood and looked so very unlikely to be right, that for a time I was tempted into a seductive looking clean path, which led to the right. However fortune favoured me, for I retraced my footsteps and proceeded along the grass-grown road. On one side, apparently very near, is the Kelston Round Hill, and on the other, a little higher up, the celebrated Prospect Stile. From this stile the most beautiful view of the surrounding neighbourhood may be seen; but as it is a little out of our direct route we proceed along the *Via Julia;* after a while we come to a stile which on my last visit was almost impassable owing to the heavy rains. These had converted the water-course (sic) into a small brook, and made me feel rather afraid that the "road" could not be that to Northstoke. However, it was, and finally the old Norman church of Northstoke appeared in sight just over the hill. The village is most picturesque and well worth a visit. The veteran litterateur, **Mr S C Hall, FSA**, paid a visit to it the year before he died, being over 80 years of age at the time. A copper beech was planted in the churchyard in honour of his visit, but this unfortunately did not thrive. Writing of this village he says *"I have travelled through all parts of the kingdom, but I never saw so pretty a model of an English village as Northstoke, and I had thought till now there were no landscapes and no delightful country lanes to equal those of my native Devon, but I must own I have been mistaken; I never saw anything in Devonshire to surpass the beauties of the remarkable picturesque neighbourhood."* Then besides its beauty it has so many interesting remains indicative of its early origin; there is no doubt that at one time it was a Roman habitation, as distinct traces of a Roman villa have been found. The earlier history of the place is lost in the midst of ages, but a little bit of folk-lore (sic) of the district, viz, that there is a golden calf buried somewhere between Bitton and Lansdown, suggests the idea that the merchant Phoenicians trading to the Cassetrides made their influence in a religious way felt.

Ye Village School

The keys of the church may be obtained from the Rector, the **Rev. F. O'Melia**, who very kindly took me over the village and showed me all there was to be seen. First we visited the old Manor House, the residence of **Mr Batley,** built a year after the Great Plague. An old fireplace in this house is interesting (see illustration) and is similar to the two fireplaces previously seen in the schoolroom at Kelston.

There used to be a stone cross in the village near this farm, but unfortunately an intoxicated man coming home from market one day collided with it and was thrown out. However, instead of punishing the man for his carelessness, the villagers decided that the cross was at fault and should be "punished" by having it pulled down, and thus another of our Somerset crosses was removed. The porch in the house of **Mr Veal** is considered good by the architects.

At the entrance to **Mr Gibbs's** house by the old-fashioned circular steps, may be seen the remains of pillars, which doubtless belonged to a Roman villa, as they were discovered when digging for the foundations of the old tithe barn during restoration. The tithe barn has been modernised, and only the old buttresses and cross remain to show its origin; but I have made a sketch from one taken by **Miss Kathleen O'Melia** as it was in the old days; a Roman duct was also discovered at the same time. Not far from the village a short time since a stone coffin was found; it was 78 inches long, 3 inches thick, the cover composed of three layers of stone, the whole weighing half-a-ton. As the remains of two bodies (probably slaves) and a horse were buried near, the probability is that it was that of a Roman general. **The Rev. F. J. Poynton** has written a paper on this subject.

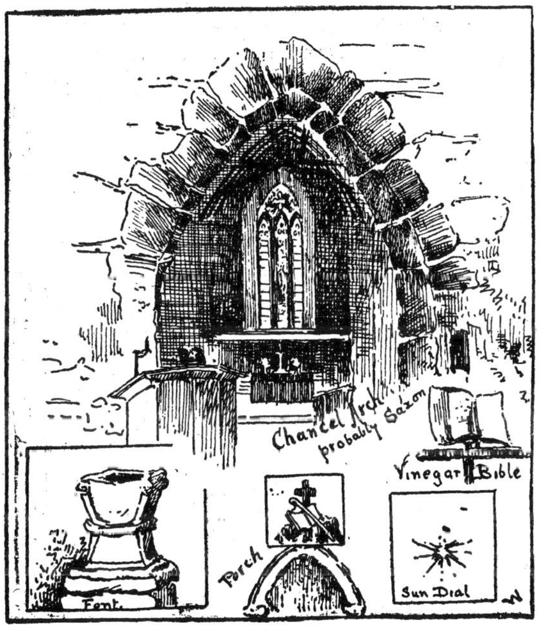

The Church has many indications of ancient origin ~ the stair turret to the tower, the Norman buttresses on the south side, marks of existence of the rood-loft in the chancel arch. The long and short work in this arch appears to be Early Norman, if not Saxon, so also does the font. In the year 800, Kenwolf gave the Manor to the Abbey of Bath. Till the dissolution of the monasteries in AD 1536, the monks held the parish under the grant of the Saxon King. The Church is dedicated to St Martin, and bears a strong resemblance to St Martin's Church Canterbury, which is modelled on the site of the oldest church in England.

An old sun-dial (sic) hidden by mortar was discovered by the **Rev. W S Calverley, FSA.** In a short treatise on Dialling, by **Edward Wright,** there is one, which resembles that at Northstoke; it stands in an upright position on a south wall, and has occupied this position from Anglo-Saxon times.

The chancel is a distinct room, and was divided from the body of the church by a wall in which were two windows and a door; no trace of the screen now exists. Thanks are due to the present Rector, who restored the church in 1878; before this it was in a most dilapidated state; for instance, the old Vinegar Bible had been used as a footstool by the children. There is only one bell, and that is a very sweet one, the others having been sold for £56 to provide pews for the higher-class parishioners.

The peace of the village was once disturbed by the soldiers at the battle of Lansdown, who tradition says came down and refreshed themselves at the expense of the inhabitants. Again, by the Roundheads an order was given that Christmas should not be kept, no mince pies eaten, and no dancing should be allowed round the Maypole. Much more might be written, but want of space forbids, and we return home down the Northstoke Lane, via Kelston Mills, across four fields to Kelston Station. In the spring, violets, primroses and other flowers are found in abundance in this lane, and will be so long as the tourist and the root-sellers allow them to remain. The return journey affords most delightful views of distant Bath and Bristol, with some choice bits for the camera or painter near Kelston Mills.

Set out below is a description of Northstoke as seen by the eyes of a poet, Kathleen F O'Melia.

Peaceful St Martin's, such a site is thine,
Thou scared teacher of the faith divine,
Whose hallow'd precepts in this rural spot,
Perchance without thee were regarded not.

There childhood Heaven's adoption first receives
There is there comfort for the heart that grieves;
There prayers are offer'd and thanksgiving made,
The dead find rest beneath thy sacred shade.

Age-honour'd fabric, would thy blessed use,
Might have acquitted thee of time's abuse.
Alas, not so, unscrupulous decay,
E'en at the church's portal will not stay.

Stoutly thou hast withstood the storm and blast,
Which oft thy aged walls have thundered past.
Within are seen the ravages of years,
Here mournful ruin at her work appears.

Who that can give, an offering will deny,
To make this relic of antiquity,
Upraised by religious hands of yore,
Worthy of its purpose and its use once more.

Blest be the donors, may their generous aid
Here, and hereafter amply be repaid;
And though their names may fade from human
sense,

Above the village like a reverend sage,
St Martin's standeth, venerable with age;
Nestled in hills, a temple quaint and grey,
Far from the bustle of the world away.

Surrounded by a wild romantic scene,
The clustering houses on the hillside green.
A picture sweet of rural peace afford,
Gathered beneath the aged House of God.

Calm haunt of beauty, dear secluded spot,
Where life exists, but its turmoil is not,
Where bounteous nature to the scene supplies,
The costly grandeur human art denies !

With radiant finger, doth Aurora wind
A crown of fire round Lansdown's brow behind,
The sun looks o'er the church tower dark and old
Flooding the village in a light of gold.

A wide expanse and beautiful as wide,
Surfeits the vision from the steep hillside;
Far, too, the sunset sweeps the valley green,
Where tranquil Avon winds his way serene

Along the west doth Dundry grey upheave,
Soft slopes that mingle with the dying eve;
And faintly gleams where vision almost fails,
The shadowy outline of the hill of Wales.

Footnote:

Just below the church, and before the first house in the village, there existed, in mediaeval times, a barn that once belonged to the Manor farm, and during excavations being carried out under the remains of the barn in 1888 a building measuring 11 feet by 102 feet with an apse at one end was discovered. Other walling was noticed close by, as were bricks and tiles, plus three bases and one capital of oolite, the dimensions of which, the experts considered, would indicate shafts of around 6-7 inches in diameter. In considering the site, it was considered that it had been well chosen, as there was a good supply of clean water, being just below the brow of the hill, the site was protected from the coldest winds of the winter, ie those which came from a northerly or easterly direction, and in addition it had the added advantage of having an excellent view over the lands to the west and south-west. Approximately one quarter of a mile to the east of the church, some interments had, during the previous year, been found on Little Down, including three skeletons, one of which was found in an oolite coffin together with a few nails that may well have been from the occupier's footwear. All of the finds are considered to belong to the Roman Occupation period.

BITTON

Distance from Bath, 6 miles

....

The village of Bitton lies midway between the sister towns of Bath and Bristol, the milestone being exactly in the middle of the village, and why is it called Bitton? Possibly from the River Boyd, which runs through it, and which "hath been variously written in different ages as Betune in the Domesday Book. Batton in other ancient records, and latterly Bitton, all of which are supposed to be contractions of, or corrupt modes of writing Boyd Town; that is the town upon the River Boyd.

The 14th August used to be a gala day in Bitton. Certain holders of land in this parish have a right to pasture cattle in the meadows, which skirt the Avon, from the Sunday after the celebrated 14th to the April following, the nominal owners having the right only to mow them. A white bull, decked in garlands, was led in with much ceremony, the others driven in with much shouting. Another custom, "Shooting the meadows," was general, and is probably of high antiquity. In modern history the name of the late Mt Wm Sommerville is connected with a custom, which will long be remembered by the small folk in the neighbourhood. On Christmas Day he promised any child who liked to come "a penny and an orange," the distribution taking place at the Paper Mills, of which the late Dr. Tunstall says, "They are worthy of inspection, more particularly the sheet of water connected with them," of which I have procured an excellent photograph. The first time the invitation was issued, no less than 250 children made their appearance, but the numbers grew to such an extent that the last Christmas before Mr Sommerville died, in 1898, no less than 730 put in an appearance, some coming all the way from Bristol, and I daresay from Bath as well. This reminds me that I have not described the route ~ a route which recalls all the pleasant recollections of my very early rambles. We take the Upper Bristol Road till we get to the Locksbrook Cemetery, and then turning to our right we walk up Newbridge Hill. We pass Partis College, and then take the Kelston road. This is rather hilly, so much so that cyclists are reminded to ride with caution, a rule I fear, not always observed. The view on each side of our road is beautiful, the well-timbered woods of Kelston stretching to our left and the village of Northstoke and the Kelston Round Hill to our right.

Church of St Mary the Virgin, Bitton

We soon come to the village of Kelston and Kelston mills, but instead if going into the village, ~ which takes a sharp turn to the left, ~ we keep to the main road, passing on route the old copper mills now used for the manufacture of flock. If our destination is to Bitton church, a short cut to the left leads to it, but if cycling or driving keep to the main roads. We are now in the heart of the village, and close to the celebrated paper mills before mentioned. One always associates mills with the "Black Country," but the paper mills are in that part of the parish called the "Golden Valley." The building itself is very graceful, and situated as it is on the picturesque Boyd brook; it is difficult to

Church Interior

conceive that it is such a busy hive inside. Thanks to the kindness of Mr Sommerville I spent a very enjoyable hour in going over the factory [see below], and seeing the paper made in all its stages. Paper being one of my useful servants, it was all the more interesting to me, especially as cartridge and writing paper are both manufactured here. First of all I went into the rag storeroom containing Spanish esparto grass, obtained from Carthagena, Tunis and other places. This grass is mixed with the rags. Another material now used for the better quality of paper is the wood pulp, brought from Norway. Then we went to the boiler room, and steam boilers were at work, consuming from 200 to 300 tons of coal per week. Our next visit was to the rag cutting room, where a number of young girls were engaged in cutting. In front of each girl is a broad curved knife like the pointed end of a scythe. The rag is drawn sharply across the bottom of the blade several times, which shakes out much of the dust. She then places it across the upper end of the blade and rips it into long shreds. The rags are then placed in the hands of sorters, whose duty is to classify them. We next go to the "duster," or, as it is commonly understood in the trade, "the Devil." This is a long cylinder of network, which as it revolves throws the rags about and practically sweeps them clean, or comparatively so. It is now time for the rags to be boiled, and here are three immense oblong spherical boilers in each of which about a ton of rags is placed. Linen rags require much more active treatment than cotton, and are boiled separately. A separate boiler is also kept for esparto grass. A good deal of soda ash and caustic is used in the boiling process. The rags are boiled by steam for about twelve hours, during the whole of which time the boilers are kept revolving, for the obvious purpose of keeping the chemicals well intermixed and the rags in constant motion. The rags are next rinsed in a long perforated machine revolving in a bed of water. The rags having been boiled and rinsed are put into an iron trough called a washing engine, or "breaker." In this trough a revolving set of steel knives works upon a set of fixed knives at the bottom of the machine, and these gently tear the rags into shreds until they are reduced to pulp. In the same trough is a cylinder covered with wire, which scoops out the dirty water at one end while the clean enters at the other. This process of washing lasts about two hours, when the pulp is emptied into another somewhat similar trough, and there mixed with chloride of lime, which has the effect of thoroughly bleaching it. It now looks like a mass of white snow. But like our own clothes, the white wants a little colouring matter; and at this period the necessary colouring matter is put in; when the rags are again emptied into the beating engine, and then finally reduced to the proper length of fibre to make paper. The pulp, after being reduced to the required consistency, is emptied into large vats in the machine house, where it is now to be converted into paper. The

next process is very interesting. The pulp flows over sand catchers into the strainer ~ a most important factor, This consists of brass plates, which are very finely cut, through which the pulp is sieved or strained, allowing only the properly prepared stuff to pass through, and retaining knots, dirt and other impurities.

Now we come to the paper making room; by far the most interesting, but the most difficult to describe. The invention is ascribed to a Frenchman, Louis Robert, a clerk in the firm of M. Leger Didot, and a patent was obtained for it by the inventor from the French Government in 1799.

The pulp descends in a regular stream through pipes, and is directed upon a mould about 10 feet in length, and is capable, by an ingenious mechanical arrangement, of receiving sufficient pulp to make paper 70 inches in width, or as much narrower as merchants desire. A "deckle strap" ~ an endless band of vulcanised indiarubber, which, being held down by rollers, forms a sort of never-ending boundary ~ marks the limits beyond which the liquid pulp cannot flow.

The mould itself consists of an endless web of fine wire cloth, which is constantly moving forward above a series of revolving rollers, whilst a vibratory motion from side to side is given to it in order to distribute the fluid evenly, and thoroughly mix the fibrous textures. Proceeding at the rate of about 70 feet per minute, and with this active shaking agency going on, nearly all the water is drained out of the pulp by the time it reaches the first pair of rollers. The paper, which is now absorbent ~ something like blotting paper, ~ takes the impress of the water-mark [sic] or any other trademark desired, and is then sized. It is afterwards rolled onto the drying machine ~ a number of hot-air or steam pipes ~ above which the paper is passed slowly over and under some 72 skeleton drums, in the interior of which are the revolving fans driving the hot air on each side of the paper.

We now proceed to the cutting machine, which is fitted with a number of ingeniously contrived circular knives, for cutting the paper into required sizes. The "Salle" is the last stage. Here the workpeople, called "runners down", are engaged in making a final examination sheet by sheet; the worst being discarded and re-made into paper, the remainder being divided into first and second quality. Then we see the glazing, and, finally, folding and packing.

One could write much more fully about this interesting manufacture, but space forbids. I must not forget though, that in 1876 the mills were totally destroyed by fire, but were re-built and re-opened, in April 1877, the new building being constructed in as fireproof a manner as possible.

From six o'clock on Monday morning to six o'clock on Saturday evening the machinery is at work night and day, and some 450 males and females, or quite one-sixth of the hamlet population, are kept in constant employment. Since the company came into Mr Summerville's possession it has been most prosperous. An old parishioner facetiously remarked that the mills were first in the holding of an Englishman, next an Irishman, and then followed a Scotchman (sic). May the Scotchman (sic) remain there and prosper, is now the wish of all who desire the prosperity of Bitton.

Mill Pond, Willsbridge

Paper mills, like the abbeys of ancient times, are always to be found on the green banks some of pellucid swift running streams, affording good fishing as well as an abundance of the best water. Roach, dace and eels etc are plentiful.

The hamlet of Willsbridge is near Bitton station, and at this place you will find almost all the wild flowers your heart can desire. I have made two sketches at this delightful spot, which in a month or two will be dressed in all its summer beauty. But talking of flowers, I must not forget to mention the interesting garden of Cannon Ellacombe, the charm of which lies in its unconventionality and innocence of the stereotyped methods and formal ways of the modern gardener. It possesses a wealth of interesting and curious plants and trees from all parts of the globe. The Vicar is an ardent and learned botanist, as those who have read his works well know. Near the Vicarage is the beautiful church of St Mary the Virgin, containing one of the most beautiful towers in the country. The late Rev. H. T. Ellacombe, and the present Vicar have done a good work in the restoration of this church. By them the fabric has been carefully preserved, and provides interesting matter for the archaeologist. One more interesting feature in Bitton is the Boys' Brigade. The present captain is Mr William Sommerville.

The present ramble brings my series to a close, and although I have not even yet exhausted the attractions of the neighbourhood of Bath, I feel that after so many walks and talks together I must have exhausted the patience of my readers. The task has been to me one of real delight, as it has opened up many beauty spots in this favoured locality quite unknown to me before, and secured the help and co-operation of many kind friends, without whose aid my task would have been an impossible one. I take this opportunity of thanking all those heartily who have assisted me, and may the links which have bound us together last long after this work has been forgotten.

Footnote:

Any of the above rambles could have been undertaken from Bath with the help of the following business and its contemporary advertisement.

CHAPTER 7 "EDUCATION" or "THE BITTON SKOOL BOORD VIGHT"

Although education for a select few has existed for hundreds of years, for most of the population, particularly in the area covered by this book, the prospect of being taught how to read and write was not an available option. Changes in local children's' education began to occur very slowly during the first half of the eighteenth century, following the arrival of such missionaries as George Whitefield and latterly John Wesley, with one of the first schools for boys aged between 6-12 opening in Kingswood in June 1739. This boarding school, based upon religious principles was created for sons of the "middle class", and however genteel their background may have been, the school regime would, by today's standards, appear to be extremely harsh, with a typical day for the students starting at 4am, for an hour of reading and praying, followed by an hour long religious service. However at this point the boys were given a rest to allow them to have breakfast consisting of milk, bread, porridge and gruel, which were served between 6am and 7am. There then followed consecutively two hours of language lessons, two hours of writing, and an hour for general studies and/of physical exercise, before being allowed an hour's break for dinner, singing and more school work. Having probably received a minimal amount of food, the boys were not allowed to slack, and were then required to spend the next three hours being taught languages, (this could include English, French, Latin, Greek, and/or Hebrew), after which there was an hour of writing and/or arithmetic including geometry and algebra and then an hour of prayer, taking the school day up to 6pm. But even then there was no let up in the order of the day, with the next hour set aside for bread and butter, plus continued studies and further exercise. The children, who were by now almost certainly exhausted, were then required to attended a religious service until 8pm, when it was straight to bed, with no talking until 4am came around again.

As far as the mid-day meal was concerned, the boys had a fairly restricted diet, which frequently included either savoury or sweet dumplings, plus the occasional helping of either boiled beef or mutton, although on Sundays there was the treat of not having dumplings at all, but were allowed a plate of cold roast beef, presumably the leftover from the school governor's table.

The following is a poem written around 1890 in the vernacular of the day, and which purports to describe an argument that occurred with the local board responsible for the school in Oldland:

My worthy Vrend,
I promised that I'd write
To tell thee aal about our Skool Boord vight;
Zo, if zo be as thou'lt excuse bad spellin,
Be zhure I doant mind the story telling.
But then thee knows I'd much prefer to spake
My mind out strait than pen an paper take;
An vrend or voe, at any time or place,
I'd ten times zooner mate um vace to vace.
Now I'll be bound thou'rt thenkin I'm a dunce,
An wishin to the pint I'd coom at wunce;
But teant no use to skould me, nor to vret
Because about th bush I'm batein yet;
Just gie mie time, an what I hev to zay
Shall be unfoulded, but in my own whay.
Zo now, ould vrend, attention if thou wilt,
I'll tell ee why th Wulland's skool wer built.
In aaiteen-vorty-vower zum thoughtful men
Saw cause to make a stir, vor ontil then,
Aalthough th vawk wer mooastly vor Dissent,
To Church skool vor their larmin chidlern went
Th raison wer' ~ I like to make it cleer,
Twas that or nothin, vor nought else wer theer;
The young uns went to skool an this ood voller
Th catekizzum thay all had to swaller!

Now theer wer many parents as disdained
In doctrines valse to hev their childern trained,

Vor in them days was principle held dear,
A theng vor which vawk now hev little keer.
Well then, my story short an plain to make,
Th skool was builded just vor conshuns' sake
An 'twer a skool, vor very zoon 'twer vound
It wer not equalled not vor miles around;
Th childern crouded in vrom var an near,
Vor parents wer right glad to zend um theer,
Th Master wer a man zo wise and good,

Who well th art ov taachin onderstood;
Into th minds ov boys ood he instil
A noble emulation vor to vill
A worthy place in life, an to this daay
Live many bright examples ov his swaay;
Her Majestie's Inspecter one became,
That wer enough to gie th hamlet fame,
An several vrom this umble villiage skool
Hev bin apinted other skools to rule;
An zum in other walks of life hev tried
Zuccess to woo, an hev not bin denied
Now in these parts, though zum thenk it queer
('Tis zimple truth as I ood make appear,) ~

Th childern wer'nt aal boys nor yet aal wenches,
Boath sexes theerfoor zat upon the benches;
Zo, as the skool wer mixed, 'twer no zurprise
The zame rule as to taachers wer thought wise.
Now 'gainst th Missis as wer theer no word
Hev I to zay, but zhurely thou hast heard, ~
Vor boath experience an history teeches ~
Th wimmen much delight to weer th breeches.

'Twer zo wie she, an as time passed away,
'Twer vound no muster very long ood staay,
An in th end, I'm grieved to make confeshun,
She managed ver to get th sole posseshen,
Ov coorse th skool went down, you maay depend
Few parents now their grown boys ood zend,

Zo they wer voorced to zend um to th Church,
Vor all their leaders left um in th lurch;
An zo th cause vor which our fathers vought
Wer overthrown, their labor came to nought.

'Tis moor than twenty year zince this wer done,
An zum be well content, but I vor one
Will never rest ontil th wrong's redressed,
An we ov our own rights wunce moor possessed.
Well, vrend, th outcoom ov this error great
It is my paainful duty now to state.

This district wunce a Liberal stronghold wer;
That 'tis zo now but few will dare aver;
An how hev th zad chaange bin brought about?
Why this th raaison is beyand a doubt, ~
In makin Tories tory skools succeed,
As in th rotten cheese the maggots breed,

Now I must tell ee how in aaighty-dree
Th vawk to hev a skool boord did agree.
Th reign ov petticooats we thought wer ended
And velt quite shower th matter ood be mended
But whether it wer witchcraft or what not
One thing is zartin, ~ we no chaainges got.
An zo at dree years' end 'twer time agen
Vor skool boord members to zelect th men.
This time we thought we'd take th theng in hand,
An them as ood do right persuade to stand;
Vive men the skool boord work ood hev to do,
We didn't mind opponents hevin two,
Zo we picked out dree men in view ov puttin
Th skool wunce moor upon a proper vootin;
Two ov um gied a pledge quite faair an straait
That this grave matter should no longer waait,
An by th tother one our hopes wer fed,
Vor zhure an zartin this is what a zed, ~
"Well, if th people thenk a chaange is needed

Their will by me shall be no moor impeded."
Now tell me, vrend, ~ thee'st got moor wit than I,
Did we do right in thenkin this reply
Vrom such a man wer pledge enough vor we,
An that on this chief pint he'd wie us be?
Alas vor honor as tis onderstood
By zum as likes to be thought wise and good!
On this pint, vrend, theer's much as I could zay,
But must defer it to another daay,
Vor if much moor I write I raaley thenk
I shall run out ov paper and ov enk.
Now vor th time th new boord had to meet
A zound mooast startling coom our ears to greet;
This was th purport ov th thengs we heard, ~
That he to whom I mooastly hev referred

Wer gwain to plaay us valse, an ood'nt gie
His vooat vor progress an prosperity,
And zo, alas! It proved, vor when a man
To tax un wie his faithlessness began,
An tried to show how high th skool wunce stood,
An that agen it might be made as good,
Th answer that a got thee'st hardly credit,
But I can take my ooath as how a zed it,
"Tis only poor vawks' childern as go theer,
Let thay as beant suited go elsewheer."
That's what a zed, an when I thenk awhile
On sentiments like that my blood do bile,
Vor worthy 'tis ov dark feudal time
When to instruct th poor wer deemed a crime;
But now thee knows 'tis thought boath right an wise,
That every child should hev a chance to rise,
An we maintain a proper education
Vor one an aal's blessin vor the nation.
Well at th meetin ov th boord I'm bould To zay that we disgracefully wer sould
Vor with two voes, an one as traitorous proved
It didn't matter what our members moved
'twer vooated down, and zo as I'm alive
Th boord might just as well bin dree as vive.
Wunce moor th time coom round vor an election,
An we moor keerful wer in our selection;
Dree men we chose on whom we could depend,
An to return um aal we did intend;
Two ov um wer as Liberals known to fame,
An one a Tory wer, at least in name;
But 'twer in names alone, vor zhure 'tis true
That not what men are called, but what they do
Proclaims their character befoor th world,
An shows which flag thay truly hev unfurled.
Well, when we went a canvassin we vound
That thay as we wer vightin had bin round,
An if what thay had zed weren't wilful lies,
At least 'twer throwin dust in people's eyes,
Thay zed to raize th rates wer what we zought,
Th plaain truth is thay be lower brought,
Vor if the skool could be made moor efficient
Moor grants we'd get, less taxes wer sufficient.
But it's too long a taail to here report

On every means thay used to gaain suppoort,
And as to tell ee all oud gie mie paain
And make mie lose mie temper, I refraain,
Well as th people's minds wer pizened, we
Vould we should hev no chance to carry dree;
Zeven names in aal wer vor the vooaters laaid,
That two ov ourn ood lose we afraaid,
Zo, vindin our desire beyand our power,
Ov two we thought 'twer better to make shower,
Ov coorse we didn't let th zaacrit out,
That ood hev made um glad I hev no doubt,
We kep our counsel 'till th race wer run,
And then we up and tould um what we'd done;
And when th vooats wer counted up 'twer zeed
That we th wisest coorse had tuk indeed.
As two good men we to the boord had zent,

Conziderin all thengs we wer well content;
Vor 'gainst us wer arraayed zum mighty voorces,
Our voes got help vrom very doubtful zoorces;
Thay stooped to actions mean, an did intrigue
Wie knights an dames of this ere Primrose League;
On powlin daay 'twer zeen suppoort thay'd crave
Vrom poor auld vawk wie one voot in th grave;
And as tha lugged um in a vooat to gie
It wer a mooast disgraceful zight to zee;
But I wunt be too hard, no doubt thay thought
That all wer vish as to th net wer brought:
I beant vindictive, but I thenk it right
On these men's conduct just to throw a light,
We've fought this battle faair an straait but thay,
Well, 'twoodn't do all that I thenk to zay;
To put it briefly, I can dare avow
Thay meant to win an didn't much keer how
Now I must ketch th pooast, an zo, ould vrend,
I must make haste this letter vor to end,
And in conclushun let me zay that though
We're beaten now, we'd hev th victors know
That this ere struggle beant awver yet,
We'll stick to um ontil we justice get;
Two men thay'll hev to mate upon th boord
Whose minds wie vacts and veggers be well stored,

And thay as still our righteous claim opposes
Wunt vind that boord much like a bed ov roses.
And while our members labor, steadfast, true,
Theer's zummat vor each one ov us to do, ~
We've got to taach th vawks th truth about it,
And I veel zhure we, nee'er shall win wieout it,
Vor out ov them as vooated half had heard
Ov our side ov the questin not a word;
Zo we must aalter that, an zhure I be
That when th people all th vacts do zee,
Thay then ool mooastly be ov our opinion,
And their true vrends ool quickly hev dominion

Now I must raaley stop, I hope, ould vrend,
Thou'lt read this letter right vrom end to end;
And much I hope that when thee'st read un droo
Thy eyes wunt ache like my poor vengers do,
Good bye wunce moor, thou'lt know th writin's mine
An I be mooast too tired mie name to zign,
But if a vrend should ax ee what it be,
Why zay as the fust letter is a

D

The earliest known schools or perhaps it should be referred to as schooling, for children of the working class, probably began around 1739, when quite incredibly the miners of Kingswood managed to club together £20 which they gave to **George Whitefield,** so that he could start schooling some, if not all of their children, and further more, they pledged themselves that they would raise twice that amount, if Whitefield could establish an actual school. Bearing in mind that £40 represented around eighteen months of wages for one man, the miners were making a substantial commitment that obviously reflected their deep desire to see their children have a better education and start in life than they had had themselves. As far as is known, Whitefield delegated the task of finding suitable accommodation to his friend **John Wesley**, and in mid 1739 a meeting room and school was established in the appropriately named School Lane, off Britannia Road. By then Whitfield had already met twenty-year old **John Cennick,** who despite his junior years had, with his high standard of knowledge and education, created a deep impression on Whitefield to such an extent that Whitefield was, without hesitation, able to recommend Cennick as the right man to become the first school master in Kingswood. Although he had impressed Whitefield, John Cennick found it much more difficult to get on with Wesley, and after serving for less than a year, Cennick left the school for what was claimed to be theological differences. Despite this obvious set back both John Wesley and George Whitefield continued in their attempt to improve the social and religious morals of the local community, and to encourage children of colliers to attend classes that quite often were held in the front parlour of a well-meaning benefactor's house, or occasionally in a communal meeting room. The problem was that very often those same children would also be expected to be at work, the sons underground with their fathers, or the girls would be sorting out coal and/or rags with their mother. With many mouths to feed, parents inevitably relied upon the few pence their older children would bring into the family budget, and were understandably reluctant to let their children have too much time off to learn their letters and their numbers. Both evangelists were of course very persuasive in their condemnation of sending the children to work, and in the early days of setting up the educational classes, the attendance was quite high, but as the years rolled by, so a gradual decline began and by the turn of the new century, the enthusiasm and studying had largely fallen into decay.

Education and benevolence were however not going to became extinct, so long as there were socially minded men of influence and wealth who as magnanimous philanthropists could exploit the situation. A number of such men had come together during the late 1790's and had together formed the "Kingswood Benevolent Society" to see if they could improve the social well being of those whom they regarded as being in serious need of such help. One of the main supporters of the society and its aims, with genuine concerns about his fellow man, and in particular, those who were seen to be at the bottom of the pile, was **Henry Hill Budgett** a newly emerging entrepreneur involved in the grocery business. He felt that the decline in the level of local education had gone too far, and that it was time to make a fresh start. He suggested to his contempories that a new school should be built with the specific aim of teaching children, not only children of the local colliers, but all children from the poor areas of Kingswood and Oldland. Mr Budgett himself was not a man to simply sit back and make suggestion, he was a doer, and eventually he succeeded with much dedication and a great deal of generosity, to have the school built and opened in Cock Road.

Henry Budgett had a great deal of sympathy, warmth and trust, which was similarly felt by the colliers, despite the fact that there was a very obvious class division both socially and financially between them. Having successfully persuaded his peers that the building of the school was not only a good idea, but that it would also bring many benefits to their workers, Henry was sufficiently radical in his thoughts to consider approaching the colliers to explain what he had in mind, and how the basis of the idea had received the backing of the fellow benefactors of the Kingswood Benevolent Society. However, more importantly he asked for the colliers help, as he had no intention of creating a school that would be forced upon the colliers and their families, with the inevitable resentment that such a situation would create. Instead Henry had the foresight to want to establish a school that was to be created out of mutual understanding and cooperation. It was not Henry Budgett's intention of looking for any financial involvement from the colliers, even had he assumed, which of course he did not, that the colliers and their friends would have had any spare cash to offer, for him the idea was much more simple, and that was to get the working class families involved with the project, and away from any lingering thoughts of hand-outs with strings attached, or charity to just make the giver feel superior to the receiver. He spoke with the passion and the humility of a man who clearly understood and respected the pride and strength of those who were in the audience, and as the colliers, their friends and their families heard his words, they became enthused with the general concept of his plans and views, which were that they should be asked and trusted to carry out the work of construction, and such was their communal enthusiasm that they unanimously agreed to give the few things they possessed, their strength and spirit, and limited time. It should not of course be forgotten that as a group of individuals they spent a great deal of their time working for their masters, dealing with domestic chores, rearing a family, and the many other jobs which needed to be done each day, and thus to volunteer to work clearing the land, digging out foundations, and building the school, after a hard days work, was no mean achievement. Typically, a collier might spend anything from twelve to fourteen hours a day working for the mine owner, who no doubt was quick to remind his employees, who it was who paid their wages, then they had to walk home, perhaps, three or four miles, to have something to eat, before climbing Cock Road, and manually working another three or four hours.

Such was their enthusiasm, that throughout 1811, they continued to push their aching limbs, to clear and level the ground at Cock Road, and then to dig the foundations, so that by the end of the year they had already started on building the walls of the school. Work was finished in 1812, and Cock Road School was opened, with Henry Budgett appointed as the school's first superintendent. On the very first day of opening, no less than 75 hopeful children turned up to be enrolled as pupils, which was far more than anticipated, and which meant the Henry needed to second his brother **Samuel** into helping with the teaching during the one day per week that the school was opened. Such was the success of the school that both Samuel and Henry's philanthropic ideas were heightened, and during 1813 they promoted and started the Cock Road Bible Society, whose objects, however well meaning, veered upon the highly pious, but equally unpractical notion of supplying a Bible to every householder in the district. The one major flaw in their idea was that it presumed that there would be at least one member of each household who could read sufficiently well enough to comprehend and understand that which was written, which of course was rarely the case, nevertheless, almost certainly in many houses, the Bible became a treasured possession, and was probably left out on display to simply impress the neighbours.

By 1816, sufficient funds had become available to cover the cost of opening the school for two or three days per week, even though the whole financial set up meant that the running and administration of the school was controlled on a very tight shoestring budget.

As the nineteenth century progressed, the benefits of schooling children from less privileged backgrounds, became more and more apparent to the forward thinking educationalists, whilst at the same time, and running in parallel, was the more general thinking that the necessary facilities, particularly the buildings, required to house those children, could not just be provided by one or two benefactors in a hotchpotch sort of way. In the long term it was society at large which benefited from the children's education and as such it should be society at large that should create the funds and to have the schools constructed. As early as 1818, plans were being drawn up to have a Church of England School established for the benefit of the children of the poor, and the general poverty of the district. However there was no financial backing for such a project, and the whole idea seemed little more than a debating forum for those who were least affected by the poverty of the district but, by voicing their opinion, they could be seen by the outside world, but even more particularly by their contemporaries, to be charitable and philanthropic, without the actual need to put their hand in their own pocket. Although a national programme of school building had been started in the late 1820's, it was not until December 1833 that authorities gave approval for such a school to be built in Oldland, which was legally brought together under a Deed dated 13th May 1837, allowing the construction work to start shortly there after. In setting up, what was to be known as St Anne's School, a great deal of assistance, including money, had been received from the "National Society for the Promotion of Education of the Poor in the Principles of the Church of England," as a result of which the school included the word "National" in its title although, fortunately for all concerned, the school governors chose not to adopt the Society's full title in the school's official name.

Thus in 1838, Oldland became the proud owner of a "National School" which was to serve the community well for some one hundred and fifty years, built, as it was, on land across the valley from the church that shared its name with the school. The stone built school, the main part of which still stands, was designed to accommodate in a schoolroom, around 200 pupils of the poor, to be educated in Christian principles according to the doctrines and disciplines of the United Church of England. In addition, the building was to include an office, toilet block for both sexes, plus a house was to built as the Master's residence, across the narrow lane that led to the school The total combined cost of these modest buildings was just £650 [probably around £540,000 by today's calculations] Although designed for around 200 pupils, within the first twelve months of opening, the school register showed that on average 124 boys, and 109 girls attended each day of varying ages, to be taught by a master, who earned £50 per annum, and a mistress, whose annual salary was £10 less than her male counterpart. Almost certainly they had their work cut out with the need to control around 112 children each, whilst at the same time cope with the fact that the children represented a hotchpotch of different ages and different stages of education and/or ability.

CHAPTER 8 "Snippets from Edward A Davis Scrap book"

A well-known and highly respected turn of the twentieth century citizen of Bitton, Edward Austen Davis J.P, kept in his scrapbook a printed copy of the "Skool Boord Vight" story as reproduced in the previous chapter No notes or comments were made by him to establish the authenticity of the story, which appears to have in fact been written by an educated person, with a sense of humour whilst making an attempt to incorporate a phonetic form of writing to illustrate what he/she considered was the local dialect. Mr Davis was born at Font Hill circa 1860, and during his lifetime took a great deal of interest in local affairs, and was, for a number of years, a member of the Parish Council, becoming in successive years vice-chairman and the chairman. For many years he was treasurer of the Thornbury Divisional Liberal Association, as well as being chairman of the Oldland and District Liberal Association.

From the many newspaper cuttings and printed articles found in his scrapbook, he obviously enjoyed keeping unimportant but nevertheless interesting fragments of information, some of which for local knowledge and interest are reproduced below:

Schoolboy's Quaint Pupil.

Round about Oldland Common everybody knew and liked **Abram Hibbs**, he was such a "character." He never had had a days schooling in his life, and frequently told those who would listen that *"I was brought up like a wild-ass's cowlt on the mountin."* However, by the time he had reached manhood, and had begun to settle down in life, his greatest desire was to be able to read and write, but he was a proud man and found himself unable to go to a teacher or the local vicar or any other educated adult and ask for help. Abram worked as an engineer at California colliery, ensuring that the engine was well maintained, and always had a sufficient head of steam to bring the coal and the miners to the surface. According to his shift pattern, Abram quite often found himself going home at around the same time as local boys were returning home from school, and it occurred to him that he might be able to fulfil his desire by learning from the boys, and in this way he could avoid the embarrassment of asking a fellow adult. Accordingly he began to put his plan in action, by walking up to one of the boys, who of course would recognize Mr Hibbs, as he would know him as the village character he was, and accost the boy with the comment:

"Well, Tommy, hast bin to school?" *"Aye, Mr Hibbs"* would come the reply.

"I'll lay thee kassent say thee letters" was the responsive challenge. *"Aw, I Can"* was the innocent answer.

Challenging the boy to prove that he could, Abram would then produce some printed-paper, and then point to individual letters, and ask the boy to name each letter. The boy was of course always right, according to Mr Hibbs, and gradually Abram would extend his quizzical probing by getting the boy to put the letters together to make a word. Having then congratulated the boy on his remarkable accuracy, Abram would, with infinite patience, and an excellent memory, gradually build up his own vocabulary, and over a period of a year or so, he completely achieved his desire.

Subsequently Abram married and settled in his new home, and with the added responsibilities he worked hard and became even thriftier than he had previously been. To help feed his growing family, he kept in the back garden, chickens, pigs and bees, as well as producing as many vegetables as possible. As was his usual practice, he would retire to bed, by 9.30pm, in order that he could be up an hour or two before it was time for him to go to work, and during that time he would ensure that both the chickens, and particularly the pigs were given their morning feed. In addition he would also prepare the next lot of pig food so that all that his wife had to do was to empty the contents of the bucket into the trough around mid-day, when Abram was at work.

Unfortunately Mary, his wife, was a poor helpmate when it came to assisting in the garden, and around the animals, and on a number of occasions, Abram would come home from work and find the pigs squeaking and chickens clucking with hunger, whilst the food, that he had prepared for them earlier that day, was still where he had left it. Nevertheless Abram accepted his wife's shortcomings quite stoically and with much fortitude, and was rarely heard to complain about his wife, although on one occasion he did say quite loudly:

"My wife is the most keerful ooman in the parish, she keerful of her labour."

Although he lived a hard and at times a difficult life, Abram was a gentle man with a Christian spirit, and a heart of gold, and was certainly not a man who would rant and rave, or cuss and swear, particularly over his wife's antics and/or shortcomings, but this did not prevent him from trying to teach his wife a lesson, which was mixed with a little bit of humour. Accordingly, whilst his wife remained tucked up in her bed, Abram decided to wait for the pigs to consume their breakfast, before placing in the empty trough the kitchen kettle. Without the kettle, his wife could not boil any water, and without any boiling water, her housework would be more difficult to carry out, but more importantly, Mary would not be able to make herself a cup of tea, a drink to which she was particularly partial. Obviously, Abram reasoned, the punishment would not last long as the moment his wife went out to feed the pigs; she would see and recover the kettle, even if she did not immediately see the funny side of the practical joke. With the stage set, Abram left his wife asleep, the pigs and chickens well feed, and trouped off, with a slight grin on his face, for a twelve-hour shift as an engine driver at California colliery.

Having completed his day's work, a rather weary Abram returned home to find a great commotion, with an upset and somewhat angry Mary turning the place upside down, complaining in a loud voice *"The kettle was lost,"* and that as a result, *"I've not bin able to h've a cup of tay."* Trying to calm his distraught wife with little success, Abram decided to change the subject, and to bring a little humour to the occasion; by casually throwing in the remark *"Did yu feed the pigs today."* Mary's reply was less than lady like, with her husband's irrelevant question doing absolutely nothing to solve her dilemma. Realising that he was not going to calm his wife until she was able to recover the kettle, and quench her thirst, Abram accepted that he was going to have to come clean and taking hold of his wife's hand with a firm grip said *"But had you remembered to feed the pigs, none of this would have happened,"* and leading her out of the kitchen, he propelled Mary to the pig sty and the missing kettle. *"oh lor"* said Mary *"I forgot them pegs today."* Whether Mary learned her lesson is not recorded, but hopefully she saw the funny side of the "Joke" once she had drunk her first cup of tea.

Christmas in Oldland during the 1830-40's

The following recollections of Christmas long ago was collected by Edward Davis, and published in a local newspaper around 1908:

"I have vivid recollections of Christmas, 70 years or more ago; I recall the wonders and delight of the presents, the joyous fireside games, and not least, keen appreciation of the good things provided. One of the events that has stood out in my mind was the visit of the Christmas Boys, and their arrival in the village inevitably caused, certainly amongst the children present, great excitement and joy. In total there were usually about four or five fantastically dressed young men in the group, each having a tin sword, whilst their clothing was decorated with hundreds and hundreds of shiny metal discs, that twinkled and tinkled as they marched to and fro in opposite directions, clashing their swords as they past each other, whilst at the same time they sang as loudly as they could a festive doggerel of one sort or another.

During the week or so leading up to Christmas Day, numerous small bands of carol singers would come to the door, with nearly all of them starting with "*Whilst Shaapherds watched their flocks etc*" whilst at the same time listening intently to any noise coming from the house that might indicate that their efforts were to be rewarded, there was after all no point in wasting breath singing your heart out, if the occupiers of the house were too mean to put their hand in their pocket. If the door was opened, and a penny or two pressed into the open hands, the household would be treated to a quick rendering of:

I wish 'ee a Merry Crismus, and a 'appy noo 'ear,
A pockut vool o' money an' a zeller vool o' beer,
An' a peg in th' sty as ool last 'ee aal th' 'ear.

From time to time an old countryman, who had during the past year rendered the occasional service to my Father, would come in to wish my Father and his family the compliments of the season, and in doing so he was usually handed a large mug of homebrewed beer. Having taken a sip, the elderly gentleman would stand up, and holding the mug in one hand, he would with the other reverently doff his hat; and then recite the following toast to the household.

Here's health to your body,
Wealth to your puss,
Heaven vor your zowl
An' I wish 'ee no wuss

Sentiments, which would be equally pertinent to today's festive celebrations.

The Gloucestershire Dialect.

In another of Edward Davis's newspaper articles, he highlighted some if not all of the local native idioms in the following imaginary conversation between two local men:

"Wheer bist gwain Jarge?"
"Why up Cockraud"
"What aater?"
"Dree baals O oosted, one white, one rid, tother yaller."
"Zam, ya young varmint, luk zharp, an' vetch th milk,
an dooant ee drap thie eer jug or I'll gie thee wot vor."

His article continued ~ In my early days I used often in speaking to a native to use the vernacular, and one particular incident has stayed fresh in my mind, as described below. A man was doing a job in the garden, and at that time we had a pet tortoise, which we allowed to wander about the garden, whilst it searched for its favourite bits of vegetation. Seeing the tortoise coming out of the flowerbed, and realising that the odd-job man had not yet seen this slow moving creature, I picked up the reptile and holding it behind me, I casually approached the old man and entered into conversation with him with the opening remark,

"Got any bugs down your way, John?"

"I dooant knaw, zir, mah be"

Was John's reply, not certain where this particular conversation was going. Pausing for a little while, I suddenly produced from behind the tortoise, which had by now mainly withdrawn into its shell. Startled by the unexpected sight of such an unusual creature, resting in the palm of my hand, John was taken aback, which allowed me to use my knowledge of the local vernacular upon him with the comment

"Hev ee iver zid one like ee"

By now John had, with a certain amount of alarm and no doubt a great deal of consternation, taken one or two steps backwards, and seeing that I had the upper hand, I could not resist unnerving old John a little more by saying,

"I wer afeared you'd hit en wi th spade."

"Aw, not I" said John, trying to regain his composure, *"I shudden hv hit en, I shud hv run awah vrom en."*

Rustic Wisdom

During the 1860's a woman from Oldland Common went to Gloucester as a witness in an important legal case. Having given her evidence in her Sunday best voice, she was then cross-examined by counsel for the defence, during which time she became very restive and agitated. Eventually, her irritation of being asked by counsel, what were to her, impertinent questions, finally got the better of her and, reverting to her normal character, she electrified the Court with the following outburst.

"Thuy tould I voor befur I cum awah vrom whoam that zum vool up here ood try an bother me out o'th truth."

Apparently even the defence Counsel succumbed to a smile, although laughing and applauding in the public gallery rather thought it was more like a sneer.

In another incident of around the same date, it was reported that in Bitton there lived a lad named Jim, who was a bit weak in the upper storey, but was quite harmless, and within his mental limitations, he would be as helpful and as cheerful as possible. However, his nature was such that he was very prone to having less than pleasant jokes being played upon him, and frequently he was the butt of those who had not matured sufficiently to appreciate that they more often than not made a fool out of themselves rather than a fool out of Jim. On one particular occasion a group of ruffians harassed and taunted him to such an extent that they eventually bullied him into having to physically defend himself, in the form of a prizefighter. Coats were taken off and Jim and his opponent squared up, whilst around them the remaining ruffians had no doubt whom they were supporting. Unable to see or understand the joke, Jim set about trying to defend himself as best as possible, with flailing arms and feet firmly fixed to the ground, he received a number of hefty knocks to the arms and body, before the protagonist forgot to duck, and was caught a severe blow to the side of his face from the whirlwind of Jim's fists. Undoubtedly a lucky blow, but it put the other youth down, and very quickly his support from the crowd, had totally subsided, and Jim was now the hero of the hour. With many "Well Done" being shouted, Jim quickly picked up his coat, before the other fighter fully recovered, and slinging the jacket over his shoulder, he pushed his way through the crowd with the comment:

"An' I'll gie out while 'tis well done."

Railway Reminiscences.

For over 68 years, Edward Davis was a season ticket holder on the GWR line that ran from Bristol Temple Meads to Keynsham, using the terrain in the days before the word commuter was coined, but nevertheless using the service so that he could travel to and from his place of work in the centre of the city. During each working day of a three-year period, he would get up at around 5.00am, wash and shave, before eating a hearty breakfast. Having done so he would put on his hat and coat, pick up his briefcase and walk, at a steady pace, the two and one quarter miles along the Willsbridge road to Keynsham Station endeavouring to arrive there at around 6.45am so that he was in good time for the 7.04am train to Bristol. En route he would have called into the local shop in Willsbridge to purchase his morning paper, and whilst he only had a second-class season ticket, he would normally expect to find an empty or partially empty carriage for the twenty-minute journey, and an opportunity of catching up with the headline news. For the return journey, Edward Davis usually caught the 6.30pm train from Temple Meads, which invariably meant that by the time he reached home, he had been away for over thirteen hours. During that three-year period, Mr Davis coped with all that the vagaries of the weather could throw at him, but one particular incident was personally recorded as under:

On one of my morning walks to Keynsham, I was faced with an element of danger as, nearing the station I noticed that the river had burst its banks, and covered many of the surrounding fields, but in particular, the road by the *Bridge House Inn* was under about two feet of water. Undeterred, that my normal route was unavailable to me, I climbed to the top of the wall that ran alongside of the road, hoping to do the *"Blondin"* trick for about 50 yards. It was a perilous proceeding, for had I fallen on my right I should, almost certainly have drowned, the water being deep, and in addition I had never learned to swim. Having very cautiously taken a few steps a man came splashing through on a carthorse. I called to him to back his horse in and let me get on, but, not halting, he shouted, *"Oh! Kip in the middle of the wall ~ you'll be aal right."* Fortunately but with no thanks to the Carman, I was able to take his advice, and successfully negotiated my dice with death.

In 1870, the Midland Railway opened their branch from Bath to Mangotsfield, so I was able to journey to work from Bitton, and thus for a while forsake the GWR, though in after years I travelled many thousand miles on its lines. I may mention that my ticket was for one year, second class, there being no third class season tickets, and no shorter period than a year was permitted. In addition to having to pay all of £8, for the ticket, I was also required to leave a deposit of £1, which was retained by the Midland railway, as long as I was a season ticket holder. This particular rule somewhat irritated me, as I could see that I had given the company the use of a very large sum on which they paid me no interest. In addition, the second-class carriage in which I was obliged to ride, ~ some would say in which I had the privilege of riding, ~ was very uncomfortable, with hard seats, and a back without any form of padding, in addition, it was so narrow that the knees of passengers sitting opposite, nearly touched mine, plus there was very little head room; in fact, a tall man could not stand up wearing his top hat. To crown it all, there was just one miserable oil lamp, which was required to serve two compartments. There was no heating in the winter, although from time to time, if you were particularly lucky, you might have use of a foot-warmer, but more often than not hardly justified the name it was given. That reminds me of an incident when I was in a train on a very cold day. A passenger put out his head at a station and said, *"Porter, have you a foot-warmer? ~ "Yes sir" ~* came the reply ~ *"but its cold"* said the porter. Being in the adjoining carriage it was quite easy for me to hear this exchange, between the passenger and the porter, and thus it came as quite a surprise when I then heard the passenger say, *"Oh! Never mind, bring it along, it will have to do"*

When the GWR was completing its conversion from broad to narrow gauge over forty-years ago, they built a number of up to date third class carriages, putting them on broad gauge wheels. Then they would make up a train consisting of some of these and some of the old seconds, and I had ridden in such a train from Bristol to Exeter, during which time I was able to enjoy the comfort of the rebuilt third-class carriages. I got out at Exeter, and stood on the platform for a moment, having noticed that the ticket inspector was busy with other passengers. As I was trying to absorb the atmosphere of the journey and the destination, I noticed that the next carriage down from the one I had just alighted was one of the miserably dirty old second-class vehicles, in which was an old countryman who evidently could not read, or who clearly did not understand the difference between second and third-class travel. With that the ticket inspector reached the window adjacent to the old man, and asked for his ticket. Having been handed a third-class ticket by the countryman, the inspector said: *"My man, you are in a second-class carriage with a third–class ticket, you will have to pay the excess."* *"Well"* replied the old man, *"I walked aal down the platform looking at the train, an' picked out th wust coach I cu vind, an' an' thought I wer zhure to be right, this mus be a third-class carriage."* The funny side of the ironic truth behind this simple and honest statement was evident to all who heard it including the ticket inspector, who continued on down the train with a very broad grin on his face.

Three Churches.

For many years in the past the following tale was told of how three local churches and the areas they served each received their own and distinctive names. In considering the probability of its accuracy, you may wish to take the story with a pinch of salt, but this is how the story was certainly told back in the less sophisticated eighteenth and nineteenth centuries:

By all accounts the threes churches at Bitton, Keynsham and Dundry were all built by the same master craftsman, a man who had inordinate masonry skills and who could calculate the required sizes and dimensions of the construction with ease but when it came to calculating the cost of both time and materials he found that he was not at all clever, to the extent that by the time that he had completed the construction of the first church he was sadly out of pocket. With most of his money lost, he dolefully commented as he left the beautiful church he had just completed, *"I'm bitten"* and having been overheard the church and the surrounding area adopted its name from this profound statement. Some few years later, the same craftsman tendered for the construction of a second church, but being much more alert to his earlier financial errors, he took advice and ensured that he would not only earn money from the second church but he would also recuperate some if not all of the previous losses. In the due course of time the church was completed with much happier financial results so that as he packed up his tools he had a large leather bag that jingled with gold, and he was heard to gleefully exclaim, *"I've gained zum"* and once again the name of the church and the surrounding was intertwined with his passing comment.

Within a year or two the same craftsman had started work on the third church, which because of its location took much longer than the usual six or seven years to build, and so by the time that all the work had been completed, the craftsman was beginning to feel his age. The financial advice he had taken many years previously had proven sound, and the old man who was extremely proud of his church building achievements, was quite content to retire, which he did with the final remark *"I've done dree."*

What better proof does one want in identifying the origin of place names? But then perhaps it is just a story after all.

Chapter 9 "Social Changes"

Towards the mid/end of the eighteenth century, modest social well-being improvements within the community at large, were beginning to take place. There was of course still a great deal of poverty, injustice, moral degradation, sudden death from sickness and/or injury, and hardship for most of the population, and no doubt the gradual changes are more likely to be noticeable as we now look back in time from a distance, rather than being perceived by those who were living there at the time. The majority of the community still had to find food for the table, live with the high mortality rate, particularly amongst their children, a factor which was just as equally true in the midst of the better off, and accept that being uneducated put them at a disadvantage, but more particularly it helped to keep them in their place, at the bottom of the pile. But gradually the wheels of change began to turn, so that by the beginning of the nineteenth century, the law of the land began to become more prominent, the criminal elements of the community had been severely pruned with many of the ringleaders having been transported, whilst local constables began to receive much more respect and help, but even so the good citizens of Oldland were not totally convinced that they were in fact getting value for money.

Possibly the gradual improvement in the reduction of local crime caused those citizens to fall into a sense of false security, or perhaps their collective memories were being dulled by the passage of time, as by 1841 they had decided that the cost of having a police force was an expensive burden that they would prefer to do without. Accordingly the following petition was organised by certain occupiers and householders in the hamlet of Oldland:

To the Worshipful Magistrates for the County of Gloucestershire, in General Quarter Sessions, assembled on the Fourth day of January 1842.
That your petitioners have observed with much concern the great increase of the County Rates occasioned by the extensive introduction of the Police Force throughout the County.
That your petitioners are deeply sensible of the expediency of every necessary precaution being taken to ensure the Peace and, as far as practicable, to prevent the committal of crime.
That in large and populous towns, a police force may not be considered disadvantageous, but in Rural Districts, your petitioners verily believe that crime is not of the extent as to warrant the interference of such force, and that the introduction of Police into those Districts of this County, has created a great feeling of dissatisfaction amongst the Yeomanry and others, whose loyalty and promptitude

in assisting the Civil powers have been found sufficient in the most turbulent times for the suppression of outbreaks.
Considering therefore, a Police Force in the Rural Districts unnecessary that the County Rates have been seriously increased by its introduction, and that in case of any popular commotion the good and loyal feelings of a great majority of the Inhabitants, combined with the assistance of the Military and Yeomanry Forces will, at all times be found sufficient to preserve the Peace.
Your petitioners earnestly pray that your Worshipful Bench will be pleased to adopt forthwith such Resolutions as will relieve your petitioners from contributing to the maintenance of the Police Establishment of this County.

Signed by some twelve upright and no doubt prominent and loyal residents of Oldland, they had very obviously conveniently forgotten their father's if not their own experience of life under the constant threat of "Mob-rule". They represented the rich and wealthy of the area who were now crying wolf, just because they thought that they could see a short-term advantage to themselves, without considering the overall problem, or how their actions, if successful, would affect the long-term future of the community at large, and in doing so they produced a petition, the whole of which was full of nothing but waffle. How much the rates had increased as a result of the establishment of a Police Force was not recorded, but fortunately for those not involved with the petition, the Worshipful Bench threw out the plea, and the police force was established.

However, back before the above petition, and or the establishment of a true Police Force was ever considered it is still necessary to deliberate upon the probabilities that whilst the punishment, for what we would today classify as minor misdemeanours, was harsh and painful and undoubtedly had a bearing upon the steady improvement in law and order, it was not the only reason, and most certainly was not even the main reason. By now there was a new wave of religious missionaries sweeping the country who were not frightened to go into areas previously shunned by community leaders, who were prepared to bring education and new religious beliefs to those who were regarded lost causes, or those who were considered to be outside of the law, or those who were considered to be uncouth, rough, troublemakers. Almost certainly this new form of religious concept, together with the creation of education facilities for the poor and unfortunate, played a greater part in structuring a new community, enabling people to lower the self made barriers of a defensively self-centred parochial group, to one which began to have a desire to belong to the greater brotherhood of man.

The conditions of those living in the area covered by this book, plus the greater Kingswood area, had not gone unnoticed by the evangelists, notably George Whitefield who, invited John Wesley to come and assist him in his work, both in

Bristol and in Kingswood. In company with William Seward, Whitefield began preaching at Rose Green, Kingswood as early as 1739, when on Sunday the 17th February he spoke in the open air to around 200 men women and children. Such was the effect of his words, and the manner in which they were spoken, those who had been in the audience on that day were so moved that they spread the word around to such an extent that by the following Sunday it was estimated that around 10,000 persons turned up to listen to Whitfield, and over the following month that number had doubled. Almost certainly, many in the audience came to see if they could stir up trouble, many came out of pure curiosity, whilst others began to feel that Whitefield was personally talking to them, something that no one in a position of authority had ever done before in a kind way. The social and collective results of the religious reformation in this area became more evident throughout the remainder of the eighteenth century, but probably grew in strength with greater momentum that was noticeable during the first half of the nineteenth century. By then John Wesley had become more and more active in his desire to reform the Anglican Church, whilst at the same time he spent a great deal of his energy challenging the evils of the Poor Law, the Penal Code, prisons, and the exploitation of labour in both factories and mines. Barred by many Anglican clergy from preaching in their churches, Wesley encouraged his ever-growing congregations to build their own preaching houses and/or chapels where they could pray in peace. Almost as though he was setting the wheels in motion, Wesley arranged to have his first preaching house, which he called the *New Room Chapel* constructed during 1739 in the Horsefair area of Bristol. Back in the Kingswood, Oldland, Bitton area, there were no less than twelve churches of the establishment erected between 1756-1845, including the Oldland Tabernacle that was built in 1811.

The religious revolution sweeping through the area mirrored that which was happening throughout the country at large and it was not just confined to the Wesleyans. In 1794, there was the first attempt to introduce Congregationalism to the scattered populace of Oldland, when a series of cottage services conducted by individual members of the Congregational Itinerant Society were implemented. For many years the Congregationalists worked on an ad hoc basis using laypersons to conduct the services, and to continue their very useful, and important work amongst the local colliers, as it was not until 1843 that their first pastor, the Rev. J Wood took up residence in Oldland.

There was, of course, already established in Oldland, a Chapel of Ease to St Mary the Virgin, Bitton. Unfortunately, no records have been discovered of the original date and/or origin of the Chapel, but it is known that prior to the Reformation, the parish of Bitton, which at that time extended across east Bristol to Lawford's Gate, was in the Diocese of Worcester. Records from the dioceses, of around 1280, make reference to the *"Bytton cum Capella de Olelond"* From this information it is safe to assume that there has been a Chapel of Ease; subsequently a church in its own rights, in Oldland for at least the past 720 years. By the late 1820's, the original chapel was in such a bad state of repair that it was becoming unsafe, and required thorough restoration. No doubt spurred on by the religious revival sweeping through the area, the local Church of England parishioners resolved to have the chapel rebuilt and enlarged, and this they were able to do by obtaining an interest free loan from the Church Building Commissioners, repayable over a ten year period. In addition, they also obtained, from the Church Building Society a grant, whilst at the same time, they organised their own subscriptions to collectively help towards the overall cost of the rebuilding. It was therefore during 1829 that St Anne's Church, Oldland was erected, being built of stone in the Early English Style. The new building consisted of an Apsidal Chancel, Nave and Transepts, with an open turret containing one bell. Seven of the windows, were fashioned in stained glass, and there is room to seat a congregation of around 350 persons. In 1830, the vicar of St Mary the Virgin, the Rev. H. T. Ellacombe, wrote a letter to the Gentleman's Magazine in which he described the old chapel in the following manner:

"The south doorway and porch of the chapel were in Early English style as were the pillars and arches in the inside. The interior was divided into two aisles, and there existed a chancel separated from the nave by a coarsely wrought screen. There was a plain piscine [a stone with a drain] *on the east side of the south doorway, and the remains of one on the south of the altar. The font was very plain, but apparently coeval with the foundations of the chapel. Most of the sittings were of oak, carved and wrought, in the old style, and open at either end with room for a congregation of around 230."*

A little surprisingly, knowing how particular the Rev. Ellacombe was for detail and accuracy was that he omitted to comment upon the fact that the old chapel had been constructed with quite its most external prominent feature, a saddleback tower, of a type rarely found in England and certainly quite unique in either Gloucestershire or Somersetshire. Within the saddleback tower were three ancient bells, one of which had been recast with the following inscription around the rim:

"Reader, thou also must know a Resurrection"

The other two bells were simply inscribed *"Fancta Anna"*

With the continued deterioration of the old building in 1819/20, and the added worry that the saddleback tower was becoming extremely weak and unstable, it was decided, some seven or eight years prior to plans being laid to have the chapel rebuilt, that for safety reasons all three bells needed to be removed. Unfortunately, because there were as yet no plans for the reconstruction, the bell appeared to be totally redundant as far as St Annes was concerned and accordingly with the ever-expanding Kingswood about to have its own parish and its own parish church; ~ the Bishop of Gloucester, had already laid the foundation stone of Holy Trinity church on the 9th June 1819; ~ it seemed a perfect opportunity for Kingswood to purloin those redundant bells of St Anne's and soon it was decided that they should be set aside for inclusion in the new church at Kingswood. Accordingly some time during 1820 or possible early 1821, the three bells were conveyed to and re hung in the newly erected tower of Holy Trinity. Kingswood's gain, sadly Oldland's loss as when the new church was built only one plain single bell was included in its design.

When the old Chapel of Ease was in existence, it was the daughter of the mother church of St Mary's Bitton, and as such did not have its own cleric, and additionally had to share the services of a clergyman with the second Chapel of Ease, St George, at Hanham Abbots. The cleric was more than likely to be the curate at St Mary's, where on most Sundays he would take the Eucharist in the morning service, and then in the afternoon travel to either Oldland or Hanham, alternating his trips so that each Chapel of Ease was open at least once a fortnight. During 1719, a Faculty was granted for burials to take place in the chapel yard, whilst in 1818, the curate of St Mary's was licensed to take services at both chapels, without being responsible for additional duties at Bitton.

Since 1830, the ecclesiastical parish of Oldland was defined, with St Annes upgraded from a Chapel of Ease to the Parish Church, however the village of Oldland Common was left in the Parish of Bitton as the south-eastern boundary between both parishes is the Warmley brook

Chapter 10 "Local Industries"

Together with the creation of the much improved social conscience and welfare within the community, which paralleled the growth of the Free Churches in the area, there were many remarkable industrial and industrial relation changes taking place, much of which can be traced back to the religious reformation that seemed to touch every aspect of life. Without realising it, there occurred a number of separate and independent catalysts that provided, not only the need and the opportunity but also the means for the manifestation of a new style of life. Beside the opening of new coalpits, and/or the deepening of others, occasioned by the introduction of new and improved pumping equipment, plus the remarkable ability of a certain **Handel Cossham** to discover, somewhat scientifically, virgin coal seams in the area from his geological investigations, there were advances made in machinery capable of producing pins and shoes, thus removing the laborious cottage industry type methods of the past. In simple terms Oldland and the surrounding parishes were being pushed into and through the nineteenth century by the start of the Industrial Revolution.

Of course as with any change, there was much opposition to the introduction of these new fangled machines, particularly by those who earned their living by producing boots or shoes or pins by hand, and who saw their way of life being taken from them. But the tide of change was too forceful for it to falter, and now that the manufacture of felt hats in the old traditional way around the Oldland Bartons, had become firmly established, and the new mechanised industries were taking up the slack, and creating employment for a considerable number of both men, women and children, the changes over a decade or so gradually became the norm. At the same time new and improved mechanisation in farming meant that more food could be produced with less people, and those who left the land, quickly found better wages, and quite often better working conditions in factories. This is not to say that in most cases the work involved, and the workers life in general, was extremely hard, tough and often dangerous. Whilst the manufacture of hats might have led to the occasional pin being stuck in a finger, or a knife cut across those same digits, boys as young as eight years of age were still employed below ground, either as a "door-boy" or as they matured to ten years of age as "tuggers," who job it was to take a dram full of coal/waste from the coal face to the bottom of the shaft. Not too difficult until you realise that the dram probably contained three or four hundred weight of material, and was connected to the boy by way of a rope through the boy's legs and hooked on a leather belt around his waist. In addition the height of the passage was probably no more than twenty inches, and thus the youth, occasionally helped by a boy pushing from the back, would have to pull the cart along on unprotected hands and knees.

The skin around the young boys waist would soon be red and sore, as would the skin over the knees, elbows, and back, with all of this work being carried out in darkness, only illuminated by a candle stuck in the boys soft hat, that is of course assuming that he could afford the cost of a candle or two, as none were provided by the employer. To strengthen the torn and braised skin, the boys were told by those who knew, to urinate over the damaged area, as a form of tanning.

Although neither women nor girls worked below ground in this part of the world, they certainly worked at the surface of the colliery as cleaners and sorters. Their work involved them standing, along a long wooden bench constructed outside in the open under what might loosely be described as a primitive shed, which was open, all-round to the elements. On the bench was tipped the material that the previous shift of miners had sent to the surface, so that the usable coal could be sorted out from the stones and any other rubbish, which quite often was mixed with the spoil as the miners struggled to fill the drams, in less than ideal conditions. The itemized stone and rubbish was put into baskets, and carried, quite often by the women themselves but sometimes by men too old or weak to work underground, to a slagheap or tip, however before any of this material was allowed to be tipped, it had first to be weighed and the weight recorded. At the end of each week, the weight of the waste was allocated to its identified shift and deducted from the total weight of material brought to the surface, as there was no way that the mine owners were going to pay their miners for digging waste, their tonnage pay was based solely on the weight of the coal they had hewn and nothing else, whether it was the miners fault or not, and more often than not it was the fault of the local geology that rarely left the coal seams free of foreign matter. Having removed most if not all of the rubble, the coal that was left on the table was then further picked over by hand so that it could be graded by size and quality, as importantly the better the size and quality the better the price. This work had to be carried out in all forms of weather condition during a twelve-hour day, by both women and their children, and quite often the very youngest would work along the top of the bench, moving from one pile to another levelling out the contents. It is difficult to imagine the pain and discomfort these females had to go through particularly on a cold frosty morning, or perhaps even worst when snow had fallen during the hours of darkness; how numb their fingers and feet must have been, and all for the princely sum of around 10d [0.04p] per day, but that was the adult rate, the girls were only paid 6d [0.02p] per day. There were sadly, no creature comforts in those days, no sick pay, no tea or dinner breaks, just long, hard, arduous, dirty and extremely uncomfortable work, but somehow carried out in the main with a great deal of fortitude, and willingness to cope.

Today we are surrounded by many comforts, and our workplace has been made much safer and more pleasant than before. Accordingly, we should perhaps spare a few moments reflecting upon the lifestyles of those mining families that went before us. Whilst the women and the girls were employed as described above the women, particularly the married ones, had in addition all of the domestic chores of life without the benefits of any labour saving devices to cope with. Just keeping the house and the family clean was difficult enough, with no running water, either hot or cold, no sanitation, other than perhaps an outside privy, and quite often that was shared with three or four different families. Then there was the need to keep a fire going all through the year on which a large kettle of water was placed to enable her to obtain a modicum of hot water. Then there was the cooking, the constant worry over obtaining sufficient food to feed the family, plus having to cope with sickness, childbirth, infant mortality, work related injury, death, let alone dealing with grumpy husbands, and irritable children, in a less than comfortable two up/two down messuage As for their menfolk, many of them were hundreds of feet below them, with the adult males laying or squatting at the coal face trying to hew and prise for the wealthy the black-gold from the bowels of the earth. Their work place would have been so confined, that they would not have had room to swing a pick with any great force, so that it would take a number of strikes before the coal was detached from its seam, and then for the loosened material to fall around their upper torso. Having hewn out the coal, the dust and the unwanted rubbish, the miner would then have to push all of this material past their legs so that other men, working behind them in a crouching position, could shovel the material away and into a waiting dram. All of this was being performed in a gloomy, shadowy dust filled atmosphere, occasionally lit by the light of individual candles held in a metal holder attached to the miners cap, or a candle that might have been perched on a protrusion in tunnels which quite frequently, were inclined as the miner followed the course of the seam. Occasionally the seam might run in a straight line for a while, but more often than not the coal bearing seams would meander up and down, according to the huge pressures put upon the surrounding geology millions of years ago. In addition, in this part of the world, the coal seams were not that particularly thick, rarely more than thirty inches, and quite often only twelve inches thick. All around were pit props, jagged protruding rocks, the general accoutrements of the early mining industry, plus of course their fellow underground workers, and physical attributes were probably only regarded as minor inconveniences, as were the day to day nuisance of having to lie on a rough hard stony floor, which chafed the skin on every part of the body, the knocks, the bumps, the cuts, the bruises, the lesions were an every day hazard accepted by the miners, as were the blue coloured scars which resulted from the healing process mixed with ingrained coal dust and blood. Such painful moments in the working day were not confined to the adults, the young boys would also be expected to carry out their duties within the confines of these hazards, controlling the movement of empty, as well as full trucks, often in complete darkness, as very few would have been able to afford the cost of a candle. The only power found underground was human power, and thus when a full or empty dram needed to be moved the young boys, some barely teenagers, would be hooked onto the dram by means of a chain that went between their legs and connected to a large leather waist belt, ~ the guss and crook ~ and on hands and knees they pulled the drams along rudimentary tracks, helped by one or two other lads pushing from behind. In addition, their even younger brothers were there in total darkness waiting for the dram to arrive so that with the passage of the dram they could open/close one of the heavy leather trap ventilating doors.

There were of course other hazards faced by all who ventured underground, roof falls being just one, but probably the one most feared was the sudden and unexpected ingress of water, which could strike at any moment, with the worst occurring when the miner accidentally broke into old and abandoned workings and caused thousands of gallons of dirty water to rush into the new workings, sweeping away all that stood in it path. It was frequently said in the surrounding area, that you could easily recognise a 30-40 year old miner by the fact that the majority were all bald-headed, with blue coloured scars around the upper part of their bodies, and scars that covered the tops of both hips from the waist down, no wonder they were regarded as being tough and unruly.

For mines such as California Pit, the primitive ventilation system consisted of the construction of a two-mile long, or there about, underground tunnel from Oldland towards Bitton, and connecting the tunnel to the base of a large chimney, which was [and still is] situated in Golden Valley. At the base of the chimney would be kept a large permanent fire, which by creating an updraft of air through the tall chimney, would allow the air to be sucked through from the underground workings, which was replaced by fresh air being drawn down the shaft at the head of the mine in Oldland. The principle behind the idea was reasonably sound, but problems arose because there were more than just one working tunnel, and those tunnels rarely if ever ran straight for any length, thus there were a number of areas within the mine, where stale air gathered and breathing became more difficult. Add this fact to a fairly high underground temperature, and you are left with yet another difficulty endured by the men and boys who worked below ground.

Whilst the mining of coal and the subsequent work involved in getting the commodity to the market, employed many persons, other industries still managed to develop within the area, one of which was the production of pins. In today's technically advanced world, we probably take the humble and inexpensive pin for granted, but to our forebears particularly the ladies, pins were a very expensive, and highly treasured item of necessity. The earliest pins known to us were made of bone, but as civilisation and man's ability to create new and improved products, the materials used to make pins gradually changed to copper, bronze and then iron. It was not until the sixteenth century that pins started to be made on the continent out of brass, and then imported into this country, but at that time there were still many difficulties in producing quality pins by hand, not helped by the fact that the manufacture of brass was highly technical and expensive. With each pin having to be separately hand crafted, and being much more ornate than those produced today, the price was understandably high, and indeed at this time ladies regarded pins as being an item of luxury. Accordingly in the main only ladies belonging to the upper classes used pins, and then they were mostly used just for decorative purposes. Such was the cost of the humble pin that during the fifteenth and sixteenth centuries, it became the custom for gentlemen of the household to give their ladies money for the sole purpose of purchasing pins, and over a period of time, the provision of this money became known as giving "pin money" a term that is now used to describe the little extra money earned by the woman for herself.

During the seventeenth century, the manufacture of pins became more industrialized as gradually their production moved away from being decorative and individually made by craftsmen, to a semi-mass production of pins that were simply functional and less elaborate than those previously produced. By now the pins were much more like the ones we use today and so very much take for granted, but nevertheless, their production was still a long and involved process, which was geared to being carried out not in factories, but in small workshops attached to or in the garden of a cottage in the area. By now, William Champion's Brass Works at Warmley had developed a means of mechanically drawing out brass wire, straightening any twists or anomalies, and cutting the wire into pin lengths, locally known as "shanks." The shanks were then put into bundles, tied and in due course distributed to local cottagers for them to produce at "home" pins for fashionable ladies. The first job to be carried out was for each shank to be held over a wheeled grindstone, which was operated by a foot treadle, so that a point could be made to one end. Once the grinder was satisfied with the work, the pointed shank was placed in a wooden tray, and either his wife or one of his children would bundle up the shanks in groups of 100, having first ensured that each shank was straight, and that all of the points were aligned in the same direction. The shanks were then weighed and re-tied, with a record of the weight having been duly noted as the grinder was paid by the weight of pointed shanks produced, and not the number of sharp shanks produced. When a new batch of shanks were delivered, the processed shanks would be collected and then re-distributed to other homeworkers who very often would be women, whose job it was to head the shanks and turn them into pins.

Towards the end of the seventeenth century, and on into the eighteenth century, pin heads were made by winding fine wire around a metal rod to form a small "cushion" of wire. This exercise was repeated hundreds of times a day and, after being carefully removed from the rod, each cushion of wire was placed in an iron ladle, which was then placed into an open fire in the cottage, or an adjoining outhouse, a fire that was needed to be kept alight and burning at a high temperature throughout the whole year, as without this process, the cushions of wire could not be annealed or toughened. Each cushion or head needed to become red-hot for this evolution to take place, and the timing of when to take the ladle out of the fire and plunge it and its contents into a bucket of cold water was quite critical. Provided this action was carried out at the correct time, the heads would have become more malleable, and could now be individually placed into a pin block, [somewhat akin to a butcher's wooden chopping block] upon which were fixed several uprights and cross pieces used as levers. One of these levers was attached to a heavy weight carrying a rod and die in its end, and this was held aloft by means of a counter balance fixed to a treadle. In the meanwhile, the operator would place and clamp into a header, a shank complete with one of the wire heads threaded at the non-pointed end, ensuring that it was positioned immediately under the heavy weight. When satisfied that the positioning was correct, the operator would, by means of using the treadle, cause the hanging weight to come crashing down onto the head so that it was literally crushed onto the shank, an exercise which probably took the trained operator no more than a few seconds, as to work any slower would have restricted the amount of money that could be earned, even if it increased the risk of losing fingers.

Quite often a number of women would, in one person's cottage or adjoining outhouse, share a block with each having a separate set of weights, levers and treadle. In the skilled hands a pin could be threaded and placed in the header every two or three seconds, and with the required weights descending on a regular basis of around ten or twelve times a minute, the resultant noise must have been quite deafening, particularly in the confines of a cottage or small workshop, not counting the obvious effects of the resulting vibrations, but of course these were days long before health and safety dictates ruled every working operation. Despite these apparent potential health hazards, aggravated by the limited amount of natural light available to them, it was said that the women were "Exceedingly fond" of heading, and not infrequently, groups of women working together would, above the noise of the hammers, be heard singing songs and ditties, which were designed or changed by the women so that the words and tune kept time with the regular thump, thump, thump of the falling weights.

As with the shanks, the headed pins would again be sorted to ensure that the points all faced the same direction, counted and bundled as the women were paid a few shillings for every hundred pins headed. Periodically, new shanks would arrive, and the bundled pins collected, to be taken back to the factory to be whitened, after which process the now polished pins were taken back to the outworkers, where the children were employed in performing a job locally known as "sticking." This involved the child taking up a small strip of cardboard, folding it in half, and then placing the cardboard on a flat surface and placing twenty-four pins in a row with the sharp end laying on the face of the board, and with all the heads uniformly level. A small amount of glue would then be carefully applied to the lower edge and open side of the board, ensuring that none of the glue went onto any of the pins, and then the strip would be re-folded to firmly hold the two-dozen pins, with their points protected from causing any harm. Back at the factory each filled strip would be placed in a box capable of taking a gross, and then each box would be available for the wholesale market.

It will be noted from the above that the manufacture of pins was very labour intensive, and accordingly commanded a high retail price and whilst those whose nimble fingers carried out the various stages of production received a pittance in reward for their efforts, the production of pins did at least provide a large amount of employment in the area, and a basis of that communities economy, although certainly very small by today's standards, its existence was vitally important at that time, but all was to change when some time during the 1820's, a machine was invented that was capable of performing all of the human tasks described above, at a much quicker rate and at a much cheaper rate. Within a relatively short space of time, pin making machines were being installed in many local factories, however these machines were expensive, and required the factory owners to invest quite heavily, not only in new machines, but also in new buildings to house these machines. Understandably individual owners were concerned about the money they had borrowed, and the competition around them and accordingly looked at every opportunity of trying to recoup their and/or the banks investment in as short a time as possible. Efficiency soon became the owners watch word, and it was quickly discovered that their machines were very capable of producing a much greater number of pins, with their production count measured not by the week or by the day, but by the hour or by the minute, and that further more these machines could, subject to mechanical problems, work twenty-four hours a day, seven days a week But possibly best of all, for the more efficient minded owners, the machines removed their huge dependency of needing a highly intensive labour force. Thus almost overnight, the homeworkers saw the dust settling on their blocks, the annealing fires go out, and the grinding wheels stop turning as they were made redundant and placed on the financial scrap heap of despair.

As the in fighting for survival between the owners began to wane, and those clever enough to see the future benefits through the midst of greed, dramatic changes to the organization and production of pins began to occur as the strongest proprietors either joined together, or had sufficient entrepreneurial skills, and financial backing to go on their own. Swept aside was the cottage industry thinking of producing a small number of pins at high prices, and in its place was the idea of mass production of utility rather than decorative pins at low prices, which in turn would increase the demand, increase sales and hopefully increase profits. Pin factories began opening in the early 1830's, with one of the largest being outside of the area, at Two Mile Hill in 1831. Here **Robert Charleton** was the philanthropist behind the company, who brought with him his Christian and humane beliefs to create a business where employees were not exploited, and whose working conditions were certainly better than most. Over the following ten years, his factory and output grew, so that by 1840 he was employing over 50 men and/or boys, and over 100 females, with none of the employed children being under twelve years of age. It was Robert Charlton's policy of employing, wherever possible, the sons and daughters of his adult workers, and quite frequently the children worked alongside one of their parents according to gender. In the main, the male members of the family were responsible for preparing the shanks, with the adult grinding the point, and occasionally coating the shank, whilst the boys would be responsible for the coating as well as carrying out the more general menial jobs, putting the pointed shanks in bundles, weighing each bundle, sweeping and cleaning around their elders etc. The boys would also be required to take the bundles of pointed shanks to their mother or their mother's friends, who would then untie the bundle and tip the shanks into an oscillating hopper from where each individual shank was delivered to a second machine. This machine had then been designed to automatically put a pinhead on to the shank, to produce the finished article easily recognisable to us today. In this way, bright new pins could be made in their thousands each working day, rather than the handful of pins painfully, but happily, produced by semi barbaric contrivances in the homes of the poor.

Some six years after Robert Charleton opened his factory, the young Victoria came to the Throne of England, and with her came, at an ever-increasing pace, the many sweeping changes of the new industrialism. Alongside these movements, other changes of a social nature were also taking place in the traditional structure of society. Throughout the whole country, past moral values, on which society had been based for hundreds of years, were being challenged, as the new force of the industrial revolution gained ground with increasing momentum. Previously accepted standards of the past were being washed away on a tidal wave of new order, whilst old licentious traditions of the Regency era were being brought into question by the new seriousness of the Evangelical movement. Many of the changes in society and its morals were confused and compounded by the genuine religious feeling and conviction that if society itself was to survive the distress and discontent of the post Napoleonic war years, then the ruling classes must set an example to the lower orders or working classes. At the start of Queen Victoria's reign, conditions of employment in all forms of industry were, often than not, totally deplorable, certainly as seen from the comfort of a twenty-first century health and safety, and working environment legislation. However, for those directly involved the conditions were accepted as normal practises and the hazards of the Industrial Revolution. Furthermore, whilst life in a factory may have been dangerous, uncomfortable, and bad for ones health, it did provide work at a better rate of pay, than had previously been experienced by the agricultural labourers of the recent past. Their working conditions were not just the by product of evil ruthless uncompromising employers, the poor conditions were aided and abetted by a Parliament which had for the past three decades or more, continued to oppose attempts to improve the lot of the working class, although it could be cynically claimed that as the majority of the Members of Parliament were either employers, or related to employers, and in any case were of the upper classes themselves, then they had a vested interest in keeping the status quo of the lower order of life. However, even the Members of Parliament could not continually bury their heads in the provable sand, and hope that the tidal wave would pass them by, and in 1833, they or certainly the members of the Whig party, approved and passed the very first Factory Act, which amongst its clauses and aims were to be found such progressive legislation as:

"the limiting of hours by women and children, in both mill and factory"

Most importantly, this Act was not a collection of Victorian platitudes for the Factory Masters to espouse for the gratification of those socially minded philanthropists who championed lost causes, it was designed to have "teeth" that included the appointment, for the very first time, of Factory Inspectors, who would visit the workplace and ensure that the new laws were not being flouted by the mill/factory owners and/or his senior management, and to ensure that the new legislation was being enforced.

During 1841, **Elijah Waring,** of the South Gloucestershire Children's Employment Commission, made a number of visits to various local pin factories in his official capacity, as sub-commissioner, and quite understandably high on his list was, as one of the largest factories, Robert Charlton's. After making his visit, Waring prepared his written report, which included,

"separation between the male and female work people in this and in other Pin Factories visited is perfect, and, the proprietors in all instances reject any potential candidate for employment who cannot bring with them a Fair Moral Character."

Such an approach and such an attitude would not be tolerated in today's so called enlightened society that would totally reject a pious and high-handed view of others integrities as simply not being "politically correct."

The well-meaning Victorian elite also introduced other rules and impositions that would not be acceptable today, and however charitable his motivations were, Mr

Charlton had his own strictly imposed work rules that were no doubt designed to improve the parental approach he adopted towards his workforce, but they were also designed to helped keep his workers subservient and in their place, and almost certainly had the irony of "don't do as I do but do as I say," about them. One such rule, that from a typical Victorian male chauvinistic way appears to have been applied more vigorously to the "weaker sex," was a 3d [2p] fine imposed on any female employee who used bad or foul language, or who sang profane songs whilst at their work place. On the other hand, Mr Charlton was full of encouragement if the female workers sang hymns, whilst at work, and apparently was very pleased when he heard the sound of well-known hymns coming from the factory, it is even possible that from time to time Mr Charlton quietly accompanied the women as he hummed the tune to himself. All the time of course, Mr Charlton was totally unaware of the fact that the lyrics of many of the hymns as they were being sung, were not the originals as a number of *double entendre* substitutions had been incorporated by his female workers, who undeniably had the last laugh on their employer. However, there was a large financial risk that they might become too bold, for if they went too far and were caught the lower paid girls ran the chance of losing ten per cent or more out of her weekly wage packet. Even the better off earners on 7/6 [35p] per week might have lost four per cent of her wage. Thus the songs were never sung too loudly, and at times there was more humming or whistling, rather than singing, particularly on the occasions when Mr Charlton was "on the prowl." This did not however prevent the female workers enjoying the "private joke" of their irreverent words at the expense of their pious but well-meaning employer.

With typical Victorian patronising ethos, pin making was accepted as suitable and appropriate employment for women, and Elijah Waring and many other men were, without doubt, convinced that the girls who were employed in such factories, were being kept out of harms way in the sense that they would remain sober, reliable and suitably chaste, and accordingly were not jeopardising their future role as wife and mother. Although his report does not express these sentiments in quite that way, the patronising element is not hard to see in his words:

"*Pin-making is carried on principally by female labour, it is light in nature, and the parties employed are generally young, there are not many mere children amongst them. Girls from 14 to 18 years are the most numerous class; whilst boys find employment in drawing and straightening the wire, before it is cut into the requisite lengths. Heading the pins, which employs the largest number of hands, is performed wholly by females, each of whom sits before a machine worked by a foot-board, or treadle, having by her a wooden bowl of pointed shanks, and another of heads; the heads being formed of compact spiral wire, sliced off by a machine not unlike a chaff-cutter in its operation. The girl then takes àn indefinite number of shanks between her thumb and fingers, and dips them into the bowlful of heads, when she generally finds each shank furnished with a loose head. She then drops the pins singly into a perpendicular receptacle in the block, under the hammer, and by a single motion of her foot rivets on the head. This is performed with almost inconceivable rapidity, and without any intent occupation of the eye. The hours of work daily are 12, with the usual allowance for meals and the whole series of operations are of a simple and easy description. The earnings of the females are from 2/6 to 7/- [12.5p to 35p] per week."*

His report continued:

There is much deplorable ignorance among the young females in these works, where eleven out of twenty-five girls cannot read, and one only has an imperfect knowledge of writing; nine do not attend Sunday school, including one who never attends any place of worship. Nothing, not positively vicious, can be more offensive to the moral sense, than the contrast, between the good looks and neat costume of many of them, and the uncouth speech, in which they betray their want of common good training; whilst on the other hand, they have excellent examples of both intellectual and religious advancement among their fellow workers, some of whom are highly esteemed as Sunday school teachers, and exercise a good influence over their compeers.

And as already mentioned above, he continued with:

The separation between the male and female workpeople, in these pin manufactories, is perfect; and the proprietors of the works will reject any candidate for employment unless she can bring with her a fair moral character."

In their simple orderly minds that routinely placed the opposite sex in the role of a second-class citizen, the majority of the upper/middle class males saw one direct and very obvious blinding fact, which was that as pins and their use was mainly, if not totally a domestic matter, and as women were born into domesticity, then there was absolutely nothing wrong with females working in a pin making factory, and that by definition it was an acceptable female occupation, provided of course they did what they were told, and refrained from using bad or foul language. However, having convinced himself of this neat tidy and extremely plausible connection, Mr Waring did not carry the same argument through to the employment of women working in the coal industry, despite the very obvious fact that the setting and maintaining of coal fires in the home was also regarded as part of women's domestic duties. The logic applied by Mr Waring, and the like-minded Victorian gentry, was that coal was much more associated with an industrial use, ie the creation of power in factories, in mines, and now in transport. As such coal had a much greater virile feel about it, and thus by definition the coal industry had to be regarded as a masculine occupation, and certainly on this basis alone it was no place to employ females. This view was firmly held by many powerful men in the country, and soon there was introduced through Parliament, legislation to implement and enforce their opinion.

Pin making, was of course, not the only work in which females were gainfully employed. Many women earned a living as a seamstress, or as a rag cutter, or as a charwoman. At Bitton a large paper mill had been established and employed up to 450 persons, many of whom would have been females, with most working in the rag cutting room, but also in the sorting, boiling and washing processes. Similarly, corset-making factories including at least one in Oldland, appeared throughout the area, as did other clothing factories, all of whom would have had a high percentage of female employees, but once again there is that underlining aspect that all of these jobs were predominately domestic orientated, and as such, the Victorians, or perhaps they should be described as the predominately male Victorians, who usually determined the views of their ladies, were relaxed about women being employed in this way.

It has already been noted that quite suddenly the making of pins, under the auspice of the miss-used description "a cottage industry," disappeared when factory machines, which were capable of producing large quantities of pins at extremely low prices, were introduced. Home workers were literally thrown out of work, or had to change their habits of a lifetime, and go out to work in these new fangled factories. As in all generations, these enforced changes came much harder to the elderly who, set in their ways, found the idea of having to lose their "self-employment" status of skilfully working in their own workshop, quite abhorrent, and many fell by the wayside as they stubbornly held onto the hope and belief that their time would come again, that the machine would breakdown, that the customers would still want to pay the extra for the handmade article, that nobody in their right mind would want to go and work in a dreadful claustrophobic factory, but as with any change, the new and progressive way won, and a way of life changed for ever. There was however, one other local cottage industry that was to last a little longer, an industry of which Oldland can be justly proud. Certainly Mr Waring would have approved of women working in this industry in view of its domestic connotations, the making of hats from wool and from animal fur.

It is uncertain that the cottages were constructed for the specific purpose to which they were used, or if the procedure was simply a way of making full use of an existing format, but many families living in Oldland, and the surrounding area lived in groups of houses that were frequently built around three sides of a square, locally known as a "barton." Towards the end of the eighteenth and into the early part of the nineteenth centuries, Oldland had an extremely good reputation for producing hats of quality, all of which were produced by women working in their own home, or possibly in the home of a neighbour. As far as can be determined, the local manufacture of hats appears to have started sometime during the 1770's or possibly in the early 1780's, but why it should have gained a tentative foothold in Oldland seems to be one of those mysteries lost to us with the passage of time. It is possible that one or two women developed an interest in hat making, or perhaps more likely that a woman, or women with the necessary skill of hat making moved into the area, and set up business. Whatever was the reason that gave birth to this embryo, the women must have been successful as within a relatively short space of time the hat making industry of Oldland had been established. The basic materials used in hat making are wool, presumably from either the nearby Mendips, or more likely the Southwolds, plus fur taken from the indigenous rabbit/hare population. Whilst the use of these local materials would seem perfectly logical and understandable, some of the hats made by the Oldland ladies, at this time, consisted of beaver skins, and certainly the owner of these skins cannot be classified as being indigenous. It must be presumed that the beaver skins were imported from Canada through the port of Bristol, but how and why they came to Oldland is not easy to explain, bearing in mind that we are not dealing with a large organisation, which would have contacts out in Canada, or a ship owner who brought the skins back to this country as a speculative venture, but instead we are dealing with small individual groups of women, who would have found the trek into Bristol quite daunting and time consuming, apart from the fact that they also needed to know when the ship with the cargo of beaver skins was likely to dock. However it was done, the fact remains that it happened, and hats made of beaver skin by women in Oldland were highly prized by gentlemen of London.

As for the wool and local rabbit skins, the process would seem that the wool would be dyed and then woven together into pieces approximately three feet square, and then each piece would be pressed and rolled on numerous occasions with other pieces of the same size until it had a thin solid form that was both flat, smooth in appearance. Separately, children collected teasels from the local hedgerows, which were then dried and stored so that the heads, and more particularly the spikes of the head, could be used to fetch or tease up the nap of the wool, and thus create felt. The material was then cut and fashioned into felt hats, some of which were trimmed with parts of the rabbit skin. Although it is probable that the initial treatment of cleaning and dying the wool was carried out by a more industrial section of the community, it is understood that the reason for the bartons, as described above is due to the fact that female occupant[s] of each cottage had a set task to perform, with the first dealing with the pressing and rolling, and even possibly the teasing, then the partially processed material would pass to the next cottage where it was cut, and shaped This was then followed by the stitching and finishing, and thus the work would pass around the barton, with each occupant making her own contribution to the finished article, the bulk of which appear to have ended up in the export market. As far as can be determined, the vast majority of the Oldland hats were shipped out of Bristol with their ultimate destination being the markets of Africa, the West Indies and America, but as with any trade, quite a few of the hats remained in the locality, and were worn by local agricultural workers, and many others.

For forty or more years hat making in Oldland appears to have prospered, and whilst it does not appear to have made any one particular person a fortune, it certainly provided a reasonable, and possibly a satisfactory standard of living, but all was to change, as around the early to mid part of the 1820's, with Britain no longer at war with its neighbours, with the Royal Navy ruling the waves, and unheard of prosperity filling the sails of social change, a metamorphose in fashion occurred, and soon the majority of hats being sold in the metropolis were made of silk. With the more expensive silk now a status symbol of your wealth, the last thing that up and coming young men wanted, was to be seen in the dreadfully outdated wool and fur hats, and orders began to dry up, not only in London, but also in America. Felt hats were of course still being sold in Africa and the West Indies, but even there the market was faltering, and as far as can be judged, very little hat making appears to have continued in Oldland after the 1850's. Intriguingly however, there was until the 1950's, a house situated alongside the stream in Court Road, Oldland Bottom that was always referred to, and known as, the *Bowler Hat* cottage Thus it is possible that even after the 1850's the making of hats, although in a much reduced format, still continued in Oldland for a further fifty years or so.

Whilst neither Oldland nor the surrounding parishes can ever be regarded as hives of industry, many and varied products have been manufactured or carried on within the area covered by this book. For example, in the adjoining parish of Bitton, there were at least two water mills at Swineford that were used for the grinding of logwood for the purpose of obtaining dyes used in the clothing industry. Additional mills, or the same mills at different times, were used for the rolling of copper sheeting and the casting and rolling of lead, whilst within the village of Bitton, the waters of the River Boyd were ponded, so that brass could be beaten into pans and dishes, and wood could be turned into paper. Warmley Brook was also a source of energy, particularly at Willsbridge where the stream was dammed, and the head of water this produced enabled a mill to be constructed during 1712, on behalf of **John Pearsall,** for the specific purpose of rolling iron into hoops, and also for the manufacture of the new and improved product ~ steel. The mill was obviously a success, as well as being profitable for the Pearsall family, in whose ownership the mill remained for a little over one hundred years. The demise of the family business occurred during **Thomas Pearsall's** stewardship when, in 1801 he took out a patent for his invention/creation of applying and using iron-hoops in the construction of roofs in place of the more traditional timber beams. He advocated the idea that as the iron-hoops weighed less and were less bulky than the thick, old fashioned timber beams, then the supporting walls/foundations need not be as sturdy, and thus time and space could be saved. His views were not simply made from the comfort of his office; he was prepared to back up his patent with money, and he spent many hours trying to persuade property developers to adopt his ideas. Thomas was pleased to receive commissions for a handful of smallish jobs, but was overjoyed when he won the contract to build a large, iron-hoop supported roof over a section of London docks. Taking as much personal control as he could the magnificence of his idea gradually took shape, and in due course the roof was constructed with a large span unhindered by supporting columns, and with a much finer tracery than could ever be achieved out of timber. Tired, exhausted but very content that he had shown the construction industry that his idea worked, Thomas returned home to Willsbridge and his pseudo castle on the hill, but a week or so later a message arrived from London to say the Pearsall's roof had collapsed, and with it went his personal dream. With his total confidence shattered Thomas was never again to put his invention into use, and by 1816 with his wealth all but gone, the mill was sold to a new owner who proceeded to convert it into a flourmill.

Up stream from Willsbridge the watercourse alternatively known in the past as either Syston or Millclack Brook, runs through a steep sided valley and then skirts the hill on which St Anne's Church stands. Just below this hill, a chemical factory was established for the production of Sal Ammoniac [Ammonium Chloride]; Glauber's Salts [Sodium Sulphate, apparently used as a laxative]; Ivory Black [a black pigment], plus other chemicals in varying amounts. Holbrow, Haynes & Company set up the business towards the end of the eighteenth century, and after it passed into the hands of various subsequent owners, the factory was closed around 1840, with the chemical production being transferred out of its rural abode, to the now more recognized industrial area of Bristol, the Netham, built on the banks of the feeder canal constructed so that ships in Bristol's harbour could remain afloat irrespective of the state of the tide. Another mile or so up stream, at Warmley Towers, was situated the largest and probably the best know site for the manufacture of metals. It is reputed that on this site the first zinc [spelter] works in Europe, if not the world, were established in the mid eighteenth century. Zinc was produced from calamine, also known at that time as *black-jack,* and the man behind the creation of these works was a certain **John Champion,** who as a young man, spent a great deal of time living in Holland, where he learned the secrets of making brass and zinc. Having decided that he had unlocked the secrets, Champion returned to Warmley around 1758, having already persuaded a number of skilled Dutchmen and their families to go with him. In this way he could ensure that the production of brass and zinc could and would be a success, particularly as his homeland was crying out for these products, ~ particularly brass ~ and having to pay high tariffs to be able to do so, tariffs that would not exist on home produced metals. Although it must have seemed quite a cultural shock to uplift their Dutch homes and relocate in Warmley, it would appear that they and their families enjoyed the experience, as they stayed and moulded themselves into the local community, and provided us with the familiar family names of *Hollister; Ollis; Craymer; Frankham and Seager.*

To produce zinc from calamine, it was necessary to build large circular ovens resembling in appearance, a glass furnace, so that the calamine could be vaporised under extreme heat, and then allowed to condense, before being cast into ingots. Champion had, within a short time of returning from Holland, a number of these ovens built in two rows facing each other so that they represented a street of coned shaped houses. In fact as early as the 18th January 1760, the Swedish Professor of Mathematics, **Bengt Ferrner,** visited the works at Warmley, and in his journal he recorded that there were no less than fourteen brass furnaces, and ten copper furnaces in two rows, plus ten brass battery hammers, a brass wire drawing mill, and a spelter works, all built around and in front of Mr Champion's own house. Mr Ferrner has also left us, in his journal, the following description of John Champion:

He is so fiery in his surveillance that the workers would hardly mention his name, but despite this he appeared to have won the absolute and complete loyalty of his workers, who were sworn never to tell, not even their wives, exactly what they did in the spelter house.

It must however be remembered that Mr Ferrner was not visiting Warmley, and in particular Mr Champions brass works for the benefit of his health, or out of idle curiosity, he was in fact part of the international intrigue of industrial espionage, he was there to spy and to try and obtain the secrets of making zinc and or brass, and no doubt made a number of attempts to elicit information from these workers, although with many of them from Holland, it is quite feasible that their English was not that good, although it is easily feasible that Mr Ferrner could speak Dutch. However the men that were there needed to show absolute loyalty to the man who had brought them and their families from across the North Sea, and provided them with secure work, and no doubt a much improved standard of living than they were previously used to. Almost certainly the fact that John Champion was, according to Ferrner, fiery in his surveillance was more likely to be a way of trying to safeguard his own interests and his own investment, than a way of intimidating his employees into silence. However, despite the best efforts of Champion and his employees, someone spoke either innocently or deliberately, as Bengt Ferrner returned to his native Sweden, a much wiser metallurgist than when he had left for his sojourn in Warmley, and was well rewarded by the King of Sweden.

Away from Mr Ferrner's possible prejudicial description of John Champion, there are indications that Champion had an enlightened paternal streak in his outlook, as besides having built the necessary furnaces, he also built a number of cottages in

Tower Lane for his workers. [see picture on page 4 of my book *Around Kingswood*] In addition he also had constructed, for the benefit of his employees and near to the cottages, one or two provision/hardware shops with a tower, and clock. [see picture on page 43 in my book *Around Warmley*] For himself, he had a substantial family residence constructed [Warmley House] overlooking a large pond or lake, which covered an area of around thirteen acres, created by damming the local brook, but being a very practical person, Champion did not have the pond built for purely ornamental purposes, but so that water could be used in the brass/zinc works, and intriguingly as a source of ice for the kitchen and the household. There being no refrigeration in those days, it was necessary to harvest the ice that formed on the pond in winter, and then to store the frozen water in a brick lined, domed roof cavern, that Champion had had built deep in the ground at the far end of the pond. Filled with ice, with each layer separated by straw to prevent the ice from becoming one massive solid block, the Icehouse became a feature of opulence and of great surprise when, on a hot dry summers day, the owner could astonish his guests with ice-cooled drinks.

Although a practical man, Champion still had an eye for beauty, as he ensured that he had his house built in classic lines, with a long sweeping drive, that ran through gardens styled in a fashion obviously influenced by his knowledge of Dutch stately homes. The gardens spread themselves all around the front of the house, through which were one or two pathways to enable the family and friends to wander through the several acres of garden and meadowland, with constant views of the reflected water in the large lake, in front of which there was a 'D' shaped pond known as "Echo Pond". When viewed from the house, near to the bottom left-hand corner of the pond there stood, across the retaining wall a boathouse that served the large lake, whilst stretching away from the lower right-hand corner on a raised causeway was an avenue of elm trees, approximately a quarter of a mile long. True to its title an echo could be heard across the water from the gardens that occupied the area between the house and the pond, but its original name of "fish pond" was equally as accurate. As far as can be determined, John or possibly his son William Champion connected the pond to a complex system of waterways that included a canal that connected Warmley Brook to the pond. The main purpose of this pond was to create a head of water that could be diverted through enclosed culverts to a number of battery mills used by the Brass Works.

The much larger lake originally covered an area of around thirteen acres and was designed to act as a reservoir for the Brass Works, but it was also designed to be ornamental. As with all forms of metal manufacture, its production caused a great amount of waste, and the Warmley Brass Works was no exception producing tons and tons of black clinker each year. Champion noticed that the clinker seemed to be impervious to water and weather, and accordingly used some of this waste to have built, in the middle of the lake, a large twenty-foot high statue depicting Neptune, fully armed with his trusted trident, rising from the bed of the lake. At the northern end of the lake a substantial dam needed to be constructed over which Champion built an ornamental arch and a castellated summerhouse, to form a neat and attractive entrance to that part of the estate. Although attractive this was not its sole purpose, as the house was firstly a foil for sluice gates built into the dam to control the amount of water coming into the lake, thirdly as a home for the lake keeper and his wife, and last but not least as a further way of disposing of waste produced by the works, in this case the black slag that was a by-product of copper smelting, which Champion, with a degree of foresight, had run-off in its molten state into building block moulds.

In addition to these water features, Champion also had constructed in the garden a grass mound around thirty-feet high and a base circumference of around one-hundred feet, plus a chequered wall garden. However his most elaborate garden ornament was reserved for the construction of a series of vaulted chambers know as Grottoes. Once again Champion needed to dispose of a considerable amount of clinker waste, and once again he allowed his fertile imagination to run riot; why dump this waste as an eyesore, were his thoughts, why not use it to bring novelty, beauty, curiosity and interest to a private section of his garden, where he could enchant his friends by taking them to a mysterious underground world of light, deep shadows and cascading water. Typical of his big ideas, Champion had a twenty-foot high arched ceiling constructed, and a copper slag block line leat to bring water into the top of the grotto from where it could tumble down over the manmade walls in small individual torrents, in which in time ferns would grow. Within the walls, niches were constructed to house statues or ornaments some of which contained candles whose flickering light cast eerie shadows around the cavern, that were possibly enhanced by smoke that was diverted from the nearby furnaces and allowed to float in the still air.

CHAPTER 11 "What Happened to our ancestors"

Although it would be extremely pleasant to report upon the good, the helpful and the normal standards of life as they relate to our non-landowning/non-wealthy ancestors, regrettably apart from baptism, wedding and death records handed down to us, the only other group of records that are likely to be available refer to the antecedent either as a victim of crime, or as a perpetrator of crime, or perhaps more precisely, a perpetrator who has been caught. This is not to say that our ancestors were anymore criminally minded than today's population, but the following reflects the different standards of how petty crime was harshly punished by those who owned property and wealth, and ignored the numerous social injustices that were an every day occurrence in their time. Many a criminal was the victim of a world that was administered by the upper classes for the benefit of their own, with a very few in that class having any form of social concern or conscience for those who were seen as nothing other than the uneducated, uncouth unclean working class. Of course they were extremely useful for carrying out all of those very menial jobs, jobs that were most often dangerous and/or dirty, with tedium spread over many hours of hardship, but after all that is surely why we have a working class, and at least they have the benefit of making us money even if one or two of them get injured or are killed in making us rich.

With such an attitude in mind the following extracts have been taken from the Calendar of Criminal Prisoners held in the Castle Gaol at Gloucester during 1789 and 1790.

Jonathan Fullwood; Convicted of felony in 1787, ordered to be imprisoned for two years and fined £10. [Roughly equivalent to £25,000]

Anne Price; Also convicted of felony in 1787, ordered to be transported ~ *beyond the Seas* for seven years

Ann Stockwell alias Harvey/Elizabeth Stringer and **Ann Davis;** Convicted of felony in 1788, all received the same punishment as Anne Price.

The calendar does not give any details of the charges laid against the above women, but the use of the word felony implies that the law regarded their respective crimes to have been serious, and probably involved violence of some degree. Also in prison waiting to be transported beyond the Seas for seven years was **Robert Bence,** but his crime was shown as wilful perjury, of course a serious matter, but was it so bad that it warranted his banishment for life from his home and family. Seven years may have been the sentence but the chances of Robert having ever made it home again is most unlikely, if for no other reason, who was going to pay for his homeward passage, that is assuming that he survived the rigours of being a virtual slave for the best part of seven long years. Robert left these shores on the 19th January 1790 aboard the sailing barque *Neptune* bound for New South Wales, and the start of a completely new way of life. As far as the Gloucester Magistrates were concerned, perjury was on a par with the theft of copper, as onboard the same ship was **Peter Payne** from Westbury-on-Severn who at the same assizes was also sentenced to seven years of penal punishment.

The *Neptune* was obviously a busy ship, as **John Teague** and **William Mishman** were also onboard with a seven-year sentence, in their case for stealing bedclothes, probably not worth more than a few pounds, as was **Jonathan Griffiths**, seven years for stealing goods to the value of 25/- [£1.25] Not only was the *Neptune* a busy ship, many more convicts were carried than might reasonably have been expected, as this ship, captained by **Nicholas Nepean,** was owned by a consortium of slave merchants, who had taken the sailing vessel from her normal duties after they had won, from the Government, the contract to convey the prisoners to the Antipodes at the low price of £23 per head. Obviously by squeezing many more convicts on board they could make more profit, and as slave merchants they were not particularly concerned that around one in four of their "passengers" never reached Australia, succumbing to one of the many diseases of overcrowding and/or poor diet whilst en route. After all the more who died on voyage the more money would be made by the owners, as they still were paid the £23 irrespective of whether or nor the convict travelled the whole distance.

In one of the dark dank prison cells, was **Rebecca Bunting**, incarcerated for the past six months, having been charged with the wilful murder of her bastard child. Certainly a very serious matter, and obviously one where the Magistrates had never heard of post-natal depression, or considered the possible trauma Rebecca may have gone through during her secret confinement. Like Rebecca, there were a number of prisoners awaiting trial, such as **William Coleman**, charged with perjury; **Robert Williams**, and **Thomas Tucknell** for stealing, from a mill owned by **George Brambles**, their master, a small quantity of meal, to help feed their families. **George Sansum,** for stealing around 50lbs of Spanish Wool from a local firm of clothiers.

Although the above named individuals have had their crime and fate highlighted, they did not necessarily originate from the specific area covered by this book, and accordingly there is set out below a list of persons who used to live in the area and who were transported to the Antipodes:

From the Parish of Bitton:

Jane Baker [39] sentenced in August 1819 to life.
John Ballsom(e) [24] a smelter sentenced in January 1829 to 7 years.
Henry Barnell/Burnell [24] a labourer sentenced in March 1839 to 15 years.
William Batman [52] a labourer sentenced in March 1824 to 7 years.
Abraham Bennett [22] a labourer sentenced in March 1839 to 15 years.
Joseph Brain [30] sentenced in March 1790 to 7 years.
Joseph Brain [24] a labourer sentenced in March 1820 to life.
Samuel Brain [22] also known as Samuel Black, a collier sentenced in March 1819 to life.
George Britton [19] sentenced in July 1815 to life.
William Britton [24] a collier sentenced in August 1833 to life.
George Bryant [27] a labourer sentenced in March 1832 to life.
William Bryant [28] also known as William Dagger, a labourer sentenced in August 1819 to life.
William Wilcox Flower [43] a butcher sentenced in March 1838 to 15 years.
William Fry [22} a labourer sentenced in August 1827 to life.
George Gingell [19] a miner sentenced in August 1837 to 15 years.
Thomas Hopes [37] a labourer sentenced March 1838 to 14 years.
Henry Knapp a labourer sentenced August 1836 to life.
James Bush [33] a collier sentenced in August 1818 to 14 years.
Sampson Cook(e) [23] sentenced in April 1817 to 14 years.
George English [21] sentenced in April 1821 to life. Bound for Van Diemen's Land, George left these shores in July 1821 on board the sailing vessel *"Lord Hungerford"* but mysteriously died on the 8th December 1821, whilst still on the high seas.
Joseph Ettle [33] a labourer sentenced in August 1818 to 7 years
Stephen Lear [21] a cordwainer sentenced March 1820 to life.
William Lear [20] a labourer sentenced in August 1818 to 7 years
George Lewis [20] a labourer sentenced in August 1830 to 14 years.
George Lucas [18] a coalminer sentenced in January 1830 to life.
David Moreton or Morton [19] a labourer sentenced in March 1820 to life.
Samuel Moreton [20] a wheelwright sentenced in December 1833 to 7 years.
William Morgan [20] a labourer sentenced in March 1838 to 7 years.
Samuel Price [19] sentenced in August 1835 to life.
Mary Ann Sheppard [28] a prostitute sentenced in April 1840 to 7 years.
Samuel Short [28] a labourer sentenced in March 1838 to 15 years.
Thomas Smith [55] a labourer sentenced in March 1819 to life.
Joseph Spicer [58] a fireman (ie a man who tended boiler fires in factories) sentenced in August 1828 to 14 years.
Edward Stone (alias Edward Bowe) [17] a coalminer sentenced in January 1830 to life.
Joseph Stone [25] a collier sentenced in May 1821 to 7 years.
Robert Wells [19] a labourer sentenced in March 1833 to life.
William White [40] a labourer sentenced in April 1830 to 14 years.
George Williams [19] a labourer sentenced in June 1840 to 7 years.

From the Parish of Oldland:

James Bush [18] a labourer sentenced in 1831 to 7 years.
Timothy Bush sentenced in March 1813 to life. This is the Timothy Bush who for some years was the common-law husband of Elizabeth Caines, and Father of James Caines Bush, and Francis Caines Bush. Elizabeth was part of the Caines family of the Cock Road Gang notoriety; James was subsequently hanged for the alleged murder of Isaac Garden just outside the *Tennis Court Inn,* whilst his brother (see below) ended up following their Father to the Antipodes.
Francis Caines Bush [19] sentenced in August 1825 to life.
George Caines [25] an oyster and cider seller and brother of the above Elizabeth, sentenced in April 1815 to life. Left these shores on the 25th August 1815, on board the sailing vessel "*Fanny,*" bound for New South Wales. If nothing else, George was a survivor, and having served his time in the penal settlement, he subsequently obtained his "freedom," a pass that allowed him to travel without any restrictions. However, George did not travel far, and within a year of receiving his freedom, he had set himself up in Sydney as a retail butcher. There he stayed for a few years before opening a public house in Parramatta, and no doubt, with happy memories of "home" still in his mind, he gave the inn the name *"The Jolly Sailor,"* almost certainly after one of his favourite local inns back home.
Samuel Caines [37] a coalminer and brother of George and Elizabeth sentenced in March 1832 to 7 years. Leaving England in September 1832, Samuel left behind a thirty-two year old wife, and three young daughters none of whom he would ever see again Like his elder brother, Samuel knuckled down to the years of hardship, whilst at the same time he self taught himself to read and write and to change his attitude on life to the extent that by 1842 he is recorded as a freeman, working as a hospital dispenser. He must have really enjoyed his new lifestyle, and been able to put to the back of his mind the family he had been forced to leave behind, as by the mid 1840's he is known to be living with Jane (no other details known of this person other than the fact that she presented him with yet another daughter, whom they also named Jane. Samuel was to live out the remainder of his life as an honest and upright citizen of the newfound colony of Australia, dying in 1883 aged 88 years
Thomas Caines [31] a dealer and brother of the above named Caines. Self styled as Captain Thomas, he terrorised the area for a number of years, although it must be said that his bark was much worse than his bite, and like many of his family there was little if any physical malice in the way in which he criminalized the area. Caught stealing five bags of grain from an inn at Cold Ashton, Thomas was sentenced in August 1817 to 7 years transportation, and within a matter of weeks he found himself on board the infamous *Neptune,* arriving in Sydney on the 5th May 1818. His transportation papers show him to be a Carter by trade, being 5ft 9ins tall with sandy hair, a fair complexion and grey eyes. Apparently he applied for a Ticket of Leave not long after he arrived, which was granted and enabled Thomas to enter into a Carting Trade & Horse Dealing business with a friend. Thomas and his partner must have worked hard and been successful as within a short ten years the 1828, New South Wales Census shows Thomas to be living in Pitt Street, Sydney and the owner of three horses, forty-two head of cattle, and surprise surprise three servants, how things had changed for Thomas. Three years later, Thomas had become an Innkeeper with licensed premises

suitably known as *"The Traveller"* situated on Parramatta Road, Liberty Plains, Sydney. Thomas fathered three children in Australia and no doubt had a much-improved life following his transportation; he died on the 9th September 1846 aged 61 years. [I am indebted to Mrs Helen Kelly of Australia for the above information of her ancestor]

Thomas Caines ~ alias Groves ~ [19] a labourer and son of Elizabeth Caines and her new partner George Groves sentenced in August 1832 to life for his first charge of theft, demonstrating how much prejudice existed against the Caines and their extended family.

George Groves, father of James. No known details of his conviction.

George English [21] no known trade, sentenced in April 1821 to life. Spent just over two months on board a hulk, before being handed over to the master of the sailing vessel *"Lord Hungerford"* in July 1821. Ship sailed for Van Diemen's Land later that month, for a six-seven month cruise to Holbart, but unfortunately George died towards the end of the voyage on the 8th December 1821.

Samuel Neads [17] a labourer sentenced in August 1825 to life.

James Rogers [35] an awl-blade maker sentenced in March 1831 to 7 years.

From the Parish of Warmley:

Elizabeth Baker sentenced in August 1832 for life.

Isaac Brain [23] sentenced in August 1832 for life, transferred to the sailing ship *Surrey* some time in early November, but died on board on the 25th November 1832 just over a week before the boat sailed for Port Holbart, Van Diemen's Land. Also on board ship was nineteen-year-old John Groose from Warmley, similarly sentenced for life; was there a connection between both youths, did one contribute to the death of the other?

John Groose [19] a labourer sentenced in August 1832 to life.

Francis Jefferies [21] a collier sentenced in April 1822 to life.

Joseph Parker [35] a collier sentenced in August 1819 to life.

Henry Phipps [22] a fish-carrier sentenced in April 1817 to 7 years

George Potter [21] a shoemaker sentenced in March 1838 to 15 years.

Dennis Rogers [20] a labourer sentenced in August 1816 to life.

James White [22] a collier sentenced in August 1832 to life.

Thomas Wilmot [31] a collier sentenced in August 1837 to 10 years.

Edward Winkworth [24] a labourer sentenced in March 1834 to life. Held aboard a hulk for some 8-9 months before leaving for Van Diemen's Land on board the sailing vessel *"George the Third"* Having suffered the privations of living on a prison ship for four months, the vessel was approaching the mouth of the River Derwent when it was caught in a severe storm that caused the ship to flounder with the loss of life including poor Edward.

During the fifty-year period covered by the above summary a total of fifty-seven men and three women are recorded as having been transported, of which just over half [32] were sentenced to life, whilst 15 received the lesser sentence of seven years, although in reality none of them had any real hope of ever seeing their family or their home again.

Although none of the above prisoners had an easy time of it whilst serving out their sentence, its is possible that those who ended up in Tasmania [Van Diemen's Land] may have suffered the worst, especially when the following description of a convict's life written around 1841 is taken into consideration:

"I had not been there many days before I was struck by the complete and abject horror of the cruelties committed by the majority of the Government Authorities in charge of us the prisoners. Basic feelings of natural humanity appeared to have been totally lost by all or most of the officers working in this dreadful penal settlement known as Port Arthur, and those who might show just an inkling of compassion are ridiculed by their colleagues, and in the worst cases are treated no better than the prisoners themselves, thus there is little wonder that within a very short space of time any new officers arriving at the settlement, are soon indoctrinated into the ways of sadistic cruelty .For example floggings are very often carried out without any legal process or backing at the whim of an officer who basically has taken a dislike to the particular individual, and usurps his power with an incredulous level of bullying, The officer designated to be the flogger is usually the most powerful office or favourite in the settlement, and is chosen not just for his size, but also because he shares his "master's" gratification in inflicting and witnessing human pain and misery. Invariably he will use a lash that is made of tightly woven whipcord, which has been saturated in seawater, before being dried in the sun. This process makes the whipcord more ridged so that as it strikes across the flesh it acts like a wire saw tearing at the flesh and inflicting an extremely painful and deep bloody laceration down to the bone. Such a flogging I have seen on more than one occasion, ~ and the crime committed by the recipient ~ the heinous one of having his hands in his pocket as he walked around the settlement!

Whilst not all prisoners were flogged, many of the transportees who arrived in the settlement spent more than half their time in a chain gang breaking stones for fourteen hours per day under the watchful eyes of officers who bullied and cajoled their charges in a totally brutal and unrepentant manner."

For those of you who are familiar with my book *"The Cock Road Gang [The Story of the Caines Family]"* you will know that Lydia Caines, the second daughter of Benjamin and Ann Caines had, when she was seventeen years of age, an illegitimate son called George Caines [aka Avery after his father]. Mr Avery may have been a married man, or his relationship with Lydia may have been casual, as he appears to have taken no part in the upbringing of his son. Some eight or so years later when Lydia was twenty-five or thereabouts, she and her son George moved in with one of her younger cousins Jasper Wilmott who at the time was believed to be around 18/19 years old, and between them they had two children, James Caines Wilmot, b1816, and Elizabeth Caines Wilmot b 1818. It will be seen that the name Caines was so powerful that the children all ended up discarding their fathers' surname, and adopting their mother's, and they were equally proud to adopt the family business of petty crime. In true fashion of the Caines family, Lydia was unable to hold onto her man, as in 1818 whilst pregnant with Elizabeth, her common-law husband Jasper was arrested along with Sampson Pow [aka Fry] for the theft, in Somerset, of a quantity of worsted hose, and not unexpectedly was sentenced to transportation for life. Lydia, like other women in the Caines family, was left to bring up three children with little or no prospects of support other than from the surrounding close-knit family. Ironically Jasper, like a number of fellow transportees prospered down-under, and when he died in July 1853 he was a reasonably wealthy man.

As for his son James Caines Wilmott, crime eventually caught up with him, and his claim to fame was that on the 28th April 1849, he left theses Islands on board the last transport ship *The Randolph"* bound for New South Wales and in due course inherited wealth, which included 280 acres of land at Sutton Forest in Sydney. [I am grateful to Shelia Payne of Sunderland for this information]

Not all criminals were sentenced to transportation, as demonstrated by the following punishment meted out to local men at the Gloucester Assizes on the 16th April 1821:

Jas Hunter six months hard labour for stealing a quantity of hay, the property of T Norman, of Oldland.

Samuel Caines, who by now was a married man with two daughters, and one on the way, was sentenced to eighteen months imprisonment, and to be publicly whipped, for having stolen two or three fowls, the property of T Waters of Oldland. To help him catch the birds, and to share the plunder was James Haskins, who received one year's imprisonment.

Francis Caines Bush [see above] who was also convicted of stealing poultry from a farm in Oldland received an eleven-month sentence of incarceration and was also to be publicly whipped.

In addition to the above, a section of the community were recorded for posterity as part of the Poor Laws, in some instances the individuals concerned are named, whilst in other instances, the information is of a more general nature, which shows society's, or more particular, the upper class's attitude to those who are the bottom of the financial pile as demonstrated below. This particular article has been taken from the papers collected by the **Rev. H. T. Ellacombe** that are now housed at the Central Library, and is a draft of an order in the handwriting of **Francis Creswick** esq. of Hanham Court who, during the reign of James II was one of the local magistrates.

"Glos: To ye overseer of ye poore of Oland [sic] *in ye parish of Bitton in said County."*
"Att the genl sessions held on ye 24th day of this instant [the next two words are illegible] *at Gloucester for ye said County, amongst other things it is there ordered that all Overseerers of ye poore within ye said County doe forthwith direct and require all such as receive any Almes from their respective parishes in ye said County, for ye time to come to weare dayely constantly certain Badges on ye upper garments to denote themselves to be such Almes folks to the respective parishes yt they doe belong to. By vertue [sic] therefore of ye sd order of Sessions yew are hereby required and commanded forthwith to give notice to such Almes folks within your parish of Hamlett,* [sic] *requiring them immediately to give obedience to ye said order of Sessions, and that on ye upper garments in the most remarkable place thereof they fixe* [sic/ *two red large roman letters there viz P.O, which shall denote ye parish of Oland, and if it shall happen that any receiving Almes in ye said parish of Hamlett refuse to weare ye same, or hereafter doth forbeare it, yet then from thenceforth forward yew are required to discontinue ye weekly or other payment that otherwise yew should think fitt* [sic] *to allow them, until they shall take or reassume ye said Badge, and this shall be your Warrant, of which, fail yew not at your peril, given under my hand and seale* [sic] *this 27th Day of April 1688."*

As can be seen from the above, apart from the normal embarrassment/distress of having to apply to the parish for financial help, the most financially disadvantaged members of society who resided in the parish of Oldland during the late seventeenth century, where now forced by law to advertise the fact by having to wear on their upper clothing the large red letters P & O so that all could see and scoff. From the parishes point of view, and even more particularly the point of view of those who had to contribute to the poor relief in the form of local taxes, there was a very important need to ensure that they did not seem to be a "soft touch," which would only encourage adjoining parishes to "offload" their poor, thus reducing their own burden. It should be remembered that, under the Poor Laws, parishes were only responsible for those who were in need and who had been born in that parish, they were not required to be charitable to the poor of other parishes. However it was possible to "try and adopt" a parish by staying in the parish for a number of years, without claiming any poor relief, and by blending in, to an extent that it might become very difficult to identify the person as an intruder. Against such persons, vigorous efforts were used in every parish to prevent the irruption of labourers from other districts, so as to avoid future charges on the poor rates, and the only way in which an intruder could legally protect himself from the sudden summary removal from his adopted parish was to obtain a certificate from his natural parish, which acknowledged that in the event that this person should fall upon hard times and become a pauper, that that parish accepted the financial responsibility to meet the poor relief in his case. Thus in an age of mass illiteracy it was important, if a little inhumane, to have a simple method of identifying those for whom the parish were responsible, from those beggars who were not, in other words the large red letters were a form of "identity card." Exactly how long these badges were worn or how well the wearing of them was policed has not been recorded, but forty years later the need to sort out the genuine claimants from the impostors still existed.

At the Justice of Peace meeting held at Bitton on the 26th January 1726, the three sitting magistrates, **Thomas Tyre, Henry Creswick** [the grandson of the above Francis] and **Richard Harte**, gave the following orders:

Matthew Rodborne, and intruder, a month to get a Certificate from Puckle Church.

Lazarus Elliot, an intruder, a month to get a Certificate from Compton Dando.

George Martin, allowed till Lady Day to get out of the parish

William Drew, allowed till Lady Day to get a certificate.

Robert Bright, allowed a week to get a Certificate from Keynsham.

Solomon Phipps, allowed till Lady Day to get out of the parish

Mary Lear, allowed a fortnight to get out of the parish

John Smith, a schoolteacher, no decision as he did not attend the hearing.

John Newman, a warrant of Contempt was issued, as he had not turned up.

Ann Seymour also issued with a warrant of Contempt.

Another twenty or so similar cases all appeared before the above magistrates on that day. Three weeks later, John Smith, the school teacher, stood before the bench, and was allowed until Lady Day to obtain a certificate, and at the same hearing a summons was granted against **Thomas Jones** for turning **Sarah Jones**, a poor base child, on the parish, contrary to Law.

Some years after the date when the above hearing was held, Henry Creswick penned the following report:

*"County of Gloucester. To wit. **Ruth Beard,** other(wise) Phipps, came this day before me, and made (an) oath, that about elven (sic) years agoe (sic) she was lawfully married to **Henry Beard**, otherwise Weston, in the parish church of Bitton, according to the ceremonies of the Church of England, and which said Henry Weston, otherwise Beard, was her first husband, and yet soon after her said marriage, the said Henry Beard sold her for thirty shillings (£1.50) to a **Nicholas Read,** a coalminer of Hanham. After a week or so she was taken to Bath, and there, before a lawless minister, she was married to the said Nicholas Read, with whom she cohabited till he dyed, which was near three years agoe. Since then she has lived the life of a pauper, and is now so poor and unwell that she is unable to relieve herself, soe that she must inevitably perish unless she is relieved. She has no contact with the said*

Henry Beard, who is the only and first husband now living.

Ruth Beard, otherwise Phipps   *her mark*

Sworn before me this   *day of*   *17..*

Signed   Hen Creswick.

It is believed that Mr Creswick decided that Henry Beard was still financially responsible for his wife, and that she should not receive any parish relief.

Although the title "Poor Rates" was in common use, the money so collected was not solely devoted to ease the burden of the poor; it also formed the source or the County Rate, or Bridge Money ~ Bitton parish paid the County £63 in rates during the 1820/21 year, and in addition it was from where parish expenses were drawn. Certainly by the end of the eighteenth century, the parish was responsible for the expense of the local constable and overseers, as well as the frequent legal costs arising out of disputes brought under the Settlement Acts, ie the establishment or identification of the person responsible for the upkeep and maintenance of any bastard children born in the parish, and as always there was a substantial level of expenditure that came under the collective heading of "miscellaneous." On the 25th March 1779, Bitton Parish paid out £2. 8s 11d [£2.35p] as general expenses incurred, by the constable, when taking 3 men by a press Warrant. A few years later on the 18th April 1785, 3/2d [0.15p] was paid to **John Naish** in respect of the supply of iron rivets and nails for mending the Stocks at Bitton.

To try and put the above expenditure into some form of perspective, around the same period of our history, Bitton Parish Overseers were making the following weekly payments to the deserving poor of the parish:

Richard Acreman ~ 4/- [0.20p]; **Samuel Prigg** ~ 4/-, **Joyce Long** ~ 2/-. **William Hawkins's family** ~ 2/-, **Sarah Brain** ~ 1/-.

As can be seen, the expenses incurred by the constable was twelve time greater than the weekly poor relief paid to either Richard Acreman or Samuel Prigg, and William Hawkins's family had less money paid to them than it cost to buy the material to repair the stocks. During this time bread was the staple diet of most of the poor to the extent that in 1795, the Gloucestershire magistrates calculated that each member of the family should be allowed 8lbs of bread per week at a cost of 1½ d or 1/- [0.05p] per loaf, thus half of the money paid to the Hawkins's family would have been spent on bread alone, leaving just one further shilling, plus any other money brought into the family, to pay for all of the other necessities of life, however sparse those were for the families at the bottom of the eighteenth century financial pile. In the parish of Bitton alone there were 39 families receiving a weekly payment from the Poor Relief fund during the 1795/96 financial year, but this number more than doubled to78 by 1814/15. If it is assumed that each family may well have consisted of two adults and say three children, then upwards of 400 persons, probably around one-fifth of the population were, at that time, receiving help of one sort or another from the "parish chest." Fortunately for those who needed help the most, society and those in authority were becoming more enlightened and saw the need to provide, clothing, bedding and even medical expenses. For example, in 1800, **John Caines** a cripple, was paid 2/6d [0.12½p] per week for food and general expenses, but in addition during the financial year a further 13/- [0.65p] was spent providing John with a flannel shirt, and two pairs of trousers. However, the generosity did not stop there, as in 1805, more money was spent on John when the overseer agreed to purchase two blankets, a bed tick to repair his bed, a jacket, and a pair of trousers shoes and stockings; poor John must have thought that he had gone to heaven, especially as the parish even agreed to pay 6d per week to have his washing done for him.

Perhaps somewhat surprisingly, medical treatment, however rudimentary it might have been, was paid by the parish on behalf of the poor, including paying from 1813, for a period of at least seven years, a retainer of £14 per year to **Dr. Wingrove,** so that he would attend the poor. Some times they would pay for the services of the local "wise woman" who was well practised in a fairly primitive level of midwifery, and who no doubt also had the knowledge of knowing herbal remedies, and was more often than not the person called out when it was necessary to wash and lay out the recently deceased. Other women from the village were paid for sitting-up with the sick and dying, or for the washing and/or disposal of fouled clothing. At other times, the overseer would allow his generosity to get the better of him by allowing for the purchase of little delicacies for the sick and dying, such as during the autumn of 1809, he agreed that a lambs head could be bought to help nourish **Ann Jones'** boy sick with smallpox. The overseers also had to deal with itinerants who needed medical treatment whilst they were in the parish as noted in 1819, when a Mrs Gill, a complete stranger to Bitton and travelling alone during the extreme cold of January, went into premature labour whilst wandering through the area. Taken to the Poor House she subsequently gave birth to a "still-born" child, and was herself very weak and unwell, as illustrated by the following entries taken from the overseers records:

1819

January 18 Cost of taking Mrs Gill to the Poor House and attending her needs whilst in labour. 1/-.

January 23 Box to bury Mrs Gill's child 1/-

January 28 Relief for Mrs Gill, including coal and candles 4/6.

February 2 Tobacco and Vitriol Nitre for fumigation in poor House in connection with Mrs Gill's illness. 2/5

February 5 Cost of nursing Mrs Gill, sitting up all night 5/-

Candles used above	*1/1*
Sundries for Mrs Gill	*1/6*

Further similar entries appear throughout the month of February and during the first week of March, although they do become less frequent.

March 8 Paid wagoner 10/- to convey Mrs Gill to London.

Not only was the local Doctor paid a retainer, the parish also paid a subscription of 2 guineas [£2.10] per year to both the Bristol and Bath Infirmaries. Money well spent as in May 1785, for reasons not given in the records, **Sarah Prigg** was taken to Bristol to have her leg amputated, and a wooden leg fitted all for £2.41p. Of course whether poor Sarah received any anaesthetic or painkillers, or was able to get around in comfort with the aid of the prosthesis has not been recorded; although the artificial "stump" must have given her some problems, as in September of that year, the parish overseer was forced to pay 1/- [0.05p] to have the wooden leg mended.

Throughout much of the eighteenth and nineteenths centuries, smallpox was endemic in the area, with some years much worse than others, and again it seemed as though it affected the poor more frequently. It also quite often led to the parish incurring costs on persons who had not been born in the parish, but had migrated to it, or were simply passing through when the illness struck. One such family was that of **John Bryant's** from Stratton on the Foss, who were in Bitton during the cold January winter of 1784, when one of his daughters became unwell, followed quite quickly by one of her brothers, and then their mother. After the doctor had been called, the illness was diagnosed as smallpox, and within a week both children and their mother were dead. Whether John or any of his other children caught smallpox is not recorded, but whatever happened, they survived and by the middle of February they were all well enough to travel, and accordingly, the local overseer made a Removal Order, and on the 2nd March 1784, paid John's distant cousin, **Robert Bryant,** 8/- for two days hire of his horse and cart to take the depleted family back from whence they had come.

In the above instance, it must be assumed that the overseer responsible for the Stratton on the Foss parish, accepted John and his family back, but quite often such matters did not go through as smoothly as one would like, which in turn led to a great deal of money being wasted in legal fees as the lawyers found more and more ways of making money out of disputes arising from the terms of the Settlement Act, even if it meant that the human pawns in the squabble were being shunted about from place to place. One such instance involved an **Ann Hicks** who, in early 1783, with her two children, one of whom was just a babe in arms, was removed from Isleworth in Middlesex to Bitton, on the grounds that the Bitton parish was the one that should be responsible for her and her children's welfare. The records do not indicate what had led the overseer to this conclusion, nor is there any clue as to why the Bitton overseer denied the claim, because as soon as Ann and her children arrived in Bitton, he submitted a Notice of Appeal against the order at the first available Middlesex Quarter Sessions. With the notice issued there was the question as to what he should do with this little pathetic family, and it was decided that they should stay in Bitton for the time being, with the parish initially paying just £1 for two week's board and lodging. The weeks went by, with the Bitton parish now paying 5/- [0.25p] per week for the maintenance of Ann and her two children until May 1783, when the Magistrates scheduled the appeal to be heard in London.

With the overseers in Bitton sticking to their principles, additional costs were then incurred, with three guineas [£3.15] being paid for a Chaise to take their lawyer, his clerk, and one other person, no doubt a witness, to London, with the same amount also being paid to bring these gentlemen back. As for Ann Hicks and her family, there was no such luxury, as they were obliged to travel to the Capital by a much more ponderous and uncomfortable wagon, that was probably also at the same time carrying freight of one kind or another to help keep down the £1.05 fare. Once in London, there was the need to consider suitable accommodation for the lawyer, his clerk and the witness, and of course for Ann and her children, and a total of £10.79p was paid for board and lodgings, plus a further £4.75 paid for food with, no doubt the lion's share being paid in respect of the lawyer, his clerk and the witness. However, all this money, almost £23 in total, was spent before the case came before the magistrates, as the hearing had been delayed by at least a whole day, but rather than twiddle their thumbs, the lawyers for both parties got their heads together, and with the lawyer for Bitton appearing to have the upper hand, those for Isleworth proposed that they accept responsibility for Ann Hicks, and accordingly the case was settled out of Court with Isleworth agreeing to pay Bitton £17.85 towards the cost of bringing the case.

Whilst Bitton may appear to have had the bulk of the costs covered by the other parish, the above £23, only represented travelling and subsistence expenditure, and thus when the lawyers fees on both sides are included, it is probable that between them the two parishes spent over £50 wrangling over who should have been financially responsible for a poor widow woman and her young family. What a complete waste of money, especially when Bitton was only paying Ann Hicks 5/- maintenance per week, and at that rate, could have done so for a further three years before they would have matched the money wasted by a principle. Sadly the story does not end there, as within two months of the lawyers settling her future out of Court, the officers of the parish of Calne in Wiltshire, paid out of their funds 75p for the cost of burying Ann Hicks' child on the 4th July 1783.

Even when the disputes did not involve the employment of expensive lawyers, the cost of removing someone out of the parish to their place of settlement could be expensive both financially and emotionally, as in the case of **James Butler.** For a number of years prior to 1821, James Butler was living with his wife and three children in Bitton, earning a respectable income as a hatter, and within the limitations of his income, and of his position in society, he and his family were content with their lot. However, all that was to change during the eventful year of 1821 when his wife became seriously ill, probably with cholera, and after a relatively short illness she unfortunately died. Now whilst Mrs Butler had been born in Bitton, and as such, the parish were able to provide some financial help during her brief malady, once she died, the rules changed because Bitton was not responsible for James, and now, with the mother dead, they were no longer responsible for the welfare (ie being sent to the workhouse for the care and attention) of the children, even though they had been born in the parish, that responsibility was now transferred to the Father's place of settlement, and that was Polstead in Suffolk. Thus without any thought for the tremendous upheaval of sending a grief stricken family to the other side of the country, the overseer of Bitton set about making the necessary arrangements of sending James and his three small children away. Not an easy prospect in any circumstances, and certainly one that was going to be a very tiring journey particularly for the young children, involving them in having an early morning, one might say middle of the night, trip to Bath by cart, so that they could board one of Mitchell's wagons for a long and uncomfortable passage to London. Once at London, it would then be necessary to travel across the Capital, to the Inn from whence Wilson's Coaches left on their way to Ipswich, calling in at Polstead some seven or eight hours after pulling away from the London inn. What happened to James and his little family is not recorded in the local records, as having paid the £12 to send them to Suffolk, the Bitton overseer had washed his hands of the case, and that particular chapter was now dead, buried and forgotten, without a stain on the Bitton Parish Councils' conscience.

The birth of children out of wedlock, ie bastardy, was a cause of much friction and considerable expense, as well as being a subject that occupied a great deal of the overseers and the constables' time, but to be able to understand the problem it is necessary to consider the national problem, and the fact that as in all cases, the situation is moulded by society's attitude at the time. In 1733, the Poor Law Act, made it clear that the supposed father of the illegitimate child would be held responsible for its maintenance, and if he refused and/or failed to do so, then the mother could ask that the Courts send the errant father to prison. In the meanwhile, the local parish would try and financially support the mother and child until the accused agreed to fulfil his duties, but on his release from prison he would still be expected to reimburse the parish their out of pocket expenses. Although much of the above seems to be relatively sensible and straightforward, it has to be remembered that in those days, there were no medical or scientific ways of establishing parentage, and accordingly, the parish was often faced with the standard dilemma of it being down to one person's word against another. Many expectant fathers were quite prepared to stand by the mother, but occasionally, for whatever reason, there may have been a genuine doubt in his mind, or simply a reluctance to pay for his fun. In addition, there were numerous occasions when the groom was rather on the shy side, and somewhat nervous about his forthcoming marriage, to the extent that there are frequent references in the poor books of men being kept in custody until the marriage, as on the 7th October 1784, when 11/6d [57½p] was spent in "arresting" **Thomas Osborn** and keeping him in custody all night and the next day before his marriage. Three years later, the parish paid out 9/6d for paying the parson, buying the ring and providing the wedding breakfast of bread cheese and beer, for the "shot-gun" wedding of **Charles Williams** and **Sarah Bush.**

For various reasons, such as the man being married to someone else, a woman occasionally had more than one illegitimate child, and as such was treated more harshly, particularly when the third bastard arrived. For example, during 1820/21, **Charlotte Brain** was in receipt of poor relief amounting to 3/9d [18p] per week to support herself and her two illegitimate children. Whether or not these children had the same father is not recorded, nor is there any reference to the identity of the third child Charlotte was carrying, but as soon as it became obvious the she was in the family way, Charlotte was arrested and sent to prison for six months, for the crime of having a third pregnancy outside of wedlock. What happened to her other two children is open to speculation but almost certainly they ended up in the workhouse, and were probably employed in the pin making industry. As for Charlotte, she gave birth in the Lawford's Gate prison, but the child did not survive, and was probably not even given a name, all that is recorded in the records is the curt note, "funeral of Charlotte Brain's bast."

The 1733 Act worked for the next one hundred years, but by 1831/32 the law was seen to be divisive on the grounds that rather than reduce the number of illegitimate babies, it was seen to promote illegitimacy and immoral behaviour, because the participants, particularly the men, were able to opt out of their responsibility, and simply let the parish "pick up the tab." Accordingly, in a peculiar logic where all the lawmakers were men, the Bastardy Clause was introduced to the new Poor Law of 1834, which decreed that in future all illegitimate children were to be the sole responsibility of the mother, until the child obtained the age of 16 years. Effectively, this new legislation categorised the mothers of the fatherless children, as widows in receiving poor relief. As such, the mother would be expected to work and fend for their child as well as for herself, with the threat of being sent to the workhouse if she failed and now, for the first time, the law absolved the named father of any financial or moral responsibility for his child. Those who were behind this new law saw their recommendations in very simple black and white, because of the ingenious aspect of the new legislation. By tarnishing the woman with implied promiscuity, treating her as a "fallen woman," and most importantly, singling her out to face the humiliation of being an unmarried mother, the message would, in due course, get across to those young ladies who were not yet in an intimate relationship and prevent them from entering into any form of immoral behaviour, hey presto! Immoral behaviour would decline, and so would illegitimacy. It was not the men who were guilty of immoral behaviour, that was the sole weakness of the women, and it had been proven ~ they do not say how ~ that forcing men into unwanted marriages was both expensive and ineffective. As far as this committee of gentlemen were concerned the root cause could be snuffed out, or certainly greatly reduced by both socially and financially ostracising these guilty women, and by doing so it would prove a much cheaper and more successful way of enforcing social discipline, and stop the rot once and for all, after all the men could not be held responsible for the woman's morals and condition.

As a result of the new Act, there was a legalised stigma and social leprosy placed upon the young girl, or the older woman, who in turn had no opportunity of defending herself or her predicament, and was therefore automatically condemned as being a promiscuous and immoral woman, a label that was probably then carried for life. Thus it is not surprising that many women very often killed themselves and their child, or sought the barbaric skills of those who would perform "back street" abortions, rather than face the shame heaped upon her by a countless number of society's hypocrites. But as society and the laws introduced by single-minded male legislators, became more and more complex, the problems that needed to be resolved by the overseers became more and more intricate, and where sympathy, if it ever existed, was left at home.

Although more often than not the illness was of a physical nature, the overseer's funds also had to deal with those members of the parish whose illness was more of a mental problem. **Solomon Fry,** was for reasons that were never made clear, unable to cope with the strain of looking after his family, and in 1828 disappeared from the local area leaving his family even more destitute that they had previously been. Some months later, Mr Fry was found staying near Shrewsbury, and with that parish unable or unwilling to subsidise him out of their poor relief, a message was sent to Bitton, basically asking that parish to come and collect him, which they did at the cost of £4. No doubt this was done on the basis that if Solomon Fry was back at home and working, then there would not be so much relief to pay out to the family. Around the same period of our history another Solomon, this time **Solomon Short** had been diagnosed, in the language of the day, as a lunatic and as such had been confined to the Asylum in Gloucester. However, some time during 1830, Solomon managed to escape from the dreary dank dark walls of the asylum, and the harsh treatment imposed upon the inmates, and headed in a general southerly direction, using his natural homing instincts. By one means or another, he was able to reach Winterbourne before he was detected, and subsequently arrested by the constable of that parish who, for taking Short to Bitton under escort, was paid £1.15p for his pains. Whether or not Solomon Short was violent or a danger to himself or others is not made clear, but the overseer in Bitton was not prepared to take any chances, and paid **Naish Bush** the sum of 3½p for making three staples, and ensuring that Solomon Short was chained to the wall of the Poor House; and then paid **George Bush** 15p for attending Short during the night, and Sergeant **George Haskins** ~ of the Bitton constabulary ~ £4 for escorting Short back to the asylum in the City of

Gloucester. Perhaps all of these precautions were well founded, as the day after Solomon Short left the Poor House, the overseer spent 17/- [0.85p] for a new window that had apparently been damaged in that building, on the other hand Solomon may have been the victim of spite or malice, as it was not unknown for a normally sane, but not always understood individual to be classified as a lunatic simply to get him or her out of the way; we shall never know what agonies Solomon Short went through because of his incarceration.

CHAPTER 12 "A Gloucestershire Woman"

During 1878, a certain Lady Stradbroke sent a letter to the Times Newspaper in an attempt to remind her fellow female peers of wealth, to become more charitable to their poorer sisters, by giving them their cast-offs. Whilst Lady Stradbroke did not use those exact words, that was her meaning when she wrote that *"ready-made clothes are an immense boon to the poor, especially for the over worked mother who has little or no time to mend and darn, and bake, and wash, and nurse the baby, much less make clothes for her husband and her children, let alone clothes for herself."*

Although there was in her letter a gracious air of patronization, Lady Stradbroke most certainly meant well, and no doubt many of her poorer sisters were not too proud to wear hand-me-downs, and to show off the refinery that was not normally part of their lives. To illustrate the life style of many poor housewives during the fourth quarter of the nineteenth century, the following is a general description of a *Gloucestershire Woman* based upon a real but unidentified woman who happened to live in the south of the County, possibly around the Kingswood-Downend area. Whilst this area is outside that specifically covered by this book, it has been included as undoubtedly there were women in similar circumstances within the book's area, even though the generalisation may have applied to more than one woman.

"The mother, who never thought about the phrase "over-worked," married at the age of eighteen, with her husband being a few months older. Throughout his life, he earned a living as an agricultural worker, and probably was never paid more than around 15/- [0.75p] for a sixty hour working week, although quantities of free cider and/or beer were provided. At seasonal times of the year, the Farmer would need extra hands, and on such occasions our Gloucestershire Woman would work in the fields from sun rise to sun set, either planting, weeding or harvesting, and for her labour, she was probably paid no more than 10d [0.04p] per day.

Within a relatively short time of her marriage, she became pregnant, but continued with her work in the fields for as long as she was physically able to do so, before giving birth to what was to become the first of her nine babies. She nursed and cared for each infant, dealing with their tantrums, their teething, their ailments, more often than not with little, if any, outside help, whilst at the same time tending to all of her other chores, such as cleaning, baking, washing, mending, being a wife to her husband, a mother to her children, and still she found time to work in the fields and to earn her growing family a little extra money. Her skill with a needle meant that she made and mended the majority of the clothes worn by her husband, her children, and herself, yet another aspect of her life that somehow she managed to fit into her day. Most days she would retire to bed between 9pm and 10pm, and awake around 4am, so that she could re-set the fire with the kindling wood brought into the kitchen the night before, Whilst the fire began to take hold, there would be water to fetch from the well or from the nearby communal water tap, and for as much of the water as possible to be heated. All being well, by now her husband would also be up together with one or two of the elder children, whose job it was to ensure that the younger children were also out of bed, and washed. In the meanwhile father would fuss around the fire to ensure, in his mind, that it was giving out the desired amount of heat, and that it would burn well into the morning if not beyond. Around the less than harmonious melee of her family, mother would, some times calmly but at other times much less so, ensure that everyone had washed behind their ears and, in the case of the children, drunk their milk, and eaten their gruel and stale bread; poured out the ale for her husband, swept the kitchen floor, aired the beds, and on at least one day in the week, carried out the weekly washing. There was then the final inspection, ensuring, as best she could, that her husband left home for work on time and in a presentable fashion, with the same going for any of the older children whose minimal education had now finished, and who were also able to go to work As for the younger children, some were sent off to receive what little schooling was available, whilst the very young children went with mother to the farm, and stayed with her come rain or shine during her working day.

In the busy harvest-time she, and those children who were old enough to be at school, or young enough to pick and carry, would be up by around 2.30am, washed in cold water, with their work clothes on and ready for the day's adventure. This usually started at just after 3.0am when they accompanied their mother to the fields to be harvested, so that crops could be gathered in, whilst the younger children gleaned the field behind the adults and the older children.

For mother, Saturdays would be a rather special day as although there was work to be done in the fields, the farmer very often allowed some of his workers to finish their working day by 1.0pm, and that meant, when it was her turn, that there was time for her to return home and get prepared for a "trip into town." Despite her busy life, mother quite often made more clothes than were required by her family, or she would mend those that her youngest child had outgrown, or even mend those clothes belonging to another person, and in this way she could help to further supplement the family income. Thus on at least two, if not three Saturdays of each month mother would be seen carrying a basket full of new and mended clothes, walking the three miles or more to a neighbouring laundress, where she hoped to sell her wares, and to buy off-cuts of material, broken garments or any other odd piece of material, which her skilful fingers and nimble mind, could turn into "new" wearing apparel, either for her family, or for re-sale. On most occasions, the money collected from her sales was greater than the money spent on the replacement material, and this would mean that mother would be able to look around the other shops. High on her list of priorities would be the acquisition of flour, and if possible mother usually tried to purchase two pecks, a dry goods measurement equivalent to about eighteen litres. Depending upon how much money was left, she would then look around for a few treats, tobacco for her husband, sweats for her children, and if she was extremely lucky in her financial transactions, perhaps a new bonnet or shawl for herself. Thus armed with her acquisitions, she could start her three-mile or so walk back home, and on the way she could make a mental note of the next list of jobs to be done.

Once the Saturday evening meal was over, and the younger children were tucked up in bed, her husband would probably stroll out into the evening gloom, with his pipe, a pouch full of newly purchased baccy, and a few loose coins in his breeches, and having done so would, in a relatively short space of time, meet up with other husbands doing the same thing. After passing the time of day, they would all begin to gravitate towards the local hostelry to sample the local brew, to quench their suddenly acquired thirst, and to discuss those worldly matters which were after all better left to the menfolk to sort out. After a couple of hours of putting the world to right, and the frequent use of that oft-heard phrase, "it was never like that in my days," they would meander home, with the firm intentions of helping their respective wives with the left over chores.

In the meanwhile, mother had planned her Saturday evening along different lines, and with the youngest children now in bed, and the older children carrying out their allotted chores, she was able to turn her attention to the flour purchased that very afternoon. First she was able to mix up a bread dough, and soon had three or four unleavened loaves cooking in the oven, whilst with the little amount of yeast she had managed to beg or borrow, two other pats of dough were proving on the shelf above the heat of the oven, awaiting their turn to be cooked. Searching her cupboards, mother would then look around to see what meat was left over, or if there was any fruit from the hedgerows that could be cooked and made into savoury or sweet pastry pies. Once the preparation of the bread, the pies, and any other use the flour had been put, had been cleared away and the wooden surface washed down with the help of the eldest daughter, Mother would then set about sorting through her basket of old clothes, and scraps of material setting aside that that needed to be washed from the clean material, which was then neatly folded and put by her chair for future haberdashery work. That done there was then the urgent need to see that her, her children's and her husband's Sunday best clothing was ready and presentable for the next days very important attendance at church. As the evening wore on and with the following day being *"a day of rest,"* mother could begin to indulge herself with her pile of clothes in the full knowledge that with the exception of the three eldest children, the rest of the siblings were now in bed, whilst her husband was sat in his comfortable chair relaxing with the quart or so of ale, brought from the hostelry. As she looked across to him, she could see in the dim light, a wisp of smoke rising from his full pipe of tobacco, knowing, in her womanly ways, that he was probably meditating upon the events of the day as he watched the dancing flames in the fire, and occasionally closed his eyes in contentment. For mother this was the best time in the week to make and mend, and before she retired to bed she would ensure that all the outstanding mending had been accomplished, and that there was at least a new pair of trousers, or a new smock-dress completed, even though by then the witching hour had passed, and Sunday had already arrived.

Being a day of rest, there was not the same urgent need to get out of bed, and for mother there was the opportunity of having a "lie-in" until at least 7.0am or even 7.30am, but with a large family to cater for, mother would still be the first out of bed, and downstairs raking the fire into life, making sure there was adequate hot water with which to wash, after all her hard efforts, she was not about to let her children, or her husband go to church with dirty hands or a dirty neck. On the kitchen table, mother would lie out some of the bread and possibly a pie baked the previous night, and there might even be a scraping of jam if the children were really lucky. Having the Sabbath breakfast, the children would be allowed to play for an hour or two, before they were subjected to the final wash and dressed in their Sunday best, with a stern warning from mother not to get dirty. At the appointed time, mother, father and their children would gather outside and then, as a family group, they walked to church, meeting their fellow parishioners on the way, and exchanging the pleasantries of a Sunday morning. For our mother there was some thing sacrosanct about attending both the morning Eucharist, and the latter Evensong, and throughout her life she was a regular attendant at church services.

Apart from the important religious aspect of attending church, which was high on mother's list of priorities, the whole ambience of going to church was, for our mother, one of the few real pleasures in her humdrum life. With little money to spend, and almost constant toil, socializing was extremely restricted, but at church, and even more importantly on her way to and from church, mother could at least talk with other women in a way that only women will understand, to chat, to gossip, to listen, to observe were all an integral part of the days pleasure, that could be carried over from one week to another, and from one woman to another, how little did men understand the needs of a sociable women.

Our particular lady, for as a woman of polite and kindly behaviour, that in reality was what she was, was strong, handsome, with a very cheerful disposition, always ready to help others, and ensuring that her husband and children always came first, an inspiration to many, and yet so modest that she found it difficult to understand the aura that surrounded her, and throughout her long life, she retained her looks and her dignity. Her legacy was that her children were well disciplined, and well looked after by a loving and considerate mother, who was able to watch them all grow up into respectable men and women each with a great capacity for hard work, loyalty and love, and many of whom were able to provide their mother with numerous grandchildren on whom she poured out her unbounded love."

Such was a Woman of Gloucestershire.

CHAPTER 13 "The Ellacombes"

It is virtually impossible to produce a book on the Bitton area without making reference to Henry Thomas Ellacombe and his son Henry Nicholson Ellacombe, two reverend gentlemen who dominated so much of the religious heart and soul of the parish and the surrounding area for almost the whole of the nineteenth century, as successively they held the living of St Mary the Virgin. It is possible to trace their roots back to the small village of Kenn, not far from Exeter, and to their family who maintain the original spelling of Ellicombe, only subsequently to be modified by the Rev. H. T. Ellacombe who, when he exchanged his Devon home for one in Gloucestershire, considered that his new spelling to be the more correct, especially in view of the fact that there was a possible connection between his family and the small village of Ellacombe that was situated just outside of Torquay.

Henry Thomas was the second of seven sons born in Thoverton, near Exeter, to the Rev. William Ellicombe and his wife, William, being the local vicar. He was obviously a man of great influence and belief, as his three eldest sons all followed into what was now becoming the family tradition of taking Holy Orders; their paternal grandfathers for the two earlier generations having previously been curates and/or vicars. Henry developed into a man of exceptional talent with very varied activities and interests, and around 1807/08, he went up to Oriel College, Oxford, where he graduated in 1812. Although he had completed his religious studies, one of his varied interests was engineering, and being unable to resist his natural impulses he devoted much of his leisure time in preparing and completing mechanical drawings, and constructing mechanical models. Whilst Henry was still at Oxford he was given, much to his great pleasure, the opportunity of being introduced to Marc Isambard Brunel, [father of Isambard Kingdom Brunel] and from this introduction, it was agreed that Henry should submit his drawings and models to the celebrated engineer. Mr Brunel was so much impressed with the delicacy, accuracy and beauty of Henry's workmanship, that he immediately offered Henry a position in his office, and subsequently, around 1814, Henry Thomas Ellicombe was made Sir Marc Brunel's personal and confidential assistant. Two years later, when Brunel was engaged in the construction of his great engineering work for the Royal Navy in Chatham, Henry was there as Resident Engineer. However, for some involved reasons Henry found himself and his services at odds with the Navy Board, and after some acrimonious correspondence, Henry left Chatham in disgust, and returned to Oxford, and his ordination studies. As for Brunel, he was quite distraught at the sudden loss of his prodigy and wrote:

"If you continue in your determinations of returning to the Church, may you, my good friend, prove as great an ornament to it as you would have been in that most arduous career in which you leave your very sincere friend, with one of his lights out."

Henry threw himself into his studies, and in the same year that he turned his back on engineering, he took his M.A. degree at Oxford, being ordained in 1816, by the Bishop of Exeter to the curacy of Cricklade in Wiltshire. However his sojourn in this parish was relatively short lived as in the following year his association with Bitton was to commence following his appointment as curate-in-charge.

It is interesting to note that whilst Henry was working at Chatham he met and fell in love with Miss Elizabeth Nicholson, a very attractive daughter of a Government contractor, and quickly decided that he wished to marry this young lady. Although no reference has ever been recorded to the affect that this relationship might have been the possible cause of Henry being forced out of his job as the Resident Engineer, it would appear to be quite plausible that Elizabeth's parents may have disapproved, or that the Navy Board were concerned that the relationship might compromise Henry's position when giving out contracts. Whether there was any connection, or that the two matters are totally unrelated we may never know, but what we do know is that when Henry arrived in Bitton, he brought with him his lovely fiancée, whom he subsequently married circa 1818. From this relationship came five daughters and just one son who was born on the 18th February 1822 and christened Henry Nicholson Ellacombe, but sadly for Henry Snr and his children, Elizabeth died at a comparatively young age. With six young children to bring up, Henry Snr turned his attention to a second wife, who in due course presented him with a second son and a sixth daughter, but tragedy was to strike again when after fourteen years or so of marriage his second wife also died, as did the second son when he was eighteen years and studying at Oxford. Henry did in fact marry for the third time, although there was no issue.

It was not long after Henry Snr had arrived in Bitton that his great interest in practical/mechanical matters was resurrected, although to start with his thoughts were less mechanical but more architectural, and in particular in church building. Whilst studying at Oriel College, he had become a close friend of John Newman and other prominent members of the Oxford movement for church design and restoration, and these connections, and his enquiring/practical mind soon led him to take a very close look at his church in Bitton. As early as 1820 he transformed the interior arrangements by sweeping away the old double pews, which in turn breathed new life into the church, although one suspects that many of the parish elders considered such changes as being little more than an unnecessary vandalism of their church.

However, Henry Thomas Ellacombe's main preoccupation as curate was to assist the vicar in dealing with the unwieldy size of Bitton Parish, and this led to Henry Snr taking up the work of providing for the spiritual welfare of those parishioners who lived in the more outlying parts of the parish, employment eminently suited to Henry as it enabled him to indulge in his interest in church buildings and could accordingly visit all of the "minor" churches situated in the parish. The first of these buildings to come under Henry's scrutiny was the little, but nevertheless, interesting mediaeval chapel of St Annes Oldland. Although in later life he acknowledged his regret at having destroyed this building, in the latter part of the 1820's, he was all for sweeping away the old building and having it replaced with the existing edifice, and thus in 1829 the new building was consecrated. Six years later in 1835, Henry was appointed vicar of St Mary's Bitton, however this did not stop or restrict his interest in church property, and in 1844, Henry oversaw the building of Christ Church, Hanham as another new parish was carved out of Bitton, only to be followed in 1851 by the building of St Barnabus for the newly created parish of Warmley.

Henry Snr was also very interested in music, and this led to him becoming particularly fascinated in the music of bells and bell ringing. He had been a bell ringer since his youth, and the more he became involved with church bells, the more he tried to reform the belfry, so as to make it as much part of the church as the nave or chancel. Having been in the parish some thirty years, he drew up a set of rules in 1848 for the Bitton ringers, and it is believed that these rules are still followed today. In addition to Henry enjoying the delights of the musical bonanza produced by the peal of bells, he was also able to exercise his mechanical abilities, to the extent he left, in his Will his models of tower bells and his collection of bells to the South Kensington Museum. Music was probably a much easier interest to share, and one that could have many religious connotations that ably suited him as vicar of St Mary's. During his early years as vicar he introduced chanting in the church, and fortunately for Henry there lived just a mile or so away, Robert Pearsall the composer of madrigals, whose work, Henry said, approaches very nearly in excellence to that of the great Elizabethan madrigalists.

Henry was also well known for his antiquarian research of Bitton, and his knowledge and interest in horticulture and gardening, and in 1867, some seventeen years after giving up the living of St Mary's he began writing a history of the manor of Bitton. Previously throughout the second half of the 1840's and beyond, he had developed a fine collection of plants as he radically transformed the vicarage garden, for many generations to come. Although he was sixty years of age when he gave up the living of Bitton and handed it over to his son, it was not his intention to retire, but instead he moved to Clyst St George where he lived and ministered until his death in 1885 at the grand age of ninety-five, having achieved sixty-eight years as an active parish priest.

As mentioned above, when Henry Snr left Bitton, his son Henry Jnr, who had lived in the village for nearly all of his life, took over the living. Born in 1822, Henry Jnr had, for the next seventeen years or so lived in Bitton quite quietly with a growing family of sisters and his half-brother. His early formative years included a formal education from his father, but at the age of ten was sent to Bath Grammar School to receive a much more in depth course of studies, increased discipline, and most importantly an opportunity of meeting and mixing with boys of his own age. In 1840 he followed in his father's footsteps and went to Oxford and gained a place at Oriel College, from where he graduated in 1844. In his memoirs, Henry recalled that when he first went up to Oxford it was by horse drawn coach via Cirencester, where there was usually a stop and a midday meal provided, and with the driver of the coach being a well-known character, the journey was usually most enjoyable. On one occasion when Henry Jnr was returning home from Oxford, the coachman, who was very rheumatic and in a great deal of pain, asked Henry if he could drive a four in hand, to which Henry replied with absolute confidence, that with a little guidance he thought he could. He accordingly climbed up beside the driver, took hold of the reins as instructed, and then safely drove the coach for a considerable distance, whilst the old coachman gave his aching limbs a rest.

In 1847, Henry Nicholson Ellacombe was ordained deacon and priest by the Bishop of Lichfield, and then took up the curacy of Sudbury in Derbyshire. However this was only an intermittent pause in Henry's progress, as in the following year he took his M A degree, and returned to Bitton, to take up, for the next two years, the curacy under his father, and then in 1850, he took over as vicar of the parish. Henry started his new post with great enthusiasm, and concern for the education and welfare of his parishioners. In an open letter written on the 17th February 1851, to the more wealthy inhabitants of Bitton he said:

By the exertions of my father, your late vicar, the school buildings are very good and substantial. For this I am most thankful, but I think few of you can be aware of the great ignorance in which large portions of the children of this parish are sunk. I speak now solely of the hamlet of Bitton, including Upton, Beach and Swinford, and almost solely of the boys. The girls are not much better, yet their condition is somewhat better than the boys, and is in a fair way towards improvement.

Of the boys I can scarcely speak too strongly, their ignorance and idleness is most deplorable ~ their manners are rough and uncouth in the extreme ~ of the common duties of civility and kindness they seem to have little notion ~ and the higher duties of truth, honesty, obedience, and the fear of God are, I much fear, little more than mere names to them. With all this they seem to have little desire to improve themselves, and we cannot but look forward with some dread to the time when such boys become men, husbands and fathers.

He then went on to say that the only remedy was to have a good daily school that not only taught the boys reading and writing, but also that which will enlarge their minds and give them a love of learning and the understanding of their duties, privileges and responsibilities as English boys, plus last but not least, God's blessing. Henry was not prepared to create just a debating society, but instead he chose to lead from the front with an announcement that within a matter of days he would be opening in the village, at his expense, a boys school with a master from Bath. However in making this statement he pointed out that he could not cope with this expense by himself, and that accordingly the main purpose of the letter was to try to find either new subscribers, or for existing patrons to increase their donations.

Unfortunately we have not been left with any records that show how well the response was to Henry's appeal, but the well built school in the village is testament to his influence and his efforts to provide for the education of the children of the parish.

Although Henry threw himself into his work as parish priest, he still allowed himself time for a personal life, and for a year or two, courted and then married, on the 5th October 1852, Emily Aprilla Wemyss, daughter of General Wemyss who had served under the Duke of Wellington throughout the Peninsular War. In total this union produced ten children, three sons and seven daughters, of whom only half survived him. Their marriage lasted just under forty-five years, coming to an end with Emily's death on the 30th April 1897. During the years that followed their marriage, both Henry and his wife lived quite quietly at Bitton, enjoying the social pleasures of living in the Countryside, with horse riding, fishing and rambling being listed amongst his hobbies. At the time there could still be found much of an old world atmosphere about Bitton, Willsbridge and Oldland, three villages almost within a stone's throw of each other. In describing the general nature of his walks around the area, Henry said:

Anything more typical of rural England as it was a century ago could scarcely be found, with the steep wooded banks, the various flowery chines, and the little thatched cottages in the village all make that remote part of the country one of the most romantic I have ever seen. Many a time we have walked along the footpath and over the downs from Bitton to Willsbridge through Oldland, so often traversed by Mr Pearsall and my father before us.

Although no events of outstanding importance appear to have occurred during his priesthood, Henry was made Rural Dean of Bitton in 1874, and seven years later he was made Honorary Canon of Bristol. Throughout his time at Bitton he took a great deal of interest in the restoration of St Mary's, and even when he travelled abroad, which he did most years, he was always on the lookout for artefacts that he felt would enhance the interior of his church. With this regard he decorated, at great expense to himself, the chancel with Italian marble, and to a slightly lesser degree, he drew all of the designs for the oak bench heads of the pews, for a local carpenter to copy.

In 1878 Canon Henry published his first book, entitled *"The Plant-Lore of Shakespeare",* which ran into three editions, and five years later published *"Shakespeare as an Angler."* Both these books where based upon subjects that he was quite passionate about, fishing, and gardening, and over a period of many years he contributed numerous papers to various organisations on these subjects. His love of gardening, and the world of horticulture was greatly helped by work already carried out at the vicarage by his plant-loving father, and by the fact that the soil and the climate of Bitton was exceptionally favourable for the growth of many exotic plants. New plants were found and introduced from his many trips abroad, and his knowledge and understanding of plants led him to publish in 1895 his third book, *In a Gloucestershire Garden,"* followed in 1902 with his fourth and last book *"In my Vicarage Garden, and Elsewhere."* One of the Canon's close friends described the Bitton Vicarage garden as under:

In making the tour of the garden ~ I mean the grand tour as distinct from minor excursions, ~ we always took the same route. Never to my knowledge was this departed from. We started at the porch of the vicarage and discussed first of all the fine old UMBELLULARIA *growing on the house and a fine plant of Berberis fascicularis. Turning to the right past the library windows and the arched doorway giving access to the vicarage lane, we came to the churchyard wall and its border and to that part of the garden abutting onto the rich Avon valley meadows. Then came the long wall on the upper side with its wonderful collection of climbers and shrubs and the narrow border at its base even more remarkable for the excellence and rarity of its plants. Every yard, often every foot, contained something of interest to discuss, something to reveal the deep and intimate knowledge the Canon had of his treasures. There is no garden in this country, I believe, that contains so much of interest condensed in so small a space. I do not know whether it was by design or not but the Canon's way of touring the garden involved one in a sort of crescendo of interest, for after traversing the long wall just mentioned you reach the warmest corner of the garden, bounded on three sides by the greenhouse, the stable yard, and the schoolhouse. Here grow Melianthus major, Diospyros kaki Corokia Cotoneasters, and a host of similar rarities ~ not as aliens struggling in adversity, but comfortable, robust, and prolific as any German in a foreign land."*

Another friend described the Canon's approach to gardening as:

"I do not think the artistic side of gardening, certainly not in the form of colour schemes and such like, have much if any real appeal to the Canon. With him the importance is the individual plant, its beauty, its health and its right position even if that puts it at odds with the neighbouring plants."

Thus the Canon and his father before him had created at the Bitton vicarage, a botanic garden in miniature, with an exceptional number of species grown in so small an area. Such was his knowledge of plants that for more than forty years until his death, the Canon devoted much of his time exchanging correspondence and plants with those who were in charge of the Royal Gardens at Kew.

Another one of the Canon's interests was local politics, and for many years ably sat on Bitton Parish Council, retaining his position well into his eighty-sixth year. In doing so he acquired even more knowledge of the parish of Bitton, and this in turn encouraged him to have a deep-seated interest in field-names. Whilst his academic interest was discovering their origin, and understanding the basis of their existence, he had a particular liking of those names found in his parish. Leaze is a very common word in field-names, he once wrote, and in my parish there are Crooked Leaze, Middle Leaze, Cow Leaze, Beech Leaze, Pigeon-house Leaze, to name just a few. The word comes from the Anglo-Saxon Lese or Leswe, meaning a pasture, ie an open field as distinct from woodland or enclosed land. In addition another word that has fallen out of common use, but still exists, as a field name is Tyning, and such examples as Long, Upper, Wall, Robin's can be found in this parish. Once again this word can be traced to its Anglo-Saxon origin of *tynen* a word that means, "to hedge in." Other words of a similar nature are "paddock," "croft" and "hayes" the later being another form of tyning. All of the fields that contain these generic names have one feature in common, which is that they all mark enclosures and originate at a time when enclosures were the exception rather than the rule. It was not so long ago in our history that the greater part of England was unenclosed, and probably as recently as 200 years or so ago, well over half of the parish of Bitton comprised of unenclosed land. And now as the nineteenth century draws to a close there is probably not a single parcel of land in the parish that is not enclosed. During my own lifetime large tracts of Oldland Common, Longwell Green and North Common, which were previously described as "common and/or waste lands" have been enclosed, mainly as a result of the Enclosure Act of 1819.Within this area there were open and commonable arable fields known as *Westfield* and *Redfield,* now fully enclosed, as is over 260 acres of commonable meadow.

..To the..

Rev. Canon Ellacombe

Dear Sir,

We, the undersigned Parish Councillors of Bitton, in accordance with a resolution which at a Meeting of the Council on October 25th, 1907, was heartily and unanimously adopted, desire to express our deep regret that you now feel compelled to sever your connection with the Council.

We gratefully acknowledge the valuable services you have rendered over a long period, you having been Chairman of the Council from the time of its institution, and we hereby tender you our sincere thanks, and desire to place on record our appreciation of the unfailing courtesy, wide knowledge, and business ability which you have always displayed.

WILLIAM ADAMS, H. G. GALLOP,
JOHN ATHERTON, CHAS. GREENWOOD,
EDWIN BRAIN, A. JEFFERIES,
THOMAS BRAIN, EDWIN MORGAN,
E. A. DAVIS, CHARLES H. NEADS,
SOLOMON FRY, W. H. QUARMAN,
J. ROLAND TORRANCE.

The Certificate of Grateful thanks presented to the Rev. Canon Ellacombe upon his retirement from the Bitton Parish Council in October 1907.

Like his father before him, the Canon developed a great interest in the general history of church building and restoration, and in particular was extremely interested in the pre-Norman church of St Mary's Bitton, a building that he was to come to know so well. According to the Canon, the exact date of the foundation of the church could not be determined with any accuracy, although certain academics considered that the origin of the church probably goes back to around the sixth century, and the fabric of the building in the main, almost certainly remained unaltered for the next five hundred years or so. Then in the eleventh century the church building was remodelled when a Western Front was added, together with the inclusion of north and south doors, and a new chancel arch was constructed within the original Saxon arch. Two hundred years later, the church building was vandalised by Bishop Button, who had a large section of the north wall of the nave removed so that a mortuary chapel could be constructed in memory of his parents, whilst at the same time a number of Norman windows and other Norman artefacts were removed, damaged and/or destroyed. Further destruction occurred during the fourteenth century when the original chancel and West Front were swept away. However this wanton act of considered vandalism did have an important reason, as it was carried out so that the existing tower could be constructed, and a new and better chancel built to replace the original. Further alterations took place during the fifteenth century when much of the south wall was pulled down and then reconstructed in the style of the day, and of course other but more minor alterations have taken place since.

Both father and son devoted more than ninety years to the spiritual needs of the parishioners of Bitton Parish, both were extremely well educated and had enormous interest in their work, and in the additional study of horticulture, history, architecture and a host of other subjects. Their very presence left an indelible mark on Bitton and the surrounding parishes, and they have left us a legacy in their writings that allow us an insight into the history of this area.

However, despite creating a good and lasting impression upon the parishioners, it would seem from his written criticism, that the Ellacombes did not greatly impress the journalist who went by the pseudonym "The Church Goer," as around 1848 he wrote an article following a recent visit he had made from Bristol on his favourite horse *John Bunyan,* and set out below are some of the highlights of that article.

"As I mounted John Bunyan to start for Bitton, I felt the cheerful influence of a warm day and looked forward to a pleasant ride out along the Keynsham road. Having reached Brislington, I passed his Worshipful the Mayor, thundering along in his enclosed carriage on his way into Bristol, whilst I had the pleasure of being able to continue on my way, at John Bunyan's pace, with my face towards the fresh air and the free country, perfectly content with myself on that fine Sunday morning.

When I threw John's bridle to the boy at the White Hart in Bitton it was, by my watch, ten minutes past eleven, but as the good people of the hostelry had not yet left home for church, I considered that I was still in time to reach the church before the start of the service. 'Hodge' said I 'have prayers commenced yet?' 'Yes sir,' came the reply, 'the bell be a done ringing.'

'How is that then, for your master and mistress, I see have not gone yet.'

Hodge shrugged his shoulders ~ a motion that said plainly as possible ~ Master and missus are too anxious to serve their customer, to afford time to serve God.'

I should hardly have known the vicarage as I passed it and the schoolhouse, on my way to the Church up that pretty little lane. In my old friend Mr Curtis's time it was a plain building; however, on the present vicar entering it as curate it was tastefully improved, but upon his becoming incumbent, it grew with his growth into a gothic edifice, with a great array of oriel windows; and on this same progressive principle, I expect to see it completed as a palace by the time he has expanded into a bishop.

Upon entering the Church, I noticed the sign "Free Seats" *painted on the wall to my left, and as a visitor I decided that that was where I should sit, however, having turned and taken a few steps and reached the pew door, I noticed, as I was about to enter the pew that the sign also read, in slightly smaller letters,* "for Women." *Posed as I was to enter this inner sanctum, I suddenly spotted this grim old spinster ~ no doubt one of the village vestals of some three score years or more, ~ scowl at me from under her rust beaver bonnet with a look that said, "You have no business here, you beant be of our sex." Somewhat disconcerted, I quickly withdrew my hand from the top of the pew door, and turning around I saw on the opposite side of the Church another painted sign, only this one proclaimed* "Free Seats for Men." *I retired to that side of the Church as quickly as my normal decorum would allow and sat inside the men only pew next to one of the local constables, hoping that my error had not been noticed by too many. As I recovered from this embarrassing and unnecessary error, my thoughts turned to the vicar, and inwardly I asked of myself, was this discrimination his doing? Was he guilty of this almost eastern segregation of the sexes in this sacred edifice? I know it is sometimes done in conventicles, but this is the first time I have ever seen it followed in the Established church, and I rise [sic] my voice against it, Mr Vicar. Besides, to be just, the practice ought to be general, as a little further up the Church, amongst the seats that were not free, there was no such "invidious distinction," and it is only with the humble that your arrangement, like the new Poor Law, interferes to separate man and wife. Whilst these thoughts chased around in my head, I was equally conscious of the fact that in the background there was an abnormal level of chanting, and I soon came to the conclusion that the vicar of Bitton was an enthusiastic supporter of conducting a portion of his service in this form. Although in the main the chanting was well done, it was not to my liking, and I felt that my ears were being accosted by two or three rough young men in fustian jackets whose ability to chant in tune left much to be desired. In addition, I understand that the organist is the self-taught daughter of the village carpenter, and whilst I believe that she did her best, to my mind, the organ of the village Church is never so appropriately played as when a village parishioner presides at it. As the service progressed I found that the vicar read the lessons much too rapidly for my comfort, and this, and the chanting helped to spoil, in my opinion, the whole service.*

I reminded myself that the local vicar was one of the most indefatigable men I have ever known, particularly with regard to the construction and/or repair of Church properties. Where he gets, or got, the money for the restoration of the mother church, or the rebuilding of the church at Oldland, or the construction of the pretty new chapel perched on Jeffery's Hill. Heaven knows, as I don't."

The Church Goer remained in St Mary's after the service ended, and in his article he noted the style of the internal architecture, and continued to make pointed remarks about the Rev. H N Ellacombe, but perhaps his comments were the creation of a journalist's mind keen to sell a controversial article, rather than writing a bland story.

CHAPTER 14 ~ Mile Stones & Guide Stones"

The Parish of Bitton is unique in the number of excellent Guide Stones set within its boundary plus a high number of preserved mile stones all of which add to the charm of wandering around the locality. Although some of the stones are set, as one might expect, along what are today very busy arterial roads, the position of many of the guide stones is more rural as they rest in the byways less frequented by today's traveller, whilst some can often be hidden by the exuberance of summer growth. For those of you who are unaware of what a guide stone is, it is a directional sign without distances carved in solid stone blocks, and usually found at the junction of two roads/lanes, with by far the largest example situated at the union of Barry Road and the Bath Road. One of the unique features of these stones is that they each include a clenched fist appearing out of a "laced" cuff, with an extended index finger pointing towards the named destination, but the matchlessness of these stones does not stop there as a close study of the individual stones will show that whilst many of the carved index fingers have the outline of a fingernail some do not, and in other cases, the laced cuff is either crimped or un-crimped, insignificant details but a fascinating insight to our past and the work of the mason.

It is probable that the guide stones were constructed before the introduction of the turnpike roads, but unfortunately unlike other markers, there is no positive evidence of when they were installed or when they were made. Based upon pure supposition, it is possible that when the Parish of Bitton embarked upon a programme of road improvement, including the construction of new roads during the 1695-1710 period that they arranged for these guide stones to be installed, certainly the carved "Gauntlet" or "Turn Back Funnel" style cuffs would seem to tie in with that period. However, by 1727 the local roads were under the control of the Bristol Turnpike Trust, and whilst it is possible that that august body may have incurred the expense of having the guide stones constructed and installed, it begs the questions why should they confine that expenditure to just the Parish of Bitton, why are there not many more such stones in the greater Bristol area, and why did they install elaborate guide stones along roads that were not part of the main arterial turnpike routes, especially as the principle reason for the establishment of the Trust was to make money from the tolls it collected. Instead it is much more likely that the Trust had the milestones installed and these can still be seen at one-mile intervals along the main road leading towards Bath.

With reference to the above named cuffs, these were a very popular male accessory of the Civil War period, and only appear to have stayed in fashion during that war and the subsequent Puritan period, having certainly disappeared by around 1720, to be replaced by a much heavier and much larger cuff. Accordingly, it is more likely that the masons employed to carve the stones would include a current fashion feature rather than either invent a new clothing fashion or to resurrect an old clothing fashion. This argument is not conclusive but it would seem reasonably convincing, but whatever are the facts, these guide stones are a unique part of our local history, and of our environment and as such, must be treasured not only for the current generation but also for the generations to come.

To find some of the more obscure guide/mile stones you will need to go to Newpit Lane, Marshfield Lane, and Golden Valley Lane as well as Brockham Hill, West Street, Bath Road and Bridgeyate; daily we pass them by and daily we do not see them, but they are there and have been there for the past three hundred years or more.

Bibliography /Sources

An Act for repairing widening and improving the several roads around the City of Bristol and for making certain new lines of road to communicate with same ~ Royal Assent 14th June 1819.
A brief history of Oldland by Miss G E Burns
A Short Guide to Bitton by C P Ketchley MA
Bristol Transported by John F Mackeson
Civil War England by Peter Young
Domesday Book Gloucestershire Edited and Translated by John S Moore
Four Hundred years of Gloucestershire Life by Anthony M Wherry, BA.
Gloucester Historical Studies IV 1970

Gloucestershire Record Office ~ Felons Register 1815-28 [Q/GC 5/1-2-3]
~ Gaol Calendars 1800-1814 QS/C
~ Petition against Police Force 184 GRO PC862/7.
Henry Nicholson Ellacombe ~ edited by A.W.Hill

Round Bath in Twenty Picturesque Rambles by Mrs Wheatcroft.
Some Coalpits in the Neighbourhood of Bristol & Kingswood by Dorothy Vinter.

The Ancient & Present State of Gloucestershire by Sir Robert Atkyns
The Changing Face of England by Christopher Trent.
The Church Goer Rural Rides by "The Church Goer"
The Heart of Mendip by Francis A Knight
The History of Kingswood Forest by A Braine
The History of the Parish of Bitton by Rev. H T Ellacombe
The Murderers of Gloucestershire, Hangings in Gloucester Prison [1872-1939] by Senior Officer Bryan White.
The Registers of Bitton compiled by The Parish Register Society 1900
The Poor Law Records of Bitton 1771-1821
Transportees from Gloucestershire to Australia 1783-1842 by Irene Wyatt
Turnpike Roads by Geoffrey N Wright
Turnpike Roads of the Bristol Region. A preliminary study.
Until She Be Dead by Penny Deverill.